The Anastasis:
The
Resurrection of Jesus
as an
Historical Event
by
J. Duncan M. Derrett

i

By the Same Author

Law in the New Testament (Darton, Longman & Todd, London)

Jesus's Audience (Darton, Longman & Todd)

Gesù insegnante (Adelphi, Milan)

An Oriental Lawyer Looks at the Trial of Jesus and the Doctrine of the Redemption
(School of Oriental & African Studies, University of London, London)

'Law & Society in Jesus's World' (in A.N.R.W., ed. Haase & Temporini,
published by W. de Gruyter, Berlin, Sec. II, vol. 25, pt. 1)

Studies in the New Testament, I-III (Brill, Leiden)

also

Henry Swinburne (?1551-1624) (Borthwick Institute of Historical Research, York)

'The Affair of Richard Hunne and Friar Standish' in J. B. Trapp, ed., *The
Apology* (Yale Edn. of the Complete Works of St. Thomas More, vol. 9) (Yale
University Press, New Haven & London)

Religion, Law & the State in India (Faber & Faber, London)

The Hoysaḷas. A Dynastic History (Oxford University Press)

Introduction to Modern Hindu Law (Oxford University Press)

Critique of Modern Hindu Law (Tripathi, Bombay)

Trans., and ed., R. Lingat, *Classical Law of India* (University of California Press,
Berkeley)

Ed., Introduction to Legal Systems (Sweet & Maxwell, London)

History of Indian Law (Brill, Leiden)

Dharmaśāstra and Juridical Literature (Harrassowitz, Wiesbaden)

Bhāruci's Commentary on the Manusmṛti (Steiner, Wiesbaden)

Essays in Classical & Modern Hindu Law, I-IV (Brill, Leiden)

Death of a Marriage Law (Vikas, New Delhi)

iii

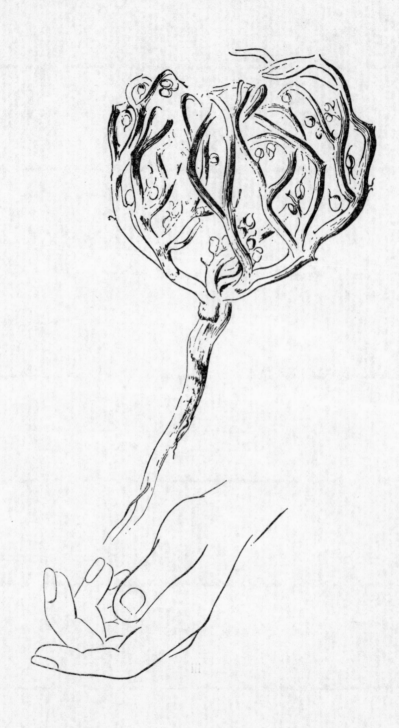

The Anastasis:
The
Resurrection of Jesus
as an
Historical Event.

by

Professor J. Duncan M. Derrett

M.A., D.C.L. (*Oxon.*), Ph.D., LL.D. (*Lond.*);
Of Gray's Inn, Barrister;
Sometime Open Foundation Scholar, Jesus College, Oxford;
Professor of Oriental Laws in the University of London;
Sometime Tagore Professor of Law, University of Calcutta;
Wilde Lecturer in Natural & Comparative Religion, University of Oxford, 1979-81.

19 82

Published by P. DRINKWATER, 56 CHURCH STREET,
SHIPSTON-ON-STOUR, WARWICKSHIRE, ENGLAND.

ISBN 0 9505751 9 4.

Set by S. C. Bloomfield in Intertype 10pt. Times.

Printed by Bloomfield & Son, Grove Road, Stratford upon Avon, Warwickshire, England.

Designed by P. Drinkwater.

ERRATA

'Escapes' requiring amendment are listed below:-

p.xiv., l.2: *hierochuntica;* l.5: with rain it *itself,* as well as its seeds,

p.17, l.1: functional-causal; l.10: effects

p.21, l.20: Lucius Lamius; l.21: experience. [M. Valerius] Messala l.31: Corfidius,

p.33, l.30 *et passim:* inchoate

p.33, l.42: *(anastaseōs;* l.35: *'I* am

p.36, n.6: Willam

p.39, l.7: Tichborne

p.44, l.20: term, 'Father

p.49, l.28: Luke?'

p.62, l.1: Christians'

p.67, n.20: manger as a stone

p.77, l.5 f.b.: disinterred

p.79, l.30: not claimed that

p.82, l.7: people. Isaac

p.90, l.32: give him approximately a week's

p.96, 1:19: *anestē;*

p.103, l.2: all this into

p.108, l.18: 'appearances'

p.109, l.5: and 'was taken up'

p.112, l.2 f.b.: 'documentation' had been

p.139. Transfer f.n.6 to beginning of 5. Renumber 7 as 6. Enter: 7. Mal. 4:2. To f.n.12 add: Gen. 22:3,5,19.

p.140: *JA* = Derrett, *Jesus's Audience*

Correct (kind reader) what thou find'st amiss;
And then it matters not whose fault it is;
For all men err, since Adam first transgrest,
The printer errs, I err most like the rest:
The faults in this by neither were intended,
But being past, they thus may be amended.

William Leybourn (1669)

TABLE OF CONTENTS

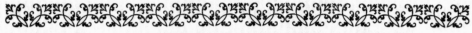

PREFACE

Did Jesus 'rise from the dead', and if so in what sense?

If he did, what meaning does this hold for faith-history and for secular history?

Secular history is what is taught as an educational discipline in schools and colleges under the name of 'history'. It intersects with faith-history at many points. While secular history seeks to discover *what took place,* as a secure basis for reflections, faith-history (which often looks as much to the future as to the past) is centred on *what was going on.* Stimulated by reports of events it projects upon them its prejudices and its expectations. Where secular history intersects with faith-history the secular historian may assist the faith-historian to base his propositions (especially theological propositions) on considerations acceptable to the world at large.

The New Testament was itself composed by faith-historians, not secular historians. Even theologians approach its contents with scrupulous care. Here I do not give conclusive answers to the two major questions I first raised, but I react to the present theological climate. The dilemma which seems to face New Testament scholars is this: if Jesus rose from the dead as the texts attempt to assure us, a breach with nature must (they suppose) have occurred; but the attitude of a public acquainted with the principles of science is intolerant of all miracles. Therefore three options are to be set up:

1) Jesus *may* have actually risen, though the secular historian cannot prove this from the confusing and inadequate sources. Something tremendous obviously happened within the tiny church led by Peter, but what it was is irrecoverable.

2) Whether he rose or not, the message conveyed in picturesque form[1] is (and was) not that at all, but a call to decision and to faith. The Resurrection of Jesus in an *as if* proposition. Those who were aware that his power survived him knew that death had not ended it.

3) The New Testament is really concerned with the timeless Messiah, Christ, Son of God; and the New Testament authors' attempt to pin him down to place and time is naïve and based on an archaic concept of historical presentation.[2] The questions we are asking are questions which the New Testament should not be pressed to answer. The so-called 'witnesses' should not be taken seriously. We can safely proceed, therefore, as if Jesus did *not* rise from the dead at all.

Over the last fifty years varieties of these options have been asserted repeatedly by theologians. In order to preserve originality scholars have rung the changes and, with equal confidence[3] and confusion, crossed and recrossed a broad path.

During the last twenty years I have pursued secular historical research into the New Testament, not excluding miracles. In each case *reminiscence* seemed to lie beneath all the stories, encrusted as they are with a patina of pious reflection and sermon-material. One must penetrate beneath the faith-history of the first two centuries to recover burnished treasures, which are no illusions, forgeries, or impostures. Of course they look quite different when freed from their sometimes childish accretions.

The reasoning behind the three options outlined above is faulty. One must know a great deal more about the world of Jesus's time, before we can conjecture what could have happened, and arrive at an order of probabilities. The New Testament, Jewish sources, and indeed common facts of Asian living must be searched into with an understanding of what these are fit to tell us. It turns out that professional theologians have consistently turned a blind eye to certain questions (e.g. what could have happened to Jesus's body?) as well as other factors relevant to the problem. The Talpioth ossuaries, for example, have been systematically ignored. In order to arrive at any of the three options above, or any others, many possibilities must be *excluded* which are commonly ignored. My present work is intended to draw the lines and possibilities for conjecture more tightly than is usually done, and to show the theological effect of a tighter construction.

*   *   *

The *mode* of the Resurrection of Jesus has never been an article of faith. 'On the third day he rose again from the dead.'[4] How he is supposed to have done it is unknown. Ignatius, writing about A.D. 100 (sixty years after the Crucifixion), wrote to the Ephesians that,[5]

> ' . . . the virginity of Mary, and her giving birth, were hidden from the Prince of this World [i.e. Satan, who would have liked to prevent them], as was also the death of the Lord. Three mysteries of a cry which were wrought in the stillness of God.'

The Resurrection itself is not mentioned: perhaps it is comprehended in the 'death', for Ignatius certainly believed in it.

A tradition to handle the Resurrection in a tangential way starts at least as early as St. Paul, who is supremely uninterested in it as an experience undergone by Jesus. St. Paul is thought to have commenced his Christian missionary work in A.D. 46 and died in 64. No doubt subsequent ages have found the question intriguing; but they have, on the whole, been preoccupied with Jesus the Saviour; his Resurrection having served as in some sense a guarantee of his saving power. As a matter of fact Jesus's saving power arises rather from his conversion of the worldly individual, by charismatic impression, into one who understands and pursues the 'will of God'. We are *not* concerned with that in this book, though it be logically prior to the Resurrection (which subserves it) and much more important.

Mark, our prime source on Jesus's Resurrection, may well have been assembling his material in Paul's lifetime. His work however is posterior to the ideas to which the Talpioth ossuaries testify (se below, pp. 124f.). His gospel bears the first so-called 'narrative' (it is not precisely such) of the discovery that Jesus's body was no longer in the tomb. He himself writes as if we should not enquire about either the *mode* of Jesus's revival, or its immediate circumstances. This has led to suspicion, from the very earliest times (see Mt. 28: 17b), that all was not straightforward, and that the church's earliest and most influential teachers had something to hide.

The emphases to be found in 1 Tim 3:16 are interesting, not to say amazing, as we shall see. Christ is not less than the mystery of God. But the true authorship of 1 Tim. is disputed, as also its date. On the whole it is better to believe that the author was a pupil of Paul, writing in his name and in the belief that his authority was available to him, as he faced problems which had not matured in Paul's time. He may have written between A.D. 100 and 110 (W.G. Kümmel, *Introduction* [1966], 272). On the other hand a strong scepticism of pseudonymous writing in respect of epistles admitted to the New Testament canon supports the belief that the epistles, apparently attributable to Paul and supposedly Pauline from early times, must be taken, in default of proof to the contrary, to be Pauline; and therefore 1 Tim. cannot be dated later than A.D. 64 (D. Guthrie, *New Testament Introduction* [1966], 623, 666, 677-83). If indeed 1 Tim. was written before 64, not more than 34 years after the events which concern us, the mystical and un-'matter-of-fact' character of the hymn which is being *quoted* in, and is therefore much earlier than, 1 Tim., is astounding.

"Christ, indeed, we confess, is the mystery of our religion:
> *He* was manifested in the flesh,
> Vindicated (i.e. declared righteous) in (i.e. by) the Spirit,
> Seen by angels,
> Preached (about) amongst the Nations (i.e. non-Jews),
> Believed on in the World (i.e. the unregenerate universe),
> Taken up (i.e. 'assumed', 'caused to ascend') in Glory."

The word I have italicised, 'He', is replaced in a great many authentic copies of the Greek text, and in very many ancient Fathers' quotations, by 'God'. This is interesting, as it proves that from very early times the equation between the Jesus of faith-history, as opposed to secular history, and God (the deity of the Hebrews) was taken for granted. Indeed the likening of Jesus to God is visible in many places in Mark himself. For example, at Mk. 5:17 we find the inhabitants of Gerasa begging Jesus to leave their territory, ostensibly because they were afraid of losing more pigs, but really because they were incapable of reacting properly to the great wonder, or 'sign', that had been achieved by Jesus in their midst. Mark deliberately alludes to Job 21:14, 22:17 MT, where the wicked, when they prosper, say to God, 'Depart from us, we do not want to know your ways!' (i.e. there is nothing you can usefully do for us).

However that may be, the hymn at 1 Tim 3 does not refer to the *mode* of the Resurrection: indeed it ignores it. The reference to a 'taking up', and thereby to an 'assumption' or 'ascension', is not only present, but is the climax of this 'creed before the creeds'. One might even moot the question whether this interest in his ascension (surfacing in popular Christian worship before St. Luke offered an actual scenario of the 'event') did not influence notions about the Resurrection. Could it have imposed some kind of pattern upon them, or required some attitude towards the tradition of what occurred on the first Easter Day? This is a major uncertainty.

There are however certain 'fixed points', which my treatment clarifies for the first time. My own tentative essays on this whole subject have as yet attracted slender attention.[6] Any further conjectures by others ought to take those 'fixed points' into account.

✳   ✳   ✳

My obligations to helpers are much smaller here than in my other publications at large, but I must mention the aptness of a suggestion of a fellow-orientalist, Mr. Philip Denwood (specially equipped in Buddhism), on the subject of the worship of relics. Again, amongst my unusual accumulation of qualifications is the fact that I was occupied with medical services (in the Royal Army Medical Corps) between 1942 and 1945. Although that did not prepare me for the electrifying advances in diagnosis of death made since 1975, it did enable me to appreciate, and utilise, the extensive and selected bibliography made for me by Miss E. Heaton of the Radcliffe Science Library (Oxford).

My original draft contained almost as much in the way of footnote references as text. For this publication, which I hope will be used as much by readers who cannot track down the references as by those who can, I have abbreviated these, eschewed discussion, and have given by way of bibliography, with a list of abbreviations, the means whereby a careful student may check everything with the aid of a qualified librarian. The standard of 'reader services' provided in our libraries has increased very markedly in the last decades, and the low cost of this book can well reflect the fact.

I refer to biblical passages often. Non-theologians easily fall into the trap of supposing that such references are merely a decoration, not realising that they are used to avoid the expense of copying out the relevant words as often as they are needed. My reader certainly should look up these references, and amongst the many modern versions available he will do well to use the Jerusalem Bible or the Revised Standard Version. When reading the text he is urged to follow the following mental drill: he should ask himself four questions in this order:

1) What is the surface meaning, and what would contemporary hearers have understood at first or second hearing?

2) What insinuations does the text hold, given the Old Testament background to its language and ideas, and the outlook of the evangelists' milieux?

3) What *use* will these texts have had in the churches where they were

intended to be recited, having in mind the confluence of pagan and Jewish traditions in those churches?

4) Retracing our steps through questions 3 to 1, what residue of *reminiscence* could have inspired the procedure of reflection, debate, research, insight, and finally composition which emerged in the texts as we have them?

Now the reader is in a position to apply his mind to the Anastasis itself, and to construct his own mental picture of it free from the imagination of the early churches, and with a perspective congenial to himself, enjoying but not being bound by, the perspective of the first literary exponents of an event unique in the history of religions.

Half Way House,   J.D.M.D.
Blockley, Gloucestershire.
May, 1982.

NOTES

1. Of very wide interest are the points made by G. B. Caird in his *Language and Imagery of the Bible* (London & Philadelphia, 1980).
2. E. C. F. Schillebeeckx, *Revelation and Theology* (London, 1967). I have never seen the young theologian's dilemma better put than by J. P. Audet, 'Admiration religieuse et désir de savoir, réflexions sur la condition du théologien' (Conférence Albert-le-Grand, 1961) (Montréal, 1962). On 'demythologising' the succinct presentation in I. Henderson, *Myth in the New Testament* (London, 1954) is still valuable.
3. On the arrogance of the socially secure but educationally immature, the late Sir Kenneth Wheare, 'On the Sin of Pride', *Oxford* 27/1 (1975), 79ff. is masterly. On scholarly pretentiousness see W. Marxen, preface to *The Resurrection of Jesus* (1970), p. 11.

   'Small have continual plodders ever won,
   save base authority from others' books.'

   Shakespeare (*Love's Labours Lost*, I.i, 86-7).
4. Tert (Hahn, §7), Orig. (ibid., §8), Ap.Const. (ibid., §9), Marcell. Ancyr. (§17), Aug. (§§33, 47), Nicene Creed (§142).
5. Ign., Eph.XIX.1.
6. My *Studies* I (1977), 95ff., 101ff., also *Con.Rel.* 1977, 232-51.

xiii

FRONTISPIECE: In the deserts of Iran, North Africa, and Palestine one may find the 'Rose of Jericho', *Anastatica Hierochuntica,* otherwise the 'Resurrection Plant'. This small cruciferous plant develops, dries, and then blows in a totally dry state over the desert. But when that most unfavourable of earthly terrains is favoured with rain its seeds root themselves, develop, and blossom; as if they had always had the advantage of a stable and favourable location. Inspired as the name it bears is, the illustration equals it. It is the work of Mme. Dorika de Winne (formerly Mlle. Dorika Leyniers), whose gracious permission to reproduce it was procured for me through the kind offices of Prof. Jean Léonard (Brussels) by Dr. A. W. Exell.

ACKNOWLEDGEMENT: Mr. Peter Drinkwater not only took a keen interest in a book which some of his profession had found unattractive, but also, in seeing it through the press, brought the art of coöperating with an author to the level of collaboration.

J.D.M.D.

COVER PICTURE:
"The Three Women at Jesus's Tomb" by Albrecht Dürer;
from *Der Ritter vom Turn von den Exemplein der Gotsforcht und Eberkeit* (Basle 1493).

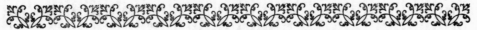

CHAPTER I

Introduction.

1. WHY 'ANASTASIS'?

I am being fussy, even pedantic, about the use of a word. Obviously 'to get up', 'to wake up', and 'to be awakened, or got up' are different. As everyone who has been unexpectedly awakened knows, the implications are very different. Yet, in poetry, or metaphorical speech, the ideas may be confused, perhaps allowably confused. In the Greek Orthodox Church the Easter greeting is 'Christos anésti', which means literally 'Christ rose'. It is correct yet the church as a whole has from the earliest times (see the phraseology of Mk. 6:14, 12:26, Lk. 7:14) had theological reasons for preferring, in most of its dogmatic pronouncements, quite a different formulation: 'Christ was caused to rise, was awakened'. This is a tendentious statement, not necessarily wrong, but possibly misleading.

Anastasis ('getting up') is the correct name for the experience Jesus underwent, and the earliest texts[1] referring to it use the verb *anastēnai*, which means 'to get up', particularly from sleep (as at Acts 12:7 *anasta*), sickness, or collapse, of which death is the extreme form. The verb *egerthēnai*, on the other hand, meaning 'to be awakened, raised up', is tendentious, suggesting the action of the awakener, *someone else*. *Anastēnai* is spontaneous; *egerthēnai* is non-spontaneous. The shades of meaning are illustrated at Lk. 11:7-8. The parable of the Friend at Midnight, which has been presented by Luke after the Lord's Prayer as an illustration of the resurrection as the climax of those things for which we should pray,[2] contrasts the action of the man in the 'house', 'getting up' (*anastas*) with the very same action viewed as the work of his 'knocker-up', his being 'got up' (*egertheis*). *Egerthēnai* can well have a suggestion of the miraculous (Mt. 16:21, 17:23, 20:19; Lk. 24:6-7 has a mixed vocabulary). Miracle is asserted by *egerthēti* ('rise', or rather 'be raised up') at Lk. 7:14, whereas the same author uses *anastēthi* ('rise') correctly at Acts 9:40.[3] The church adopted the second verb, *egerthēnai*, in reference to Jesus's experience as a *second thought*. That was not so absurd: Is. 26:19 LXX ('The dead shall arise'), and the play on words we find at Jn. 11:23-24, confirm that both *anastasis* and 'resurrection' *could* be implied by *anastēnai*. The church thought itself entitled to utilise the ambiguity; but for the modern reader the confusion has been a source of misunderstanding.

Certainly an analysis of *theological* references to revival of the dead shows that *anastasis*, linguistically merely a 'getting up', is most commonly used[3a] metaphorically of the reviving of the dead, resurrection. It is not surprising that it was the earlier term applied to Jesus. *Egerthēnai* on the other hand had always a wider background, and, though applied to resurrection, retained its secular uses. On the other hand it is certain that Jewish non-Christian works in Greek prior to A.D. 70 were able to depict God (who makes the dead live: 2 Kngs. 5:7) raising

1

a person from the dead with the use of that second verb. So in the valuable *Vita Prophetarum* (in a state free from Christian interpolations), Jona 5: πάλιν ἤγειρον ἐκ νεκρῶν ὁ θεὸς διὰ τοῦ Ἠλία, 'Again, God raised (men) from the dead through Elijah' (referring to 1 Kngs. 17:22).[3b]

'Resurrection' itself is a technical term referring normally to something which has never actually happened! It is an imaginary entity which lies in the future according to some religions. It is something about which no one can pass a conclusive opinion. Therefore no one can say, seriously, whether the *anastasis* of an individual is an example of it. On the other hand the idea conveyed by 'resurrection' is not *less* than *anastasis:* it is very much more. It implies a revival which leads immediately to an unbounded, an endless existence, whether in bliss or otherwise. And it is *collective* (below, p.32), that is to say it is the experience not of an individual but of a sizeable group. Jesus's Anastasis is *prima facie* not resurrection.[3c] I insist (except in the Preface above) in calling Jesus's experience by its original and correct name, in order not to confuse it with the imaginary entity, *even if he, for reasons of his own, wished to profit from such a confusion.* Whereas resurrection has acquired a theological patina, *anastasis* by itself is an objective term, carrying no implications. As we shall see (p.33), the idea arose, at a crucial point in our story, that Jesus's Anastasis was not merely an *anastasis* such as that of the persons whom he had revived or his apostles subsequently revived and was not merely an *example* of resurrection, but *was* Resurrection. In other words the religious belief in Resurrection was forcibly hooked onto a historical *anastasis* of an individual. This highly individual treatment of religious entities can hardly be attributed to any Tom, Dick or Harry. Nor can it be attributed seriously to mere 'lapse of time'. As we shall see, actual people believed it before Paul wrote any of his epistles or Mark assembled his gospel. My own suspicion is that it was Jesus's own idea, and since it is of a piece with his autonomous treatment of the cultural archives of his people (I mean scripture and legend) there need be no doubt but that such an attribution has plausibility.

However, in spite of this theological brigandage, appropriating the Resurrection, the great hope of the Pharisees, to Jesus—a notion which did not prevent some from taking a very different view of it (p.129)—I persist in calling his experience Anastasis and to avoid further confusion I shall keep the two terms carefully apart.

2. OUR SOURCES.

Fortunately our sources are very confined. That does not mean that they are not discordant. We must be grateful that they are. Some speak of Jesus's Anastasis, some of his Resurrection. Some say he *was* (implying that he still *is*) Resurrection, others that at his death on the cross resurrection took place in favour of the Just (Mt. 27:52). These discrepancies are proof of the very wide difference of opinion that emerged during the first century about the nature of Jesus's revival. A wealth of ideas and theories accumulated around a unique event. There was room for the differences, not because any Christian then doubted that he had revived but because there were quite different ways of assessing, and therefore of describing,

2

the significance of the event. Had Jesus himself delivered a theological lecture defining and explaining what he was about and why, few if any of these discrepancies would have occurred. It is plain that he did no such thing. My conjecture is that his time was short, he knew it, and had other, more practical, things to do.

No credence is to be given to the false (late) endings of Mark's gospel (below, p.135). No credence is to be given to the apocryphal gospels, such as the Gospel of Peter,[4] nor to an over-publicised document supposed to be a letter of Clement. We are left with the four gospels, with the extremely important passage at 1 Cor. 15 which deals with 'appearances', and with scattered references and allusions in other epistles. Very few scholars will agree with me that there is independent information in the *Testimonium Flavianum* (below, p.107), but there is. Until an alternative explanation comes to hand for the unique formulation which appears there, I take it to be an ancient report of Christian belief by a non-Christian. Even though it may not be the genuine work of Josephus it is interesting and suggestive.

If we wish to have recourse to the practices and ideas of the time we must take advantage of rabbinical sources also, which fortunately have raised, for me, no problems of interpretation. No doubt where it comes to rabbinical interpretations of scripture, on the other hand, there is a considerable variety of opinion, and one cannot pontificate about *the* 'Jewish' understanding of the sacred text. But we shall do the best we can, and fortunately the path is broad.

3. THE INTERPRETATION OF OUR SOURCES.

One of our first tasks is to recognise what our sources are. For many centuries the believing Christian took all the New Testament material and harmonised it, understanding that it was profitable for him to believe the harmonised whole, more or less literally. Since the Enlightenment (particularly in eighteenth century Germany) sceptical opinions have been heard continually, and they may now be regarded as commonplace. The average English schoolboy has heard of the so-called 'Resurrection', and he may accept it as pure myth, or he may keep an open mind. Those who purport to believe in it are not noticeably different from others, and this carries some weight with him. He is prepared to take the Crucifixion more seriously. Unmerited suffering is within his comprehension if not also within his experience.

It is only in the last half-century, and particularly in the last quarter century that it has dawned on scholars—and so very gradually percolates through to the parish and the school—that the New Testament epistles are concentrated theological treatises in a cult language appropriated to an established sect—a language not adapted to handling mundane matters, and that the gospels are written in a peculiar style of neo-scriptural Greek, impregnated with Jewishness, which has no profane counterpart. The style only partly corresponds with edifying writing put out by non-Christian Jewish scholars, thinkers, and propagandists of the period; and it shows marked differences—largely in the direction of restraint.

The style is in fact the result of a process of mixed story-telling and propaganda, which itself results from certain overwhelming convictions. Those convictions were valued by and enjoyed by groups of these sectarians assembled as congregations and participating in festivals which implied pilgrimage. The first was that the man Jesus of Nazareth had come into the world to save sinners by urging them to repent, by announcing the immediate arrival of the Kingdom of God, and by giving his own life as a highly meritorious act to atone for the wickedness of his fellow beings. In this capacity Jesus was not merely a Christ (i.e. one anointed, inaugurated or initiated by God, e.g. Saul) but *the* Christ, or 'Christ'—we are not to look for another. The second was that 'Christ' was anointed with the Spirit (i.e. the Holy Spirit)—and so, of course his actual anointing with oil at Bethany (Mk. 14:3ff.) was of more formal significance than real. The Spirit made him not merely *a* prophet but also *the* prophet whose coming had been foretold centuries before (Deut. 18:15-18). Contemporaries were convinced that a true prophet must suffer (Lk. 13:33) and, like Isaiah in the legend, be murdered. Joseph the righteous[5], who was sold by his brothers into Egypt, prophesied to them, after they were reconciled to him, that God would *twice* visit them (and their descendants): the first visitation had been Moses' act in rescuing the Israelites from Egypt: the second visitation was that of the coming of Jesus (see Gen. 50:24-25). Thirdly the anointing with the Spirit gave him the power of the Spirit which equated him, *tanto quanto,* with God himself. The Son of God promised by God at 2 Sam. 7:14 had come, and 'son' implies imitator and representative. Some ways of referring to God in the Old Testament therefore could unhesitatingly be attached by his followers directly to Jesus without at the same time assenting to the current Jewish uses of the same traditional scriptures. This tremendous, and highly embarrassing, notion was present before any gospel was composed.

Fourthly everything which the Spirit had dictated and achieved in the Old Testament was *co-authentic* with the sayings, doings and experiences of Jesus. Hence every reminiscence of Jesus not only *could* be transmuted into a proclamation of those beliefs, but ought to be so transmuted if its true potential was to be brought out, and justice was to be done to it. Yet the result would be a reformed religion, not a variety of contemporary Judaism.

The beliefs are summarised for us in a creed (c. A.D. 51) reappearing in Rom. 1:1-6: 'From Paul, bondsman of Christ Jesus, emissary (or ambassador) by appointment, set apart for the gospel of God—a gospel announced beforehand through his prophets in the holy scriptures, the gospel concerning his son who was descended from David (according to the flesh) and declared (according to the Holy Spirit) Son of God by a mighty action in that he *rose from the dead* [or 'by way of an *anastasis* of dead (persons—collective)] (*ex anastaseōs nekrōn*), Jesus Christ our Lord, through whom I received the grace to be emissary to all nations to bring them to obedience and faith for his Name's sake, amongst whom you too are called to belong to Jesus Christ . .' So Paul's belief, in passing.

In the gospels we are faced with two basic types of communication—there are variations on which we do not need to dilate now. The first basic type is pseudo-narrative. It purports to tell a straightforward story of an action, e.g. Walking on the Water, or a piece of teaching (e.g. the Parable of the Sower), or a controversy scene (e.g. the Debate on Resurrection), or a prophecy (e.g. the Fate of the Temple). But, as 'excavations' have proved on numerous occasions, the

4

deceptively straightforward narrative, with its typically Jewish idiom, 'Behold', is loaded with allusion to scripture, so that the passage appears to fit into the stream of utterance of the Holy Spirit, timeless. Mark treats his material in this way even if it originated with Jesus himself, as some items obviously did, viz. the Temptation in the Wilderness and the Vigil in the Garden of Gethsemane.

This led the way to a much freer handling of the material by his successors, Matthew, Luke, and John. Any material not found in Mark, or in the Sayings source (called 'Q') or in the compendium of largely parabolic teaching of Jesus which was acquired somehow by Luke (called 'L'), is to be attributed to the fermentation of curiosity, meditation, and religious research which went on after Mark had become a liturgical medium (this included especially a deeper study of the Old Testament). Mark's very success was his undoing—in the sense that he was superseded by more luxurious efforts. The later evangelists' inventions were not pure uncontrolled composition, but tended to hang from tenuous hooks. This is the second type of basic composition.

The post-Anastasis 'appearances', which are highly varied, exemplify this type of communication. They are thinly disguised commentaries by the three later evangelists on the puzzles left by Mark, basically rejecting Mark's decision to make the women's stupefaction the high point of his gospel, and thereby sacrificing an artistic feature which they have by no means replaced. Christian festivals at the Sepulchre were interrupted by political and religious intervention and Mark's climax was no longer convenient. For these appearance-stories there is no known source. It is not a question of embellishing tradition. The stories communicate not what Jesus said or did, but what the later evangelists' churches had come to believe he must have said or done: they are communications from those churches through the evangelists to us. But the technique is similar, save that Mark himself as well as the Old Testament, and some para-biblical legend, provide the text upon which a commentary is being woven. This is what is meant by saying that they are almost entirely secondary.

St. John improves, so far as we know, on material similar to Luke's, or at any rate on one or more gospels of similar range and quality. As we shall see he says plainly what people believed a half century before him. As time went on therefore the interpretation of gospel tradition invaded the text and began to assume the place that tradition itself formerly had. There is more than a suspicion that what is really the evangelist's or his church's reflections reappear as narrative. St. John's meditations on the older gospel material are written out for us at large, so that we can see for ourselves how he went to work. He may well have had independent sources of information, but if so there is no proof that he used them in the part of his gospel dealing with the Anastasis. His work on it, however, is characterised by earnest meditation on information we ourselves have.

How are we to unpack or unwind the evangelist's own contribution? We must find out what the author is trying to tell us, and then try to guess what stimulated him. Where the material could easily have been derived from some known source relating to Jesus's ministry we are on sure ground. The evangelist is inventing, his mind triggered by a recognisable stimulus.

5

The Anastasis of Jesus seems to have set off several phenomena at the time: stupefaction on the part of the ladies which is historically plausible (p.62), anxiety on the part of the males (Mt. 28:17b, Lk. 24:11-12), curiosity on all sides as to the event's meaning (p.128). The Asian mind (of which the Hebrew is an example) does not behave in all respects like the Western. This is a fact which is seldom emphasised as it should be. When Westerners differ they hammer out their differences like the blacksmith fixing two pieces of hot metal. Neither is really satisfied with the accord when the compromise is made, but both are glad that conflict has ceased. A formula is found that can enable the parties to work together without loss of prestige on either side.

The Asian mind does not work in that way. When Asians of roughly equal prestige differ, possessing different insights, both are right! The two versions would be set down side by side with no serious attempt to harmonise them. Where a Western mind would eliminate the incongruous or arrange the alternatives in an order of priority, the Asian conglomerates all. An example of this is to be found at Lk. 24:1,10. Luke was a Greek, a Westerner, but he was steeped in Jewish learning and considered himself an apprentice of the Hebrew civilization. He starts by saying that 'to the tomb there came (ladies) bearing *aromata* (spices) which they had prepared', and much later we are told, 'And they were Mary Magdalene and Joanna and Mary the mother(?) of James'. One could be forgiven for supposing that it was some misguided elegance that postpones the names of the ladies to that point, where in fact Luke insists that other women joined them in conveying information to the apostles. As a matter of fact Luke has found it difficult to understand Mark's report at Mk. 15:47 of two named ladies and at 16:1 (the next verse) of three named ladies, only one of whom obviously corresponds, suspecting an inartistic suture, and has joined two traditions, or two versions of one tradition together, and proceeds in that way because he has an incidental purpose to pursue (p.110).

An attempt to study the lowest common denominator of the post-Anastasis appearances would be rejected by their own authors as much as by modern 'redaction critics'. The latter take the view that the appearances do not directly relate to any event behind the 'curtain of redaction' (i.e. an editor-author's own mind), but express only the state of intention at the time of composition, stage by stage. They are, in short, adaptation of 'theophany' (an individual experience of the divine), God's revealing himself actively to man after the style of Old Testament theophany. The authors themselves, who would perfectly understand this bizarre explanation and see much good sense in it, would reject my common-denominator approach, on the ground that each story is active as a whole, and that there never was a common pool of stimuli, a common pond-bed, as it were, in which, like lilies, each passage grew.

But our present technique is different. None of the 'invented' passages, to which the post-Anastasis appearances belong, arose without stimulus expanded with insight, and it happens that if you add these recovered stimuli together they do tell an intelligible tale. The burden of proof then shifts upon the objectors to show that the tale is false in itself.

6

The stripping down of invented passages is much harder than the stripping down of the other major type of communication. The latter is after all built on reminiscence, if doctored to make it part of a substitute 'holy scripture'. The former may be conceived in the first place as a continuation of that holy scripture. The secondary nature of these passages is obvious when one realises to how large a degree they are built out of débris from the authentic pre-Crucifixion material! The curiosity of the churches mounted, and the want of genuine reminiscences of those very few days Jesus lived again gave rise to fabrication. The want of the genuine gives occasion for the production of the counterfeit. That fabrication was done, however, by highly-skilled people in full view of the most critical audience any author has had. It is entitled to our respect, and no talk about 'redaction-curtains' must hinder our appraising it.

4. MARK'S METHODS.

Doubly dependent as they were on Mark, the others, heirs to his major ideas, force us to be frank about what Mark hoped to achieve. They after all, and particularly Matthew, prolonged the line Mark had drawn.

It was never Mark's intention to compile a retrospective diary of Jesus or to draw up a biography, least of all one that would let us into his self-development. Even the soliloquy and the extraordinary conversations in the Garden are an editor's depiction of a traditional story. Mark's ability is shown in his attempt to reveal God's plan for Israel working out relentlessly, in spite of appearances and by means of the most unlikely media. The school, or sect of John the Baptist is superseded and the promised Saviour comes on to the scene to enact a Redemption, parallel to, but finally completing, the Redemption by God (through Moses) of the Israelites from Egypt. Popular fancies, biblical themes, and legendary elements coalesce and cohere in the life of Jesus. Mark is a historian steeped in theology. Consequently many factual details are given to us not because they are facts but because of the load of implications under which we find them labouring —seen, of course, with the eye of faith.

The centurion testifies to Jesus's being truly a son of God (Mk. 15:39) not because a Roman centurion said so but because testimony is wrung from a most unlikely quarter—inadequate testimony on all accounts, but testimony. Irony runs right through the gospel, like a dye. The Temptation (Mk. 1:12-13) is where it is not because Jesus left a testimony of his reasons for not taking up secular opportunities available to him (as I do not doubt he did, it was very congruent to his message), but because in his own person Jesus must relive the experiences of Adam after the Creation and the Israelites in the Desert of Sinai. When Matthew and Luke take up this hint—and they must be following a common source here— irony has gone a stage further. Satan offers three boons to Jesus, who rejects them as offered, knowing that he will, at the end of the day, achieve all of them in a way Satan himself could not foreknow!

Mark does not hand on some scrap of tradition because it was true, but because it was meaningful. Judas Iscariot is remembered by name because Judah sold his brother Joseph out of envy to the Midianites and Iscariot means

7

'Business-friendship/love'[6] The man at Gerasa is remembered to have been there because the Hebrew root from which 'Gerasa' (now a ruin by the southern tip of the Sea of Galilee) could be fancied to come means 'take possession', as in 'spirit-possession'. Simon of Cyrene is remembered as the one who carried the Cross, because Simeon the Patriarch most desperately wanted Joseph killed, not sold, and the Hebrew root QRH, from which Cyr- with an ending meaning 'me' could be fancied to come, means at one and the same time 'to meet somebody by accident' and 'to fit something (or somebody!) with a (construction-) beam'![7] Perhaps he was viewed as a 'son of the prophets' as at 2 K. 6:2? The disciples of John the Baptist buried their master's corpse (Mk. 6:29) not because they did so —as we can be sure they did—but (in part) because Jesus's disciples did *not*. And so on. The ladies are asked not to be stupefied when the Young Man speaks to them (*mē ekthambeisthe*: Mk. 16:6) not because they were stupefied ('dithering') (*exethambēthēsan*: Mk. 16:5)—as no doubt they were—but because such stupefaction was appropriate to those who, in their perplexities, receive a blinding impression of the divinity who reveals himself (Mk. 9:9,15). And stupefaction, not cool comprehension, is the correct way to receive the news that the body was no longer there.

The Young Man himself, I suspect, is not there because there *was* a young man—as no doubt there was. He represents the theme of fulfilment. As we shall see, only the *young man* has the insight (Mk. 14:51) and therefore the fruition must be his also (Mk. 16:5). It would be as well to suppose that no piece of information is in Mark simply because it was authentic tradition—so much has inevitably been left out. Every piece worked for its position in the gospel, and some passages worked hard.

Take for example the *ladies* at the tomb. First their identity: Mary of the Tower (Magdala), Mary the mother of James the Younger and Joses/Joseph, and Salome (whose name means 'My welfare' or 'My peace') were required in the story, as told, to watch the Crucifixion (Mk. 15:40) as well as to visit the tomb. Mary the 'Magdalene' was reputedly cured of possession by Jesus (Lk. 8:2) and was subsequently his follower (a pattern well known to anthropologists). But neither she nor her companions were disciples in the conventional sense (a male preserve)—they looked after him and no doubt after the inner company of male disciples with him. They were affectionate strangers. Next, one of them was the mother of a Joseph, and not only was Jesus regarded officially as a son of a Joseph, but he trod the path of the Patriarch Joseph. Matthew picked this up from the mere name 'Judas Iscariot', and developed it hugely with legendary material, borrowing the scene of Pilate's wife from the *Testament of Joseph* and the behaviour of Judas partly from the *Testament of Zebulon* and that of *Gad:* the material in the *Testaments of the XII Patriarchs* was based on ancient *haggadah* (legend) surrounding the authentic book of Genesis, and therefore was a fair quarry for an evangelist.[8] To return to the *ladies*, they were where they are because they were, as women, 'second-class citizens' and thus they were highly suitable: they were the first 'contacts' of Jesus to receive the message that he had passed the barrier of death, he who was, during his lifetime, exceptionally sympathetic to women.

It is no accident that women have figured largely in his cult ever since. The climax of Mark's gospel is a recitation actually fitted to an Easter pilgrimage to the Sepulchre in which women could well have played the major part.

I must now deal with the anticipated objection that serious and responsible persons cannot have composed their enormously important works placing such irrational importance in relatively trifling items of fact, e.g. a young man was dressed in white. This underrates the oriental mind. An orientalist would find no difficulty here. Let me relate something that happened only a while ago. A Japanese religious organisation started a mission in London and sent, strangely, as their pioneer a young man we can call 'K' who was slow-witted. Unsympathetic critics called him feeble-minded. After three years, by which time he had broken a path for a much abler man, he was sensibly recalled. The abler man later requiring a helper, many names were put forward, amongst which persons senior to K, and, of course, much more intelligent, were short-listed. When it came to the selection a question was asked about his performance in England. There were only two pieces of information. He had passed the most elementary examination in English. And he had pruned my apple trees, which bore a good crop the following year. The directorate convened, the matter was discussed. K's turn arose. He had passed an examination in the church's college. Good. What had he done in England? He had passed the English examination. Good. And he had succesfully pruned apple trees. *What? Pruned? Which* trees? *Apple* trees! By an unanimous decision it was resolved that K return to London without delay on an enhanced allowance; and so a highly coveted opportunity was won to the chagrin of all his competitors. The resolution was taken by a Board of Directors, every one of whom is a businessman, the identical folk who are at present laying waste the industries of the Western world! I am afraid Europeans are very far from understanding the mentality of such men.

The evangelist hears that the beam of the Cross was carried by one Simon, and he says, 'Of course, it would be a Simeon', and he hears that the traitor who denounced Jesus to the hierarchy was a Judas, and he says, 'Of course, it would be a Judah', and then he hears that his name was 'Business-friendship', and he writes 'he betrayed his Master with a kiss'. Now I have shown my reader how the texts are to be understood, not merely with a footling 'antiquarian' interest,[9] but in order to retrace the steps of the authors who are widely believed to authenticate an enduring fragment of truth.

Mark's methods are particularly well illustrated by 1:16 ('for they were fishermen'). Jesus, who was domiciled in the land traditionally allocated to the tribe of Zabulun, goes to the Lake of Galilee to recruit fellow-workers. Zebulunites are traditionally merchants and therefore interested in partnership (cf. Lk. 5:10). The eastern seaboard of the Lake belonged to the tribe of Naphtali, who were traditionally swift bearers of good news (Gen. 49:21) and that tribe traditionally had a monopoly of fishing in the Lake with nets. Mark 1:16 is there not because Simon and Andrew were fishermen—indeed they were, and Jesus went quite a distance to recruit them because they were—but because Mark wants to show the scenario formerly laid down by the Holy Spirit gradually unfolding itself[10].

If such techniques were used at the outset of the story we shall not be surprised to find them at its climax. Take the Last Supper. Mark makes it abundantly clear that it was at the Last Supper that the fact of Judas's denunciation (*m^esîrâ*), or betrayal as it is usually called, was settled, announced, activated (Mk. 14:17-21). John is even clearer about it. He goes to lengths to emphasise the point, with the 'sop' (Jn. 13:21-28). The particularly Jewish phenomenon called *m^esîrâ* (denunciation of a fellow-member to outsiders to be destroyed by them) is essential to the story of Salvation (as I shall explain: p.120). And the great *m^esîrâ* of Jewish scripture and legend was the sale of Joseph down into Egypt. It was concocted when 'they sat down to eat bread' (Gen. 37:25). The evangelist seems to have put two and two together; but it is quite possible that Jesus himself was not merely *aware* of a parallel, but actually created it, in which case his remarkable dramatic sense was at work.[11] The modern theologians' habit to reject any procedure to which they themselves could not have been parties is anachronistic and unrealistic.

The question of Mark's date arises. I take the view that he wrote about A.D. 50, whereas modern scholars generally assume A.D. 70-75 to be much more nearly right. Their reasons are many, including 'Latinisms' and material suggesting that Mark wrote for Romans. These latter are mare's nests and I shall waste no time on them. The chief reason for the late dating is Mk. 13. The predictions of a cataclysm in that chapter are said to prove that he must have written after the First Roman War was well advanced. But this ignores a fact which ought to be well known. Attacks on the Temple[12], and messianic movements, including ecstatic-apocalytic manifestations, were on the one hand accompaniments of political unrest, in particular that caused by foreign rule, and on the other portents of God's movement within and on behalf of his people. That a powerful charismatic leader should *not* foretell vast upheavals in language reminiscent of the Old Testament prophets would be strange. Mk. 13:1-2 is actually about the destruction of the Temple, but it is clear that this is afar-off, impending yet not specifically predictable (vv.7,20,33). Jesus rightly sees the prophetic predictions as of permanent relevance. The actual destruction of Jerusalem in A.D. 135 would not exhaust such predictions! Of *every* generation it is true that 'this generation shall not pass away until all these things be accomplished'. 'Woe to Jerusalem' was, as we know, not a call to be made only *after* her fall. Quite irrespective of any rational predictions Jesus may have made, his own charismatic movement carried with it just such outbursts. Political attacks on the Temple caused ecstatic manifestations; ecstatic manifestations would predict the fall of the Temple (cf. Mk. 14:57-59). For the evangelists this was especially valuable as they believed Jesus to be a perfect substitute for the Temple—a belief which naturally arose after the Anastasis.

If we do not date Mark early we have no time for the development of Matthew, Luke, and John (who is not, in my view, an early evangelist) before Ignatius testifies to fully-formed Christian doctrine, and the first papyri begin to appear, showing that the material was circulating widely. And Paul's baroque theology will have presupposed the use of a sober 'narrative' in liturgy well within his own lifetime.

1. So Hooke (1967), 29, 31, 50-1, 107, 116. Lindars (1961), 65, 66 n.2 requires revision as unduly influenced by Hos 6:2 LXX (where of course *anastēsometha* does occur).

2. Derrett at *Donum Gentilicium. Fest. Daube* (Oxford, 1978), 78ff., reprinted at *Studies* III (1982).

3. On the roots see Fascher (1941), 166ff.; Schnackenburg (1967); Delling (1970); Evans (1970), 20-5; Spörlein (1971), 31-37; cf. Knox (1944), 20 n.1.

3a. Fascher, Spörlein (above); B. Rigaux at Kremer in Dhanis (1974), 181.

3b. C. C. Torrey, *Lives* (1946), 27.

3c. Schubert in Dhanis (1974), 207-8.

4. ix-x. Text at Aland, *Synopse,* 498; translation in M. R. James, *Apocryphal New Testament* (Oxford, 1955), 92-3.

5. H. W. Hollander, *Joseph as an Ethical Model in the Testaments of the Twelve Patriarchs* (Leiden, 1981).

6. *Downside Rev.,* Oct. 1979, reprinted in *Studies* III (1982). I ignore the Syriac root SQR as it is not known to have had the use 'envy', 'hate' at our period (I am obliged to Dr. Sebastian Brock for drawing my attention to it).

7. Ibid. The people of Cyrene, who fancied that the twin gods, the Dioscuri, were their protectors, would be just the people to carry a beam, or an arrangement of beams, since that was the symbol of the Heavenly Twins.

8. Ibid., and see n.5.

9. As suggested by Prof. D. E. Nineham, 'New Testament interpretation in an historical age', *Explorations in Theology* I (London, 1977), 145, commented upon unfavourably by Prof. N. Lash at Horbury & McNeil (1981), 189-90.

10. *N.T.* 22 (1980), 108-137, reprinted in *Studies* III (1982).

11. *J.S.N.T.* (1980), 2-23, reprinted in *Studies* III (1982).

12. E. Schürer, *History of the Jewish People* II (2nd edn., Edinburgh, 1979), 606, n.60 refers to *B.J.* 1.347, an incident of the time of Herod!

CHAPTER II
Current Notions about the Anastasis.
A Negative Picture.

To Mark as to Paul (who says so) there was no question but that Jesus rose from the dead. The faith of Christians depended on it, and not upon some existential hypothesis. That knowledge had even acquired a poetical shape well within a generation of the Crucifixion! Christ was the 'first-born', not of some existential hypothesis, but 'of the dead' (Col. 1:18, 1 Cor. 15:20, Acts 26:23). What was not so clear was the point of Jesus's rising — or had it multiple points? To the average man it hardly proved a distinct thing — while to a believer it could prove almost too much. To Paul (as we saw) it was an essential. But to the evangelists who succeeded Mark it disagreed with all previous expectations including those for which (in their own accounts) Jesus himself was responsible.

When Jesus said, thrice, that he would 'rise again' (p.79), the phrase in its context meant that, despite the rough handling he would receive as a victim of $m^e\hat{sira}$, he would awaken after three days, i.e. participate in due course in bliss (p.105), which anyone would suppose referred to resurrection, i.e. *the* resurrection. He would, as it were, be justified then by God.

Let no one say that the evangelists have no sense of humour. At Mk. 9:9, shortly after the first prediction of the Passion (Mk. 8:31-32), Jesus, having revealed his identity through the experience of the Transfiguration, tells the three disciple-participant-witnesses not to divulge what they had seen, 'until the Son of man gets up (*anastēi*) from (among) the dead'. The hearers then solemnly debated (so we are told) what it meant, 'to get up from (among) the dead', as well they might. With gospel irony Mark tells us something withheld from *them*. It was as if Jesus was quoting from Zeph. 3:8 LXX ('therefore await me, says the Lord, until the day of my Anastasis unto [or for] testimony'), a text which literally promises *God's* coming to visit Jerusalem at the Last Judgement, and also his opening the way for gentiles to worship him with a single mind! From Mark's point of view Jesus's Anastasis is predicted by him as God's *rising up* for the punishment of Jews and redemption of all nations. The joke is on the disciples, who are shown guessing that Jesus meant merely the resurrection, pointing out, rationally, that they themselves might not be still alive to divulge anything, since (even) Elijah must come first (Mal. 4:5); Popular ideas linked the return of Elijah with the (subsequent) coming of the Messiah, and the arrival of the World-to-Come. When Jesus answered (9:13) that Elijah *had* come (presumably in the shape of the Baptist, but one wonders?) their perplexity continues. There was no popular expectation (as we have seen) that any messianic figure would undergo *anastasis*.

Jesus's Anastasis, therefore, did not correspond with what was conveyed to the inner group of disciples after the Transfiguration, nor to the disciples at large in the three predictions of the Passion. What he told even the three chosen witnesses of Jesus's true, 'transfigured', glorified identity — during and after their trance experience—neither prepared them for what happened nor offered any explanation—in retrospect—for what did happen.

Mark's gospel, therefore, emphasizes, not the Anastasis itself, but the path to it, and the cosmic significance of it, concentrating on the Redemption-aspect, on Jesus's teaching (not so scarce in Mark as is usually thought), his blue-print for an Age still to be born. Mark leaves out the details of the Anastasis, for they were not vitally important. The churches for whom he wrote may even have been in doubt which elements of tradition were reliable, edifying and theologically conclusive. The facts—the chief of which was known to every Christian—had stupefied all persons actually concerned. Thereafter they could review Jesus's life on earth and piece it together in an intelligible pattern. Then it became, for the first time, compelling. That much, indeed, the churches could accept; and they were sufficiently relaxed to see in some widespread pagan notions (to which they were heirs before their baptism) some virtue of which Christianity, in its world enviroment, could take advantage.

The modern reader thus finds no direct statement in the gospels that Jesus revived in the tomb, came out, and took up the threads of his work. Peter, about whom so much *is* said, is never depicted as having certified those details. No witness is led forward to proclaim that he saw the Risen Lord shortly after his revival, saw him in the ordinary sense of the word 'to see'. The well-known statement of Paul in 1 Cor. 15 is equivocal (p.97), and it is therefore as easily set aside by some as it can be recruited by others as a prominent piece of corroborative testimony.

The leading modern treatments of the Anastasis lean heavily towards the negative. Professor Macquarrie, after mentioning how the modernist E. Le Roy rejected the miraculous stories of the empty tomb and claimed that 'the resurrection possesses reality of the highest order, though this can be known only to the life of faith within the Church, which is Christ's body,' passes to the scientist, Bishop E. W. Barnes. He wrote on the Resurrection as a great essential truth of Christianity, but one 'which is quite independent of the question as to whether the body of Jesus was reanimated after his death. What matters is that Christians shall feel a spiritual power in their lives, which they can rightly interpret as that of the spirit of Jesus revealing, as in his teaching in Galilee, the wisdom and righteousness of God.' Marquarrie admits that 'the question of an adequate theology of resurrection is an open question', [1a] and it is obvious that such an open question gives professional scholars a most attractive scope for speculation and debate. To them the conservative position taken by L. Sabourin in the traditionally-orientated volume *Resurrexit,*[1b] 'the bodily resurrection of Jesus is not only historically secure, it is a theological necessity' (1 Cor. 15:17), is a provocation.

Let us suppose a traditional-conservative scholar being asked, 'How should one teach this to a confirmation class, composed of sceptical youngsters?' If he replies, 'Teach them that Christ was raised by God in the tomb' he is only rephrasing the question in other words. Evasion and prevarication are the inevitable consequence. '. . . In the last resort Christians believe in the risen Lord and only by implication in the Resurrection.' The nature of the event which caused the Easter faith is taken by scholars to be incapable of being contained in any historical narrative, especially one which presupposes an exploded cosmology.

When D. F. Strauss came to consider the case for Jesus's revival he could not bring himself to overcome practical objections: where did he lodge after revival; what was the air like in the tomb; why assume such a thing anyway? Bultmann was very downright: 'The resurrection itself is not an event of past history. All that historical criteria can establish is the fact that the first disciples came to believe in the resurrection . . . the historical event of the rise of the Easter faith means for us what it meant for the first disciples — namely, the self-manifest-ation of the risen Lord, the act of God in which the redemptive event of the cross is completed.' Two much more recent writers have come up with an intri-guing idea, the vacuity of which escapes both of them: 'The historical fact is that the apostles put a question to everyone: "Are you too prepared to believe that Jesus rose from the dead?" '; the upshot of the historical event, whatever it was, is that man is challenged to say whether he believes. Wilckens says, 'We are not doing justice to the truth of the original testimony and the experiences transmitted in the testimony if we only establish that what the New Testament reports narrate as events, did "historically" actually take place . . .' One feels that if proof of the actual Anastasis of Jesus came to hand academic theologians would grieve: their ingenuity might be devalued and their freedom might be infringed.[2] The discovery of the Talpioth ossuaries thirty-five years ago found them unable to adjust to an increase in factual data. Schillebeeckx says of the resurrection that it arose from the conviction that sins had been forgiven. John the Baptist's mission survived him; why should not Jesus's? Consciousness of having been saved [how?] gave rise to the notion that, in a sense, Jesus 'rose again'; Easter means 'being converted.'[2a] Rochais puts it somewhat differently: 'to believe in the risen Jesus is to affirm that the promise of God has found its fulfilment in him; that the messianic era and the End of Time have been inaugurated; and that in him all Scripture has been accomplished. The meaning of the Jesus-event was not confined within the limits of his terrestrial life . . .'[2b]

To some, 'We have no means of knowing what would count for or against the declaration that Jesus is risen, and granting our empirical attitudes, we would say that it is not an empirical assertion. . . The statement "Jesus is risen". . . does not signify a movement from a sense-content statement, "He appeared to me", to an empirical assertion. It is a movement to an "end-word" statement which is verified by the conduct of the man who uses it.'[2c]

We have come a long way from 1920 (immediately after the First World War) when an influential and gifted clerical teacher (Henry Major) was accused of heresy and an inquisition into him instituted because what he taught conflicted with the credal formula, 'I believe in the resurrection of the body'.

Yet it is hard for the scholar to deny the Anastasis outright. When that is done clearly and honestly, as Professor W. Marxsen did, one is persecuted by churchmen, who realise that if the doctrine of Christ's rising from the dead is denied by their functionaries church-taxes will be endangered. Marxsen was able to retain his university post, but lost a great deal of sleep over the conservatives' tactics against him. He insisted (as he informs me) that they should debate the problem with him in public. This would have compelled them to expose *their* notions of the Anastasis, and this they were not prepared to do, and so he out-manœuvred them.

How they would have fared had they accepted the challenge is shown by the comparatively conservative scholar, C. H. Dodd. He wrote 'I should be disposed to conclude that while the general tradition held that Christ "rose from the dead" (commonly understood to mean that he emerged from the tomb in which his body had been laid) it preserved also a genuine memory that on that Sunday morning his tomb was found broken open [*sic*] and to all appearances empty. At first the discovery was disconcerting and incomprehensible; later it was understood to mean that Jesus had in some way left his tomb. Whether this meaning was rightly attached to it, and if so in what sense, is another question, and one which lies no longer in the sphere of the historian. He may properly suspend judgement'.[3]

As things stand teachers have to teach and students have to learn matter which is neither historically verifiable nor capable of falsification: *and at the same time it is agreed that Christianity is a historical faith in the sense that it stems from one event in history, namely the Anastasis!* It is in the light of the Anastasis that every part of the New Testament was written! And yet no one can explain it. This is most unsatisfactory. For scholars claim as the one decisive and distinguishing characteristic of Christianity over against other religions a fact which, when defined by themselves, turns out to be a void or a question-mark.

R. R. Niebuhr (1957) says, 'the resurrection of Christ does not violate Nature but only death (!). It epitomizes the original creativity that informs all history and underlies every conception of Nature'. Equivocation, prevarication, and mystification abound. Ved Mehta[4] says, after a little enquiring around, 'there are very few theologians today who believe the Resurrection actually happened', a discovery no doubt comforting to a Hindu. One cannot quarrel with Eberling,[5] 'It is unworthy of Jesus and of the Christian faith to dodge the issue here, whether by making a *sacrificium intellectus* along with weighty assertions of what you do not understand, or by deceiving oneself and others by means of apologetic and dialectical tricks or by making do with a phantom faith, in resigned or superficial mood'. Rationalistic and naturalistic attempts to explain the Anastasis are quickly condemned,[6] but equivocal statements take their place,[7] or prevarication.[8]

The outlook of Marxsen is perhaps typical of our age. It was the faith of Simon Peter which constituted the church.[9] This outlook keeps close to the texts and relies on their evidence that early Christians believed (Lk. 24:34) Peter 'saw' the Lord.[10] Their belief in Peter's subjective vision was the foundation of the church, in accordance with the saying, 'Thou art Peter, and upon this Rock I shall build my church' (Mt. 16:18).

H. Braun says, 'The decisive turning-point (for Jesus's authority) is the conviction, on the part of his dependants, that he did not remain in death after his death on the Cross.' It was only in course of time that 'the Resurrection' (in which Jesus shows the way to the disciples) 'was understood as an actual coming out of the tomb.'[11] What caused that conviction no one knows!

An existential view of the Anastasis is that it is a summons to each man to renounce the security of this world and rise with Christ here and now to his own real existence. The Easter events have no other meaning, *whatsoever they may have been* (!). To faith facts are in the last resort matters of indifference (!). It matters less what we believe than who *he* is in *whom* we believe. Professor E. Schweizer says, [12] 'Jesus without Easter would be a dead Jesus, a figure of the past', but, as to the Anastasis, what he says amounts only to this that it is nowhere proved, but that Jesus probably appeared to his former disciples from heaven, as the exalted Lord. He says, ' . . . proof cannot be given of Jesus's resurrection. Here, too, very much as in the crucifixion of Jesus, God exposes himself to scepticism, doubt and disbelief, renouncing anything that would compel men to believe . . . All the accounts show unequivocally that the discovery of the empty tomb did not awaken anyone's faith; this was done by the risen Lord himself, who encountered his disciples.' '. . . the assurance is based only on Jesus himself, the risen Lord.' All the New Testament witnesses understood Easter primarily as a call to service, 'unexpected and uncomfortable.'[13] Here, if I may be allowed to say so, we find sermon-material invading the interpretation of the texts, a phenomenon recently adverted to by Professor N. Lash.[13a]

Schweizer's outlook is as popular and widely welcomed as it is subtle and plausible: 'Even the first Christian community did not gain its assurance of the resurrection by learning of a demonstrable miracle that had taken place and repeating a proposition about it, but by living under the dominion of the risen Lord.'[14] Resurrection is 'communion recovered after the cross, which is annihilating violence.'[14a] This is widely welcomed because it links the student (soon to be a curate or a high-school teacher) with the earliest church. His problems were theirs.

A more refined equivocation is offered by R. C. Ware,[15] who shows us where we stand with these 'plausibilities' without technical aid.

Since Jesus is an historical figure, one cannot meaningfully speak about his resurrection at all without recourse to historical facts. Since we are concerned essentially with religious experience, not every interpretation which accounts for historical data is for that very reason a 'correct' interpretation. If the abstract models of interpretation are to be expressive of living relationships, they must represent concrete models of experience. It is true that historical research can only provide the raw material for the intuitive discernment of faith. But where, one wonders, is the 'raw material', the experience which warrants discernment of Jesus' resurrection? Here . . . lies the categorical limitation of conventional theological conceptions. All the studies . . . virtually reduce the resurrection itself to a formal sign of an abstract, transcendental event. The sign is either left to stand as an unknown causative factor or else it is filled in retrospect with theological-soteriological and functionalkerygmatic significance. For the functional-casual view, resurrection is ultimately a formal category derived in the history of ideas from the imagery of Jewish apocalytic as a sign of God's meta-historical action in Jesus. Likewise, exegetical studies and theologies which see in the "appearances" revelatory encounters or disclosures of the Crucified and the Risen One in effect only deduce the resurrection and postulate it as cause or at very least *sine qua non* for the origin of resurrection faith. At best such theories are always one step removed from the reality of resurrection itself.

Ware himself prefers not to abandon the Anastasis but to consider the 'resurrection' as a symbol, an energic factor which affects transformation, and the symbol is not postulated or deduced, but itself appears. A revolutionary new relationship of man to God occurs: faith in the earthly Jesus and in the God 'Abba', Jesus's preferred style of addressing the Deity, is transformed into resurrection faith in the God 'Who-raised-Jesus-from-the-dead'. The symbol has created a new image. Jesus's own life and history contained a revelation to the disciples,[16] and the Anastasis completed it.

We are left, then, very much where the form-, source-, and redaction-critics would leave us. Virtue has been made of necessity. 'The Easter experience remains basic — the encounter with the risen Lord.'[17] 'The apostles are Christ's messengers, who have been called by visions of the risen Lord.'[18] 'Jesus's messianic claim was confirmed by God when in the resurrection he created him Son and King of the end-time.'[19] But what was 'the resurrection'? If it never occurred God could have confirmed nothing by it? And if the apostles' ability to react to the encounter with the risen Lord, who never rose, was God's confirmation we are going round and round, effect constituting cause and cause giving birth to effect, both of them imaginary.

My sceptics are prepared to believe that the first Easter set a curious sect on its feet — but there have been many curious sects. Now the miraculous is so useful as a means of getting a sect going that it would need to be invented if none had presented itself (see the intriguing story at Acts 8:18-19). But (I reply) the invention is, in this case, not satisfactorily accomplished. A forger never leaves his dupes in doubt as to his meaning. Yet the Anastasis is nowhere proved by a verbal 'fake photograph', as it were. Admittedly one possible explanation is that it did not occur, and that the whole thing was a hoax: in which case it is a mystery how it stood up in the face of constant Jewish ridicule. Another is that everyone knew it occurred, but their energy, intellectual and emotional, was absorbed by reacting to it, and making sense of it.

A minor parallel is the Virgin Birth. It seems to have been a somewhat banal physiological event[20] (births from women whose hymen is still unbroken are by no means very rare). It too is not noticed in so many words by Mark. It seems to have obtained significance through the matching, perhaps rather a laboured matching, of events with a pre-existing scriptural pattern (Is. 7:14). That notion was itself the result of a Christian interpretation of scripture. The full poetry of the event could not be brought out safely until after the persons concerned were all

17

dead, and so unable to promulgate on their own a gloss on the event which could embarrass the poets.

NOTES

1. The credit of observing that Zeph. 3:8 LXX appertains to the Anastasis of Christ belongs to H. Michaelis (1720!), since forgotten.
1a. Macquarrie (1971), 383. The citations are taken from Macquarrie, 185, 250.
1b. Dhanis (1974), analysed by Sabourin, 'The Resurrection of Jesus', *Bibl. Theol. Bull.* 5 (1975), 262ff., 293.
2. D. H. van Daalen, *The Real Resurrection* (London, 1972); Strauss in Reumann (1970), 120, 358; Bultmann at Bartsch, *Kerygma* (1953), I, 42; Koch (1959), 283; Léon-Dufour (1974), 207; Wilckens (1977), 131-2.
2a. Schillebeeckx (1979), 379, 391-4.
2b. Rochais (1981), 189.
2c. P. van Buren, *The Secular Meaning of the Gospel* (Harmondsworth, 1963), 136.
3. Dodd (1971), 167.
4. V. Mehta (1965), 34.
5. G. Eberling, *The Nature of Faith* (London, 1964), 63.
6. Künneth (1966), 28.
7. Clark (1967), 95.
8. Evans (1970), 180 quoting Pannenberg, 174, quoting V. A. Harvey on K. Barth.
9. Marxsen (1970), 96.
10. Cf. Enslin (1953), 53, Gils (1962), 5-43. Protests against this approach: O'Collins (1973), 34. But it persists: Pesch, *Simon-Petrus* (1980), 49-59.
11. *Jesus. Der Mann aus Nazareth und seine Zeit* (Stutt./Berlin, 1969), 151-3.
12. E. Schweizer, *Jesus* (Eng. trans., London, 1971, 1978), 190.
13. Ibid. 48-50.
13a. Horbury & McNeil (1981), 183ff.
14. Ibid., 50.
14a. Dumas (1981), 590.
15. Ware at *Hey .J.* 16 (1975), 184-5.
16. Ibid., 185, 188-9, 192.
17. O. Betz, *What do we Know about Jesus?* (Eng. trans., London, 1968), 103-4.
18. Ibid., 105.
19. Ibid., 114.
20. Derrett, 'La nascita di Gesù . . . ', *Con. Rel.* 1972, 221-5 and references there given, reprinted at *Studies* II (1978), 33ff.

18

CHAPTER III

Anastasis in the Ancient Western World.

Mark does not show us the point at which Jesus rose. His aim is not secular history. As if at a tangent, he brings us within reach of that which he does not show. He falls short of showing us the sun's rays, through smoked glasses. But at the same time he does more than that: he shows the effect of whatever happened upon those nearest to it. Perhaps that coincided with his church's reception of that news. Small wonder that modern critics, even the arch-sceptic R. Bultmann, praise him for his 'restraint', whilst inclining to believe that nothing objective happened to Jesus which was — in itself and by itself — of any consequence. So they concentrate on a void. It has not occurred to them that Mark may have had an excellent reason for not claiming in so many words that Jesus rose, or had been revived, a reason quite other than a simple want of trustworthy evidence that he rose or had been revived! If there was one such reason it could also explain why Paul also, our earliest literary witness of what was believed about A.D. 35 in Jerusalem, blurs the image of a most vital element in the faith he was disseminating.

Death was taught by Greek moralists and philosophers as no evil in itself. On the contrary the only death complained of by the philosopher was that of a promising child, or of a youth in full vigour, and he was not a little ashamed even of that regret. Death was welcomed if it was a release from troubles, torture, sickness, senility, or despair. Some said life was inherently troublesome and that for many, if not most people, it would have been a boon not to have been born at all. The Greco-Roman world was used to teachers who taught that death should not be feared — only a dishonourable life, or a life that had not been lived to the height of one's natural potential.

The idea of *return from death to life again* was not inherently agreeable, and surely offered nothing to the serious person. Of course one could have fun with the notion, and legend obliged. Hermotimus, honoured by the people of Clazomenæ, wandered after his death and reanimated his body from time to time.[1] Transmigration of souls was widely believed in. Æsop experienced one, so we are told,[1a] and Herod believed that John the Baptist had undergone one (Mk. 6:14 and parallels), a fact to which we must return (p.97). Perhaps the poet could use the idea of return from death — and indeed the creative mind could find some value in it. That a lover might wish his beloved to return, like Eurydice, from the dead, was as beautiful as it was reasonable. Alcestis, too, might return at the poet's command. Whether the beloved would have the same eagerness, given the chance of an even choice, is not enquired into. No doubt lovers have the privilege of transcending death in a poetical sense.[2] But in a civilization which believed in bliss for the good and torment for the wicked after death, return from death could be an embarrassment. Naturally, for it rarely occurred. But occur it did, as it still does: and every-

19

one knew it, as we shall see.

Meanwhile the concept of periodical death and rebirth was known: the deities of nature gave expression to the belief in the rhythmic decay of winter and the revival of spring. But this has nothing to do with our subject, and the dying and rising god of fertility cults, e.g. Adonis, has no contact with primitive Christianity. As for Attis there is something to be said (p.131). On the other hand the Hellenistic world was quite familiar with the desire for immortality. Immortality is the transcending of physical death and perpetual survival as a person. Not only philosophers sought to prove that that was the soul's right. Immortality however, even though it could be obtained by sacrifice and devotion to a deity that proffered it, had nothing to do with physical revival from death. On the contrary, one who revived from death denied thereby that he had qualified for immortality, at least this time round.

The scientist of the ancient Western world knew two interesting facts he could not account for: (1) persons declared dead did sometimes revive, and (2) there were specialists in the art of knowing when the apparently dead were capable of being revived. An exorcist might add this peculiar skill to his accomplishments.

Valerius Maximus, writing between A.D. 27 and 31, was a contemporary of Jesus, though, of course, a thoroughly Roman person. He reports two interesting cases. Acilius Aviola, believed to be dead both by physicians and members of his household, was laid out at home for a period and taken out for cremation. The fire touched his body and he called out that he was alive and sought the help of his 'pedagogue' who happened to be the only person who stayed after the pyre was lit. He could not, however, be 'withdrawn from Fate' because the flames completely surrounded him (as they should, of course). Evidence was forthcoming, too, that when a gentleman of prætorian rank, Lucius Lamius, was on his funeral pyre he too cried out.[2a] Valerius comments that such instances throw light on Plato's creation, Er the Pamphylian, who lay for ten days on the field of battle, of whom more later.

Aulus Cornelius Celsus, who was born about 25 B.C. and lived during the reign of Tiberius, wrote on medicine. A passage directly bearing on our subject deserves to be reproduced here:[3]

I know I may be asked, if the signs of impending death are certain, how are we to account for the occasional revival (and recovery) of patients given up by their attendants? There are reports of individuals who came to life again (*revixisse*) actually during the funeral. A man who justly bears a great reputation, Democritus, laid down that there were no sufficient indications even of actual death in which physicians might have complete confidence. In consequence he never admitted that there were definite indications of impending death. In reply I might go so far as to say that certain approximate indications are adopted which commonly deceive unskilled physicians, but at any rate not experts. It happened to Asclepiades [a medical man of the first century, possibly Celsus's contemporary] that he met a funeral procession and detected that the 'deceased' was actually still alive. It would be a mistake

20

to attribute a fault to the art of medicine which is really to be laid at the door of its practitioners. I may however tentatively add that medicine is a *conjectural art,* and the characteristic of a conjecture is such that, though it very often serves, at times it deceives. One is not to reject as an indication that which answers in innumerable cases, simply because it leads one astray in perhaps one case in a thousand.

I may interject here that no one pretends that Joseph of Arimathæa (of whom much more later) or his servants were trained in medicine; they will have relied on the expert knowledge of the centurion and crucifixion party, about which we can form no close estimate. What is interesting is that those experts (according to St. John [19:34]) applied a test which was, until recently, regarded as sufficient even by physicians in the case of suspected death, though not in a case of hysterical paralysis.

Pliny the Elder, a sober, meticulous, and indefatigable collector of facts on every conceivable subject, assembled his material at considerable pains between A.D. 50 and 77, i.e. during the lifetimes of Mark and Matthew, and therefore of the apostles who were always capable of monitoring the gospel as it developed. He has provided a chapter devoted entirely to revivals of the dead:[4]

Aviola, an ex-consul, revived on the pyre, and, since the heat of the fire prevented succour reaching him, was cremated alive. Lucius Lamina, an ex-prætor, is said to have had a like experience [M. Valerius]. Messala Rufus [c. 103-27/26 B.C., a most respectable person] and numerous others relate that Caius Ælius Tubero, who held a prætorship, was brought back (alive) from the very pyre. *This is a condition of mortals.* We are born to such curiosities of fortune as this, with the result that one should not believe even in a person's death . . . To this topic belongs the splendid Greek work of Heraclides [390-310 B.C.] concerning the woman recalled to life after being lifeless for seven days. Varro [the famous antiquary and literateur, 116-27 B.C.] also reports that when he was boundary commissioner at Capua a man who was being carried out (for cremation) in the forum, returned home on his own feet. The same thing happened in Aquinum. Also that Corfidus, the husband of his own mother's sister, came to life again after his funeral had been arranged and subsequently took out the funeral of that same funeral-arranger! He adds marvels which could usefully have been given in their entirety. There were two brothers Corfidii of the equestrian order. It happened that the elder appeared to have expired, and when his will was opened the younger was found to be appointed heir and took charge of the funeral. Meanwhile he, who appeared to be extinct, clapped his hands, summoned the attendants, related he had just come from his brother, who had commended his daughter to his care, and revealed furthermore, where he had buried some gold unknown to everyone else, and asked that he should be borne out in the same funeral rites which he had been preparing. While he was passing on this information, his brother's servants rushed in and announced that he was dead, and subsequently the gold was found at the spot indicated.

21

The case of the Corfidii is of particular interest, but I postpone discussion of it for the present. At the end of the passage Pliny himself says, 'there are also cases of persons appearing after burial — save that our subject is the works of nature, not prodigies'.[5]

Diogenes Laertius, who seems to have lived in the third century A.D., repeats[5a] the reference to Heraclides and the lifeless woman, *apnous*, 'through whom Empedocles obtained glory by sending away alive a dead person' (*aposteilas tēn nekran anthrōpon zōsan*).

Lucian, who lived between A.D. 120 and 180 and had a superficial knowledge of Christians, was familiar with this phenomenon and plays with it. He introduces in one place the physician Antigonos who asks the question: 'What is remarkable in that? . . . I know of a person who rose again (*anastanta*) after the twentieth day(!) from his burial, and I attended him both before his death and when the man rose again (*epeidē anestē*)'.[6] In another of his works Alexander of Abonuteichos claimed to have raised (*anastēseie*) several deceased persons.[7] The reader will have noticed the Greek verb used here, cognate with *anastasis*.

Apuleius, who was born in A.D. 125, tells the story of Asclepiades (above). Unguents and spices were prepared for the corpse. The physician stopped the cortège. He handled the body and detected life. 'He lives.' Some mocked. The heirs vigorously objected (a point worth remembering)! Drugs later recalled the dead to life.[8] Apuleius is a great writer, and he would use no theme for which his public was unprepared and which it could not thoroughly enjoy.

Philostratus, though by no means so great a writer, wrote a famous biography of Apollonius of Tyana, a near contemporary of Jesus. The work was published in A.D. 217 and is known to contain some authentic reminiscences of the East amidst novelettish inventions.

> Here is another of Apollonius's wonders. A girl ripe for marriage seemed to be dead, and the bridegroom was following the bier bewailing the frustrated marriage. Rome joined in his mourning, because the girl's house happened to enjoy consular status. Apollonius happened upon their grief, and said, "Set down the bier, for I shall stop your tears for this girl." He next asked what her name was. The crowd supposed he was about to deliver a speech, in the style of a funeral oration to excite lamentation. But all he did was to touch her, saying something over her obscurely, and awakened (*aphypnise*) the girl from her apparent death. The child uttered a sound, and returned to her father's house, like Alcestis returned to life (*anabiōtheisa*) by Heracles. Her family presented him with a million and a half, but he said it should be given to the child as a dowry! Whether he found a spark of 'soul' (*psychēs*) in her, which had escaped the notice of her attendants — for it is said it was raining and some vapour was given off from her face — or he warmed up and restored a 'soul' (*psychēn*) that was actually extinct (*apesbēkuian*) that was as mysterious a problem for those present at the time as it is for me.[9]

The request for the girl's name, and the 'obscurely' uttered words suggest that Philostratus thought some exorcism was involved. The ability to recall the

22

supposed dead to life is already a sign not of a well-trained physician as compared with amateurs, but of a peripatetic holy man. The religion associated with Lao Tse knew that a true sage could arouse the dead. Many cultures selected this as the height of magic. Tradition had it that such powers existed amongst Jesus's pupils. Eusebius, writing in or about A.D. 311, speaks of the apostle Philip. His daughters are said to have told Papias that the *anastasis* of a dead person occurred in Philip's time (*kat' auton*) 'and other marvels besides'.[10]

Such revivals are actually attributed to Jesus himself with circumstantial particulars. There is the case (so Matthew and Luke believed) of the daughter of Jairus (Mk. 5:22-43 and parallels), that of the son of the widow of Nain (Lk. 7:11-17) (cf. Exod. 23:20-21, 26 and below, p.127), and of course that of Lazarus (Jn. 11:1-12:1), to which we shall return (p.52). Peter is credited with such a miracle in favour of one demonstrated as indubitably dead (Acts 9:40); and a rather feeble attempt is made to attribute similar powers to Paul (Acts 20:9-12). That nothing better is forthcoming is good evidence that he did not develop a practice in that direction.

Proclus (A.D. 412-480) commenting on the *Republic* of Plato, to which we shall return, mentions one Kleonymus who was taken out for burial on the third day (the Greek burial custom) and revived.[11]

It is time for us to turn to imaginative uses of this rare, but well-known phenomenon. If someone is put on the pyre as dead, revives and goes home, nothing is more likely than that he should be asked about his experiences, and for advice — for it was a normal practice to ask the dead to answer hard practical questions (p.78), to help with love affairs,[11a] and to execute curses and spells. What could be better than a case of one who died and has actually returned? The story of the Corfidii (above) illustrates all this, whatever the manner in which one accounts for the story itself. It proves the sort of thing that was expected in the time of Christ. This is emphasised by the tale of Galienus, which appears, with circumstantial detail, at Pliny VII. 178-9. Galienus had been killed by having his throat cut at the orders of Pompey. The executioner had not worked well, and Galienus revived, insisted on being taken to Pompey, uttered some predictions and died. The implication is that one who has visited the other world can make useful and credible predictions.[11b] Here was a tale which evidently had been built up out of some accurate, but less dramatic reminiscence; but it is excellent evidence of what was expected at that period.

The celebrated philosopher Pythagoras is credited with absurd behaviour by one Hermippus, who lived long before Christ and is reported by Diogenes Laërtius (8.1.41). Pythagoras stayed in a cave, to give the impression he had died, emerged, claimed he had returned from Hades, and amazed neighbouring rustics with his bogus experiences there.

On the other hand there is no instance of a person returned from the dead whose experiences have improved him, or anyone else. Tennyson actually complains at Lazarus's silence![12] And Lucian had fine fun with his story of Menippus, who went to the Underworld and returned 'prophesying' in verse after recently communing with Euripides and Homer![13] Menippus does have some quite sensible remarks to make, all the same, e.g. that the status of the dead below as between themselves is not related to the relative splendour of their tombs, etc. The proposition that people returned from the world of the dead, in the manner I have been describing, are not expected to be believed in any matter of importance is, however, made by Luke himself at Lk. 16:31. And, apart from that, all that have done so died a further death in due course and stayed dead (as far as we know)!

The possibility of utilising the notion of a return from the dead had been exploited extremely thoroughly by Plato. His *Republic* (380-370 B.C.) was one of the more widely read books of antiquity and the story of Er (his own invention: cf. Lk. 3:28) was widely known in the time of Christ.[14] Unlike the story told to Alcinous in which Odysseus goes to Hades and enquires from the prophet Teiresias[15] — a theme every schoolboy who had studied Greek knew (and many who had not) and was copied by Vergil a half-century or so before the birth of Christ and much later by Dante — Plato's Er provides a single profoundly moving account of the judgement of the dead, and the fates of the judged. Er's opportunity to see for himself the effect of behaviour in this life on the destiny after death is utilised in a sustained creative effort. Coming at the end of the *Republic*, which is a solid book in the field of political science, the myth made a profound impression. The story went that Er was ordered, down below, to be a messenger (*angelon*) to mankind (cf. Lk. 16:27-31). He arrived in the Underworld, and returned, in the following way. He was slain in battle. It appears the usual scavengers, whose methods are none too nice, were negligent (!) and when the corpses were taken up for mass cremation or burial on the tenth day already (obviously) decayed, he was undecayed, and having been brought home, at the moment of the funeral (!), on the twelfth day as he lay on the pyre, revived (*anebiō*), and after revival related what he had seen there below.[16] In his Phædo (113a-115a) Plato had evidenced the immense curiosity the sage of his time would feel as to the fates of the dead, once within the gates of Hades.

Only in imaginative literature, though of the widest dispersal, do we find such good didactic use made of the temporary journey to the world of the dead. On the other hand romantic literature has made the most of dramatic revivals. The theme of revival in the tomb has endless possibilities.

Chariton, who is thought to have been a contemporary of Jesus,[17] a writer from Aphrodisias in Caria, wrote the affecting tale, *Chæreas and Callirhoe,* typical of a genre of literature, full of incident and sensation, of which a very well-known second-century example is the work is Xenophon of Ephesus.[18] Chariton utilised older models, and there is no reason to suppose his story original in point of themes. In this novel a young man was accused of causing a young lady's death. Her relatives bemoaned her and in due course she was buried in a cave-tomb in a remote place. A kind tomb-robber opened the tomb and after admiring the young deceased was proceeding about his normal business when she revived (ἀνέπνευσεν, ἐλάμβανε παλιγγενεσίαν: the romantic style gives an indication of the tone of the whole).[19] The further adventures of the young couple do not concern us. The revival in the cold tomb was the centre and pivot of this affecting story.

So attractive was the notion of a young woman's revival in the tomb that the same idea, with elegant variations, was taken up by Xenophon.[20] The enjoyable productions of these predecessors of Fielding have a glow all of their own, of romance, adventure, and the picaresque. In order to appreciate the importance of this growing literature, devised for young adults who then had a mental age of our adolescents, it would be desirable to consult the entrancing work of Ben Edwin Perry as well as the scholarly thesis of Reardon. No especial attention is paid there to the 'revival in the tomb' motif, but the latter is of course very ancient. Alcmene, a somewhat unpleasant figure of ancient mythology, somehow died a natural death and was buried solemnly. None the less Zeus thought she would make a good wife for Rhadamanthus, the judge of the dead, and to that end commissioned Hermes to steal the body. Hermes opted to leave a stone in place of her, which was duly found when the Heracleidæ opened her tomb. The stone subsequently figured in her hero-cult. Information on this interesting sequence of events was available for at least half a millennium before Antonius Liberalis[21] and Plutarch[22] recount it.

On the whole revivals in the tomb have been the preserve of young women. One is interested in youth's refusal to stay in the tomb: and in the novels of Chariton and Xeonophon they live on into not less intriguing futures.

Young men, however, are not necessarily exempt from corresponding adventures. Youth must have its tribute, whichever the gender. In *Chæreas and Callirhoe* the hero, Chæreas, is with a party who have been sentenced to crucifixion. Each goes along carrying his own cross (42,7: ἕκαστος αὐτῶν τὸν σταυρὸν ἔφερε), and Chæreas carries his cross (τὸν σταυρὸν βαστάζων) and is prepared to be erected on it. Mithridates, the ruler, himself in love (or supposedly in love) with Callirhoe, finding that Chæreas was a friend of hers, orders him to be taken down from the cross. The others were actually nailed up, but by good luck, the stand-by of the novelist, Chæreas was not yet completely fixed on to it (4.3,5: ἐπιβαίνοντα τὸν σταυρόν), so that the hero could be rescued for the happy ending essential to the genre. It was on this sort of matter that, not the kitchen-maids, etc., of **Alexandria,** Ephesus, Antioch and Cyrene, were fed, but the bright young sparks of the Hellenistic world, including the unromantically married. Pornographic aspects had their own rôle to play in such an 'adult' environment.

It need hardly be argued at length that the depicting of an actual revival, e.g. by the intervention of an angel (on the model, say, of, e.g. Acts 5:19-20, 12:7-8, which evidently consist with a popular genre), could not do the gospel the smallest good in Hellenistic circles. It must be a failure if it is unconsciously assimilated to the popular theme of 'raisings' done by charismatic power rather than medical expertise; if only because no holy man caused Jesus to rise from death. There was no evidence whatever to hand that he preached about the denizens of hell, though it was believed in due course that he went there! A legend soon grew that Christ went down and harrowed hell. That proves a natural penchant had to find vent, and consequently did so. As far as we are concerned all it shows us is that there was *no* evidence that he communicated anything about the underworld—on the contrary all the appearance stories concentrate on his *not* taking his attention off the needs of *this* world; while angelic messages insist that he is not to be looked for among the dead. In other words he was not 'safely put away in the tomb', which is what some people evidently would have preferred; and on the other hand no one was to consult his spirit in the vicinity of his tomb (a contemporary practice: p.78). There was therefore no question of a parallel with Er: any attempt to provide one would be dismissed as a feeble imitation of Plato, whom contemporaries were (as we have seen) quick enough to refer to when an actual revival was reported. If a dramatic finding of Jesus alive had been the climax of the story a romantic edge could hardly have been avoided, with endless amusing conjectures, and the verisimilitude of the tale would have been sacrificed. Since Mark had already contrived a Christian counterpart to the widespread myth of Divine Marriage at 5:21-43 all females could have a symbolic rôle.

My suggestion is somewhat complex. Mark may well have stopped as most scholars are satisfied he did (16:8) not merely because his churches may have had their uncertainties how one might proceed: on the one hand the women did not find Jesus there (he was not there, after all) and it would have been unseemly to suggest (to reassure the curious) that they did so if they did not; on the other hand the development of a festival at the Sepulchre more or less determined his climax for him, provided he did not actually connive at a tomb-cult.

As I understand it, male members of the band of disciples had seen Jesus, and everyone knew it. However, the pressure of curiosity from convinced Christians a few years afterwards caused first Matthew, and then Luke and John to regret Mark's decision and consequently to revise his treatment—with great artistic loss as a result. Amongst other defects an anti-climax was unintentionally created. The later evangelists actually depend on the earlier in this process (p.101), so that a persisting curiosity eventually fuelled a chain reaction.

Meanwhile we must not lose sight of an entirely mundane aspect. A modern detective pursuing such a question, where first-hand evidence is lacking, would ask himself, firstly whom did it profit that Jesus should be dead, and why? The 'envy' theme which is so prominent in the gospel—Pilate knew it was out of envy (cf. Acts 7:9) that they delivered Jesus to him (Mk. 15:10, Mt. 27:18)—has its own background, and must not be taken as the sole operating cause. And secondly, whom would it have profited that Jesus should revive, and be reported alive; were there any who would lose by that; and finally what relation would there be between those that would lose by his revival and those who profited from his death?

It must be borne in mind that a holy man can be a source of profit to his disciples (an easy living for them, I am sorry to say), and there are two kinds of dead holy men. There is the holy man whose tomb works miracles (he is highly valuable still to its custodians), and there is the holy man whose tomb does not. In the latter case the disciples are poorly off, unless they can find members of the charismatic's family to retain and prolong his charisma. This means give-and-take (not necessarily bargaining) between two parties having competing interests. Mere revival from the dead interferes with the market in these matters and introduces unpredictable complications. Small wonder the ladies at the Sepulchre found food for thought. The news, when it reached the disciples, would have several implications which they could not ignore.

Hellenistic laws seldom placed the widow in the order of intestate heirs. Therefore the male relations of one who revived would be very interested. Any property, in the case of a childless man, would pass to his nearest agnates, and if he were estranged from them and had affectionate pupils I should take it for granted that a lawsuit would ensue, with pickings for orators if the estate was worth the contest. If a man revives from the dead some of these persons will have the effrontery to demand his estate on the ground that he was divested by death. The Roman law, in its practical way, took this seriously. Jurists of the earlier imperial period replied to anxious enquirers that if such an eventuality materialised the man would be conclusively presumed not to have died at all. This was a pragmatic solution to a problem which they had no difficulty in visualising, with Pliny the Elder behind them.[23]

If that line of thinking had been pursued, at any rate by Romans, Christ must have been presumed not to have died on the cross, and therefore his death could not, by any stretch of imagination, be seen as a propitiation for sins, nor could he seriously be visualised as obedient to death, as, legend insisted, Isaac was obedient to the knife (pp.34-5). This would contradict at a stroke the elaborate theology upon which the Christian story of salvation was constructed. It was not Christ's natural, but his unnatural death that was salvific. The result will be the same, whether my reader agrees with me that the bizarre programme leading up to the Cross was Christ's own idea, or whether he takes the view more approved in some theological quarters that it was a piece of quick-thinking by his disciples in need to construct (as a compensation for losing their master prematurely) an Anastasis-Ascension-Exaltation myth. A presumption of his never having died on the Cross would be fatal to all of it. The background to Mark's composition is therefore much more involved than has previously been suspected.

Notes

1. His soul *diegeiren to sōma*: Apollonius Paradoxographus, *Mirab.* 3 (? 2nd cent. B.C.) (O. Keller, *Rer.Nat.Script.* i, Leipzig, 1877).
1a. Plato com., *C.A.F.*i,619; *Plut., Sol.*VI.2.
2. Plut., *Mor.*761F-762A, 764F-765A. Cf. Test. Gad. IV.6 (love wants to call back those in the grip of death).
2a. *Fact. et dict. mem.* 1.8 (de miraculis), §12.
3. *De med.* II.6, 13-16.
4. *Nat. hist.* VII.173-9.
5. ibid., §.179.
5a. VIII.67.
6. *Philops.*26 (Loeb edn.)
7. *Alex.*24.
8. *Florid.*19.
9. *Vita Ap.*IV.45.
10. *Hist. eccl.*III.39,9.
11. *In remp.*II.114.
11a. Lucian, Philops.14.

11b. One who looks into hell will have a lot to tell (ibid., 24); a dying man tells such tales (ibid., 25).
12. *In Memoriam* 31.
13. *Menippus or Necromancy*.
14. Plut., *Mor*.740B. Clem. Alex., *Strom*. V.710.
15. Hom.,*Od*.xi.88ff. Ps.Lucian, *de Astrol*.24.
16. *Rep*. X.614.
17. *Der kl. Pauly*, s.n., also A.P. Papanikolaou, *Chariton-Studien* (Göttingen 1973), 161, 163. K.Plepelits, *Chariton von Aphrodisias Kallirhoe* (Stuttgart, 1976), 8 (c.A.D. 50).
18. Anthia, having drunk a mock-poison, is rescued by pirate tomb-robbers, her lover believing that her body was stolen by them.Xen.Eph. 3.8,1-5, 3.9,1,8 (text Papanikolaou, 1973; trans. Turner, 1957, p.38).
19. *De Chaer. et Call*. 1.4,12, 5.1, 6, 8-10 (text Blake, 1938, trans.Blake, 1939).
20. Note 18 above. Hengel (1977) utilises this literature at pp.81-2.
21. *Metamorphoseon Synagoge* 33 (c.A.D. 100-150), quoting Pherecydes (mid-5th cent., B.C.)
22. Plut., *Mor*. 577E. Pausanias, *Des.Gr*.9.16,7.
23. Justinian, *Dig*.1.3.4,6 gloss (ed.Lyons, 1627,i.34), XXIV.3,31. Julius Clarus *Sent*.III §Test., qu. 86 (*de raro contingent*.)

CHAPTER IV

Anastasis & Resurrection in the Jewish World.

Such embarrassments as we have just studied were by no means the end of the matter. Hard and fast legal presumptions of the Roman type were alien to the Jewish world to which Jesus and his immediate associates belonged, even if they were operative in Tarsus, Corinth, Alexandria and other places which Mark can be presumed to have had in mind while writing. On the contrary the fact of revival from death posed, to men who knew the psalms, many interesting questions. For example there is Ps. 40:2, 'He brought me up also out of the horrible pit . .', as contrasted with Ps. 88:4, 'I am counted with them that go down into the pit . .' He who does not see corruption (Ps. 16:10, '. . neither wilt thou suffer thy Holy One to see corruption') is not necessarily one who has not died: death has, for some reason, not mastered him. Indeed the pious *did* not see corruption; this was a matter of faith, though never verified (so far as we know) directly. Similar notions persist in the Greek Orthodox and Roman Catholic worlds to this day: the non-putrefaction of a corpse signifies the holiness of life on the part of the deceased.

There are many diverse elements making up awareness of survival of death. Numerous optimistic notions made themselves felt in the times of the Maccabees, of the first martyrs for the faith of the Jews. In order to demonstrate the care we must use in disentangling them let us examine Mk. 6:14-16 which has been tampered with at Mt. 14:1-2 and Lk. 9:7-9. The Marcan passage runs:

> Now King Herod heard of it: for his (Jesus's) Name had become manifest, and they said "John the Baptist *has been raised from the dead* (*egēgertai* [not *anestē*] *ek nekrōn*), and therefore the powers are at work in him." But others said, "It is Elijah!" Others again said, "It is a prophet like one of the prophets." But after hearing this Herod said, "John whom I beheaded, the same has been raised."

Matthew paraphrases, stating that Herod pointed out that John the Baptist had risen from among the dead, while Luke shows that Herod had his doubts, as if the theory did not appeal to him.

The evangelists' irony is no doubt at work again here (p.7), for *ēgerthē ek nekrōn* ('he was raised from the dead') expresses the way the church settled to formulate *Jesus's* experience. John did not experience resurrection from among the dead. But the passage is evidence that a Hellenized Jew could well believe that a holy man's spirit, 'awakened' from the dead, could return, inhabit another body, and so transmit to it a power it otherwise did not possess. Of course Mark is laughing at Herod and his contemporaries (Matthew calls them his slaves): the power of Jesus did not come from the Baptist at second hand, nor was he Elijah or even *the* prophet of Deut. 18;15-18 (cf. Jn. 1:21), but the embodiment of the Holy Spirit itself at least from the moment of his baptism. The passage, however, confirms that the phrase *ēgerthē ek nekrōn* ('he was raised from the dead') did *not* necessarily mean a bodily *anastasis*, a revival from physical death. Transmigration of souls was no new idea to Jews. Spirits were thought to be able to move about and achieve things without any such implications (as we find at Lk. 24:37.39). 'Christ rose' *Christos anestē* could therefore be different from *Christos ēgerthē*, 'Christ was raised up', and we do well to watch the nuances carefully, in spite of the deliberate confusion that occurs.

1. ANASTASIS.

Jews who spoke Greek used the word *anastasis* in two senses: (1) revival from death, and (2) revival to participation in the resurrection (below). Thus the *Testament of Job,* which like the *Testaments of the XII Patriarchs* was written about the time of the gospels or somewhat earlier, speaks[1a] of Job's future resurrection (it will be remembered that Job is one of the prophets who most clearly visualised resurrection: Job 19:25-27): καὶ ἐγερθήσῃ ἐν τῇ ἀναστάσει 'He shall be raised at *the anastasis*' (cf. Job 42:17a LXX). The general resurrection of the just is referred to. So at Jn. 11:23 Jesus predicts to Martha, 'Your brother shall rise again', but Martha replies (*v.* 24), I know that he shall rise again *at the anastasis on the last day* (ἐν τῇ ἀναστάσει ἐν τῇ ἐσχάτῃ ἡμέρᾳ) (alluding to the idea voiced by Job). Then Jesus makes the extraordinary remark (*v.* 25), which we must eventually unwind: '*I* am the Anastasis and the Life!' The resurrection is likewise called (at Lk. 14:14) 'the *anastasis* of the righteous'. Here is no question of Hellenistic difficulties in visualising life after death.[2] It is a question of vocabulary. *Anastasis* could refer (p.2) to the *mythical arising* at the last trump. As Ps. Sol. 3:12 puts it, 'But those that fear the Lord shall arise (*anastēsontai*) to everlasting life, and their life shall be in the light of the Lord and shall never fail'. The *virtuous* are entitled to immortality, as we find from Wisd. 5:15-17.

Meanwhile this second sense has nothing to do with the location of the body. In Hymns 10 and 17 the Qumran sect expressed their belief that corpses gnawed by worms would rise from the dust (1 QH. VI.34, XII2). The soul of Job (Test.Job.ch.52) was immortal, going to heaven while his body was put in a fine tomb mined underground (*hyponos* 53:7). The children of Job went to heaven immediately due to Job's *merit*, their bodies also being taken up (39:11-12, 40:3).[3] The soul is immune from death, while the body 'sleeps' (Ps.Phocylides, 105). As we shall see, one can be in heaven while one's body rests in a grave, and fancy has even added a third stage, whereby a bodily assumption into heaven occurred. God no doubt revives the dead (p.35), but actual release from Hades is not to be looked for once one has entered it (Wis. 2:1). A novelettish touch appears in the Test.Abr. (ch.18): God sent the spirit of life to Abraham's servants who had died and they were 'brought to life again'.

We return to the first meaning of *anastasis* (revival). Because precipitate burial was the normal practice,[4] it was the rule to visit graves for three days after burial, counting inclusively. The technical term for this visiting was evidently (in Greek) *theōrēsai* ('to inspect'), and this is the term Matthew uses. Mark omitted it as superfluous, since the ladies were going ostensibly to anoint a body they had presumed (without proof) to be dead, but Matthew is almost certainly right: even Mark's story alludes to a pilgrimage visitation of the tomb (p.9). For the women it was especially desirable to visit Jesus's tomb because the burial was hasty and inadequate by contemporary standards: the unguents were needed for the body's regular desiccation, not merely as a matter of honouring the dead. However one motive for visiting graves (apart from ritual mourning, which was particularly significant in this controversial case) was to check that the body had *not* returned to life.

One may go out to the cemetery for three (not 30)[5] days to inspect the dead for a sign of life, without a fear that this smacks of heathen (Amorite) practices. For it happened that a man was inspected after three days, and he went on to live twenty-five years; still another went on to have five children and died later.[6]

The Jewish evidence of grave-visiting[7] is not to be dismissed as 'late'.[8] The purposes behind it stretch back indefinitely. The burial of Ananias and Sapphira (following the precedent of the burial of the sons of Aaron at Lev. 10: 1-6)[9] are famous examples of precipitate burial, but it is notorious[10] that burial took place on the day of death if time permitted.[11] It was etiquette to keep one's parent for a day if possible, but this was an obvious concession. Job was buried on the *third* day (*meta treis hēmeras*) because widows and orphans insisted on the delay (*Test. Iob*. 53:6-7). Jews relate their normal practice to Deut. 21:23 which by an incredible coincidence is the very verse whose implications inspired Joseph of Arimathæa to bestir himself that very evening (p.56).

Some scholars have argued that, apart from Mark's lack of interest in secular history, the ladies' visit to the tomb of Jesus as depicted at Mk. 16:2 = Mt. 28:1 was hardly in order to anoint the body as indicated, since it was impracticable to anoint a body three days dead.[12] This is not necessarily true, since these fluids can be poured, but in any case the body was in a kind of refrigeration-chamber. Matthew rightly emphasises that their mission bore the character of a routine visit of inspection, the Sabbath (a day of compulsory joy) having detained them in the interval. One cannot carry spices for the dead, who are already buried, on the Sabbath. It is important to grasp that after three days the features change and the body is no longer recognisable.[13] The hovering spirit gives up the attempt to return, and goes where it may.[14] A tomb thus needs to be inspected for three days inclusive of the day of burial. If a particular deceased has been duly visited, and the tomb is finally closed, he can be presumed only to 'stink' on the fourth day (Jn. 11:39) and is indubitably dead! Jewish belief in this matter is evidenced strikingly at Rev. 11:9,11, where the author, steeped in Jewish idiom and imagery, sees two prophets, dead *three and a half* days, revived by a spirit of life sent by God and called by a voice from heaven, 'Ascend hither!'.

2. RESURRECTION.

The body at the resurrection of the just will be raised up as the bones rejoin and form the original skeleton by the power of God (so Ezekiel says: below) The Sadducees, no unimportant party in religion or the state, denied, on the whole, that there was any resurrection to look forward to. Even at the time of Paul's trial before the High Priest it was possible to throw the Sanhedrin into confusion by claiming that the gist of the accusation was belief in the resurrection (Acts 23:6-7). The belief in resurrection was no doubt extremely popular; it was fostered as an article of faith by the Pharisees, who linked it with the conception of the Kingdom of God and the World to Come—all three being purely hypothetical ideas.[15]

But not only the Sadducees doubted the resurrection. There were other quarters in which there was less than enthusiasm for it. The Qumran sect, to whose writings, recently recovered, we are highly indebted for a realistic vision of life and thought in the period in which we are interested, concentrated on the building of a model state, on preparing troops suitable for the coming holy war, and on plans for the rebuilding of the Temple to provide correct worship of God within a pure sanctuary and city. That they looked forward to a non-terrestrial paradise is not impossible. Hymn 10 runs (as Vermes translates), 'Hoist a banner, O you who lie in the dust! O bodies gnawed by worms, raise up an ensign..'[16] But nothing is based upon an enthusiastic assertion of the resurrection. The Second Book of Maccabees certainly expresses the hope well known to students of Christianity (2 Macc. 12:38-45). But the *Testaments of the XII Patriarchs,* a book which must remain prominent in the 'background' of early Christian theology, gives extraordinarily little attention to the subject. The Testament of Judah does indeed say[17] 'And after these things shall Abraham and Isaac and Jacob arise unto life, and I and my brethren shall be chiefs of the tribes of Israel (cf. Mt. 19:28) . . .' and later 'and they who were put to death for the Lord's sake shall awake to life . . .'[18] And the Testament of Zebulun says, 'For I shall rise again in the midst of you, as a ruler in the midst of his sons . . .,'[19] and the Testament of Benjamin, 'And then shall ye see Enoch, Noah, and Shem, and Abraham, Isaac, and Jacob rising on the right hand in gladness; then shall we also rise, each one over our tribe, worshipping the King of heaven . . . then also all men shall rise, some to glory and some to shame.'[20] But relative to the quantity of instruction and exhortation contained in this book these expectations are marginal, as indeed they are terminal where they occur.

In 2 Bar. 30:2 we find the idea that those who die in the *hope* of the Messiah will be resurrected. Admittedly the resurrection plays a greater rôle in Judaism after the Roman Wars, and this is proved by the extraordinary frescoes of the third century synagogue at Dura Europos (now in Damascus) devoted to Jewish spiritual history in the light of the resurrection as described by Ezek. 37:12-13.[21] But this does not prove that any such preoccupation with the theme characterised Jewry as a whole in the first half of the first century. In any event the Jews who believed in the resurrection in any of its forms which are evidenced for us had no *individual* occurrence in mind.[22] Even the revived 'saints' in Jerusalem (Mt. 27:52-3) who have given such embarrassment to scholars, were introduced by

Matthew, who sees Jesus's death[23] as releasing the righteous dead, as a *collective* experience. Individual resurrection was unknown.[24] When the resurrection comes no doubt the bodies will participate.[25] but it will be a group event, with the bones (as it were) sorted out.

3. CONFUSION OF THE TWO.

One may well ask, then, what of individuals who enjoy bliss while their bodies remain on earth? Lazarus (Eliezer) in Abraham's bosom was apparently not buried, but that is the author's artistry (Lk. 16:22). The Rich Man in the same story was buried and was in hell at the same time (16:22-23). The actual position of the body was irrelevant for this purpose. A number of pious persons, whom we have seen listed above, including Phineas, went bodily to heaven. On the other hand the penitent thief is promised bliss with Jesus (p.84) though both of them were in their graves, the former not being *raised* in any sense whatsoever. Luke, the literary genius, never related individuals' fates with the common fantasy of what would happen at the End of Time.[25a]

The admittedly tendentious Heb. 11:35 leads us to reconsider the miracles done by Elijah (1 Kngs. 17:22) and Elisha (2 Kngs. 4:34-35): these were gifts of their dead sons to their mothers through a process of *anastasis,* granted to them because of the exceptional merit of the miracle-workers (ἔλαβον γυναῖκες ἐξ ἀναστάσεως τοὺς νεκροὺς αὐτῶν). But though no one suggested that with those boys resurrection had commenced, the Dura frescoes prove that the son of the widow of Sarepta (1 Kngs. 17)[26] was seen as some kind of earnest of resurrection or intimation of it. A hope had begotten a myth.

From what we have already seen it is clear that Jews, typical Asians, could hold inconsistent ideas: (1) the bodies of the just await the general resurrection in their tombs, when all will be raised jointly; (2) the especially holy may be resurrected first; (3) the exceptionally holy may be 'taken up' to heaven bodily; (4) certain individuals may enjoy bliss in Abraham's bosom whilst their bodies decay; and (5) though sceptics may define the miracles of Elijah and Elisha as instances of *anastasis* (revival from incohate death), religion teaches those two instances as God's method of intimating that resurrection is not mere fantasy. Granted that Jews in the Hellenistic world were inclining to substitute immortality for resurrection, personal desire for immortality did not obscure the common hope.

That is how it comes about that in this intellectual environment a revival not achieved by a physician, exorcist, or holy man could be taken as a prototype of resurrection. Whatever Jesus's Anastasis might *be* it might be presented as *resurrection.* Thus in Acts 4:2 Peter and John annoyed the Temple administration *and* the Sadducees by proclaiming '*the* rising from the dead' (*tēn anastasin tēn ek nekrōn*: here obviously meaning resurrection) as occurring in the electrifying instance of their deceased master. At Rom. 1:4 (as we have seen) Paul speaks of Jesus as having been defined as Son of God as an outcome of (not 'from the time when') 'rising (not *the* rising) of (or from) the dead' *anastaseōs nekrōn*: a deliberate ambiguity). Jesus's Anastasis was (by this time) resurrection. No wonder the fourth evangelist later makes Jesus say, *I* am *the* resurrection (11:25: *ego*

33

eimi hē anastasis)'. Ignatius believes in the bodily presence of Jesus with the disciples *meta tēn anastasin*, 'after *the* resurrection' (Ign., *Smyrn.* 3).

Let us go back to the list of five inconsistent ideas which we found among Jesus's contemporaries. In none of them does revival from death, as a medical phenomenon, play any part. Indeed it is inconsistent with them all. At least by the time Paul has seen Jesus's experience as resurrection, and John has seen Jesus *as* Resurrection, a powerful equation has been forged, for a new element has appeared. Resurrection and actual Anastasis have been brought together. It remains for us to conjecture how this was done; and to achieve this we must give our attention to a very important but mythical person.

4. THE CASE OF ISAAC.

I shall be asked at this point, what of the case of Isaac? Vermes (1961) and Spiegel (1967) have given prominence to Isaac, and they are right. Some have questioned whether it is really important for our investigation[27], as recent study has exaggerated the significance of the gap in time between the Crucifixion and the details of the Isaac *haggadah*.[27a] The church in fact utilised the mixed biblical and *haggadic* (legendary) background of the Isaac story in relation to Jesus, and it remains an important part of the scriptural, cultural background to the story of Redemption, as we shall see.

The biblical story of the so-called Binding ('*Aqêdâ*) of Isaac (Gen. 22: 1-19) [27b] is a moving example of a theme found in more than one culture (in India it occurs with the story of Harishchandra and Sunashepa), that to secure firmly that which is most desired one must be willing to surrender it, sacrifice it. The verbal and thematic content of the story of the Binding was closely studied in ancient times. The scene forms part of the central and most prominent feature of the Dura frescoes, which we know are about the resurrection.[28] It figures in the Beth Alpha synagogue mosaics very prominently. The Jews were proud of Isaac well before the time of Christ. The biblical tale was developed and expanded with the aid of *haggadah*, so that the slightest hint in the Hebrew text was accounted for and exploited.

Isaac, preparing himself, trussed up like a lamb, for his father's knife, had no idea that he would be redeemed by a lamb. But 'lamb' and 'son' are kindred words in Aramaic (*taliyā'*). The ram which was providentially available at Gen. 22:13 was a lamb.[29] The lamb could be seen as a precursor and 'type' of the paschal lamb:[30] it was a 'lamb of God'. The word for the sacrifice of Isaac, '*aqêdâ*, specifically relates to the tying up of the sacrificial lamb.[31] Ingenuity with Gen. 22:13 discovered something interesting. In ancient times the Hebrew letters corresponding to D and R were easily confused. Scholars sometimes read words with both! The Masoretic Text has 'YL 'HR (a ram behind): it was also read as 'YL 'HD (the one and only ram) and 'YL 'HRYT (the ram of the End Time). It was thus pre-existent, the lamb for the ultimate atonement![32] The Beth Alpha mosaic clearly shows it tied to a *tree*.

To return to the story: the most comprehensive research into the history of the story of Isaac makes it clear that Isaac was actually killed with the sacrificial knife.[33] Isaac died *twice*: Abraham lifted the knife to slaughter him *twice*.[34] As a result of his willing submission to these extraordinary proceedings, to his father's obedience to God's unexplained command, Isaac was revived, and after a period in heaven (during which he went to school with Shem, who seems to have run an academy), returned to life to beget Jacob and through him all Israelites. This is not so incongruous as it sounds: the Jews in general, unlike the Greeks, thought of soul and body as a unit and if God restores life to the dead (as the Second of the traditional Eighteen Benedictions of Jewish liturgy assert) the body is no less a participant than the soul and any deviations from this are wanting in perfection. Thus the tombs of the patriarchs are empty. Meanwhile the merits of Isaac survive for the benefit of all his progeny. Remembering the sacrifice of Isaac God offers the resurrection to his descendants.[35]

It is clear that the ram which was slaughtered, and subsequently burnt in Isaac's stead, was not merely a substitute for Isaac, it *was* in some sense Isaac. Yet Isaac himself was the first person to experience (mythically) resurrection. Isaac is therefore the outstanding exception to the two propositions that *anastasis* need not be resurrection and that resurrection must be a collective experience.

To this the obvious reply is that when Isaac revived after his death on the altar his 'resurrection' *was* the corporate experience of all his descendants. Without Isaac there would be no resurrection. And this is part of the traditional explanation of Gen. 22:18 (God's promise to Abraham: 'and in thy seed shall all the nations of the earth be blessed, because thou hast obeyed my voice'). Through the Jews, descendants of Isaac, the World to Come can be offered even to gentiles, for Abraham, himself a proselyte, is the father of all proselytes.

Isaac is therefore the one case—albeit a fictional one—of an individual experiencing resurrection, and continuing to live on earth with an earthly body, dying naturally, and being buried thereafter (Gen. 35:29). Isaac is the exception that proves the rule. The rabbis connect Is. 33 with the '*Aqêdâ*,[36] and Is. 33 is of great interest in connection with the Anastasis (below, p.104).

About the time of Christ a notion existed that the Messiah would be approved of by God as Abraham approved of Isaac. Test. Levi XVIII 6 reads 'the heavens shall be opened and out of the shrine of Glory shall come upon him sanctification with a voice (cf. Mk. 1:11!) of a father as from Abraham the father of Isaac'. Now why should Abraham bless Isaac? Obviously because he was obedient to the knife! And this is solemnly associated with the Messiah, whom the author of the *Testaments* believed would come from the priestly, not the princely tribe.

The sacrifice of Isaac plays its full part in the theology of the Redemption (p.123). Paul mentions the 'precedent' of Isaac with emphasis. Gal. 3:16, 'Now the promises were made to Abraham and his descendants, literally "his issue". It does not say "and to his issues", referring to many; but, referring to one, "and to your issue", which is Christ.' In the epistle to the Romans the point arises thrice. Rom. 4:19-25:

'He (Abraham) did not weaken in faith when he considered his own body, which was as good as dead . . . and the mortification of Sarah's womb

35

. . . That is why his faith "was reckoned to him as righteousness' [i.e. merit] (Gen. 15:6). But the words "it was reckoned to him" were written not merely in reference to him but in reference to us also (cf. Rom. 15:4, 1 Cor. 9:10, 10:11). For it will be reckoned to us who believe in him who raised up Jesus our Lord from among the dead, Jesus who was surrendered for our sins and was raised up for our justification.'

The topic arises again at Rom. 9:7-8:

'. . . not all are children of Abraham because they are his descendants but "Through Isaac shall your descendants be named (Gen. 21:12)." This means that it is not the children of the flesh [including Ishmael] who are the children of God, for it is the children of the promise who are reckoned as descendants.'

The implication is brought out at Rom. 8:31-34, where reference is made to Satan's attempt to interfere with the sacrifice of Isaac (p.83).

'. . . if God is for us, who is against us? He who did not spare his own son but surrendered him for the sake of us all, will he not freely give us all benefits along with him? Who will accuse God's elect ones? [Not Satan, for] God is the acquitter. Who condemns? [Not Christ the judge, for] Christ who died, and, more than that, was resurrected, he who is at God's right hand, is in fact our advocate.'

The importance of faith in this process is emphasised by the author of the epistle to the Hebrews (11:17-19):

'By faith Abraham offered up Isaac when he was put to the test; he was in the process of offering his only son though he had received the promises, for he himself had been told "through Isaac shall your descendants be named (Gen. 21:12)." For he reckoned that God was able even to raise from the dead: and thence, figuratively speaking, he did get him back.'

NOTES

1. Josephus the historian probably believed in it, since he refers to it in favourable sense: *BJ* 2.163, 3.374, cf.Ap.2.218.
1a. 4:9.
2. Hengel (1974) I, 196-202. Manson and Barrett at Duthie (1979).
3. Rahnenführer (1971); Philonenko (1968).
4. Mishnah Sanh. VI.5 j.Hor.III 48a. Burial rushed because of onset of Sabbath: b. Shab 94b, Ket.20b.
5. An incorrect variant reading. Zlotnick, *Tractate 'Mourning'* (1966), 11-12, 135. Tos. Shab. II,10,b. Shab.32a.
6. Tractate Semahot VIII.1. Tur, Yoreh Deâ § 394. Lockton (1924), 28 n.1, 32 n.1. William (1949), 204-13.
7. Brüll (1874), 51-2; Perles (1861), 352; Klein (1908), 41-3; Grundt (1868), 22. S. Lieberman in *Wolfson Jub.Vol.* (1965), Eng. sect.II,495ff.

8. As Bode (1970) 15 and n.2.
9. *Studies* I, 201.
10. b.Zeb.100*a*.
11. Mishnah, Sanh.VI.5, etc. as in n.4 above.
12. Campenhausen (1968), 58; Evans (1970), 76-7.
13. Jellinek. *Bet ha-Midrasch* I, 96-105. Wünsche, II (1907), 53, 55. b.Shab. 151*b*, Midr. R., Gen.LXV.20 (on 2 Chr. 13:20), b.Yev. 120*a*. Cumont (1949), 36-7 Spiegel (1967), 112.
14. Wettstein on Jn. 11:39. Hertz (1960), 34-7. Freistadt (1928), 53-72, 73-89; Schmitt (1949) 168, 171; Metzger (1957), 118ff, 121; Nötscher (1954) 313-19; Dupont (1959), 748 disagrees. Campenhausen (1968) 46 n.12 traces the idea in A. Meyer, C.Clemen, J. Leipoldt, and others.
15. See n.1 above.
16. Vermes (1977), 51.
17. 25:1.   18. Ibid.4.   19. 10:2.   20. 10:6-8.
21. Riesenfeld (1948).   22. Wünsche (1903); Marmorstein (1915); Schubert (1962); Seidensticker (1967); Schnackenburg (1969),16; Nickelsburg (1972); Keller (1974).
23. Jeremias (1971), 309.
24. O'Collins 1973), 31.
25. Schubert (1962), 191, 206, 214. Evans (1970), 16 n.35.
25a. So. J. Dupont, 'L'Après-mort dans l'œuvre de Luc,' *Rev. théol. de Louvain* 3 (1972), 3-21.
26. *Studies* I, 148.
27. The contribution of the myth of Isaac to Pauline doctrine has been exaggerated according to Stanley (1961), 260-1, but Spiegel (pp.81-6) does not doubt it, and he is right.
27a. P. R. Davis & B. D. Chilton, 'The Aqedah: a revised tradition history', *C.B.Q.* 40 (1978), 514-46, conclude that there was no pre-Christian Aqedah. They are rejected at Horbury & McNeil, *Suffering* (1981), 13-14.
27b. J.-L. Duhaime at *Science et Esprit* 33 (1981), 135-6.
28. Enc.Jud.VI (1971), 285, fig.15. Riesenfeld (1948); Garte (1973); Simon (1952), 31-44; Kümmel (1965).
29. Jeremias (1935). S. Lieberman, *Greek in Jewish Palestine* (N.Y. [2]1965), 197.
30. Jub. 18. Midr. R., Exod.XV (on 12:2), ibid.XIII.15 on 22:8. Mek. on Exod.12:13 (Bo. 7). Moore, I,540. P.d.R.El.29 Midr.R., Num.XIII.19. Jeremias, *Z.N.W.*57 (1966), 216-19, a propos of Test.Jos.19:8 is wrong. He is misleading at (1971), 309. Is. 33:10 is associated with Isaac. 1 Cor. 5:7. Vermes (1961), 215.
31. See Mishnah, Tam. IV.1, cf. b.Shab.54*a*. See Jastrow's *Dict. of Talm. Babli* ad v.
32. Spiegel (1967), 78, 95.
33. Jos., *de Macc.* 18,219 (*holokautōmenon*), 4 Macc.13:12, 18:17; Job 18: 2-19; 4 Macc. 16:20; Targ. ps.Jon.,Gen 22.
34. Spiegel, ch.10. Midrash on Gen. 22:15 ('a *second* time').
35. The second of the Eighteen Benedictions blesses God who revives the dead: *bāruk 'ātâ yhwh mehayēh hamētîm*. Billerbeck, *Kommentar* IV/1,211. P.d.R.El.XXXI. Midr. Haggadol (1947, 354) on Gen. 22:9e. b. Men.53*a*.
36. Mann, at the Seder concerned. P. d.R.El.XXXI. Midr. Haggadol (as above). Midr.R., Gen.LVI.5. b.Hag.5*b*.

CHAPTER V

Anastasis in the Modern World.

Apart from public and private worship and religious discourse it can hardly be said that resurrection, once so interesting to the Pharisees and to other pious people in Jesus's time and afterwards, or immortality, which interested pagans then and afterwards, plays any role in our daily life. To a highly individualistic people the idea of any collective experience (if at all prolonged) is unattractive. It hardly enters into our thinking; though fear of retribution in some other 'world' for sins committed in this life is not so uncommon: it is one of the few truly religious experiences commonly felt, due to the operation of conscience, which is part of our genetic inheritance. If there are people who believe in resurrection, it will fairly readily be agreed that this is not in any sense a description of 'resurrection' (that X believes in it) but a description of the mentality of the believer (it is a condition of X to have such beliefs).

But *anastasis* is not at all rare. It has no moral or theological content or significance *whatsoever*. It is ridiculous to pretend that those who have revived from clinical death have prepared themselves or others for dying! If the lady who snored in her coffin (below) told, on her revival, that her husband had been committing various crimes unknown to anyone, and if her testimony were solemnly taken down and pursued with independent enquiries, that would be a different matter. But this never happens. And there are enough examples for us to be clear about it.

Legislation from pre-Christian times until recently has tried to prohibit burial, especially cremation, before 72 hours from the time of death. By 'death' of course I mean death signified by the absence of pulse beat. Such was the decree of that prince of ideal legislators, Plato.[1] About A.D. 190 Rabbi (R.Judah I) introduced it as imperative for Jews, though we know that the custom of tomb-visiting for three days was much older. Death could not be certain until after some delay.[2] The same caution inspired Renaissance rulers.[3]

Forestus[4] (a celebrated medical man of the late sixteenth and early seventeenth century) goes into detail about mistakes made in spite of the greatest care. Traditional methods of ascertaining death, such as a shallow dish of water on the abdomen, and a mirror to the nose, fail. There was a case where a family tomb (Italian style) was opened to receive a new occupant and a figure was found moved some distance from where it must have been laid.[5] Such discoveries, e.g. a skeleton crouched by the door, leave an indelible sensation. Precipitate burial is everywhere reprehended, and in many countries prevented. Few of the States of the United States permit burial or cremation until specified tests have been applied twice with an interval of 24 hours.

In the famous case of *Srimati Bibhabati Devi* v. *Ramendra Narayan Roy*[6] the facts were established in 1946 at the conclusion of many years' judicial investigation. The ruler of a small Indian state died of serious diseases and was carried, as the custom was, to the bank of the river Ganges. There, on his funeral pyre, he was revived by a heavy shower. He was rescued by some fakirs who were camping nearby, travelled with them all over India, was subsequently recognised and then (naturally) rejected by his widow and other persons who were, by then, heavily interested in his estate. His identity was established, eventually, to the chagrin of all except the lawyers who handled this so-called Indian Tichbourne case.

In 1947 Jellinek published a work devoted to the cause of improved life-saving techniques. His survey is based exclusively on reports of actual cases. A frozen person revived from death after six hours, but died some hours later after intelligible speech; a dead man coughed in the mortuary; deterioration into death takes place if no resuscitation is operated after the first inspection. After electric shocks aggressive resuscitation is called for. In 1877 a revival after *burial* took place, which electrified the Paris medical faculty (then the premier in the world), which caused a circular to be issued by the Académie de Médecine. During a cholera epidemic a woman was buried without proper formalities; exhumed for a legitimate purpose she was found to be alive and died on the following night. The professors of Paris admonished the profession that they should be more careful.[6a]

M. Nemiroff of the University of Michigan Medical Centre recently made a special study of cases of drowning in very cold water after hearing of only three or four isolated cases of survival after prolonged immersion. One particular case he presents was an 18-year old student who seemed dead after nearly 40 minutes trapped in his car in an icy pond. He was blue when recovered, *with no pulse and a glassy stare*. An attempt at resuscitation was abandoned; he gave an involuntary belch; his rescuers renewed their efforts aggressively; and he was rushed to hospital. One does *not* learn that he regards his experience as miraculous, though his mother could have definite ideas on the subject. He made a perfect recovery and completed his college course very creditably. Of thirteen people who were submerged in Michigan for at least 4 minutes, *two* died and *two* suffered permanent brain damage, but *nine* recovered. 'There is some brain damage even in those who recover', says Dr. Nemiroff, 'but this is reversible within the first 24 hours'. The cold contracts the peripheral blood vessels, reducing the flow of blood, the heart rate slows, and oxygen is shunted to where it is needed. In warm water the drowned are likely to suffer irreversible brain damage after about 4 minutes. All this is apropos of the need for the speedy rescue and aggressive resuscitation of the drowned.

In the natural sciences research goes on in the same area simultaneously in various countries and from various points of view. Nemiroff's study was not alone. Since absence of oxygen for the provision of hæmoglobin and the functioning of the brain is a prime source of brain-death, studies of *anoxia*, or, where the supply of oxygen is extremely attenuated, *hypoxia* are increasing. The possibilities of revival are precisely the source of the interest. There is no anoxia so complete as when the person has been drowned. The navy is naturally interested, and no effort is spared. F.St.C. Golden, of the Institute of Naval Medicine (Gosport) writes, in "Problems of Immersion", 'Attempts at resuscitation should always be made in apparently dead hypothermic victims regardless of the period of submersion and only abandoned if still unsuccessful after rewarming had occurred'. The last I have seen of an astounding series of studies[6b] is that of J. Pearn of the Department of Child Health, University of Queensland, 'Neurological and Psychometric Studies in Children Surviving Freshwater Immersion Accidents'. All the children studied were drowned, and suffered anoxia for considerable periods. Brain damage was measurable, but in the case of younger children, more easily repairable. Anoxia was repairable over as long as five years. The vast majority of children studied had been subjected to vigorous resuscitation, and survived without *any* defect. 'The outcome, for a child and his family, after a freshwater-immersion accident, is obviously very good even in cases when the child is apparently dead when rescued.' One can reassure parents provided that the child is breathing spontaneously *within an hour of the rescue!* But there is something even more astounding, which baffles all researchers. The medium I.Q. of the survivors (110) is significantly above that of the general population! The group of survivors appears, therefore, to be in some way self-selecting. But only absurd explanations are offered for this, and at once rejected, e.g. that children of parents with high I.Q.'s are mentally prepared for, and experienced in conditions suitable to drowning, above their contemporaries! It is possible, but not proved, that children revived after drowning receive some mental advantage from their period of anoxia.

Recoveries after clinical death continually occur. No one claims that any is miraculous. A friend of mine relates how he drove his mother in his car, found her to be dead, and covered her up; and when she had been in the mortuary for a while she revived—an undertaker's nightmare. A recent newspaper article by a physician, apropos of new ideas about the treatment of the recently drowned, relates, '. . . there are sources of error. Overdoses of drugs and severe cold can depress brain stem function to give the appearance of death. For that reason old people may sometimes appear dead when they are actually hypothermic, and it is an explanation of why a young woman who was found on a beach and given up for dead came to life when she "warmed up" in the mortuary.'

One notices the public's greater interest in the revival of 'young people'. Few would not welcome a young woman's revival, but many are relieved when old people die.

There are societies which are not averse from hastening the departing, when the flame of life is low. An old woman in Normandy Is., New Guinea, had been ill. Her relatives pronounced her dead, and when the Rev. Dr. Brownlow pointed out that she was still alive they insisted on proceeding with the burial: 'her head and throat were dead, and that was sufficient'! The missionary called to the mourners to cease lamenting, and to lift the woman out of the burial chair. With great reluctance they consented, and she survived until the following morning (much to their disgust).[6*] In the Syria of a half-century ago when people fell into a coma they were at once given up for dead and lamenting began much as at Mk. 5:38 Often the wish is father to the thought.[6†] The celebrated sculptor

40

Benvenuto Cellini was given up for dead, but while his shroud was being made and a very insipid sonnet (which survives) was being written to lament him he suddenly revived: 'Many of my friends crowded in to behold the miracle . . ., and among them people of the first importance . . . My brother-in-law . . . arrived; he came from Florence for the inheritance; but as he was a very worthy man he rejoiced to have found me alive . . .'[6‡]

If someone has an actual interest in X being dead rather than in a deep coma, he will rarely consider that the latter must be excluded. That has a bearing on our problem. There *was* a person, Joseph, with a keen interest in Jesus's being not only dead, but dead in time to be buried before the Sabbath commenced at sunset. As we can see from the unauthentic insertion at Mk. 15:44, very early students of Mark were concerned (as well they might be) at the chronology. Was not the timetable far too tight? They wanted to be reassured that Jesus was taken down *dead* notwithstanding the haste which they knew (only too well) was quite uncharacteristic of Asians.

Recent examples of revivals include Ruth Young (*The Times* 14 Ap. 1972); an event near Trivandrum, 24 Jul. 1972 (*The Statesman* 29 Jul. 1972); the person whose revival is discussed in *The Daily Mail*, 7 Oct. 1972 (on p.15); and Rose Hanover (*The Sun* 17 Ap. 1973), who snored in her coffin. I was alert for examples during a relatively short period, and there have been others since.

The incidence of severe comas of various origins, brain damage due to accidents and drugs, and the practice of organ-transplant operations have stimulated increased interest in the distinction between incohate (clinical) death, i.e. death formerly all too easily certifiable by a physician, and brain death. The latter may occur very much later if a person falsely certified to be dead revives and, as is all too likely to be the case, is neglected in consequence of the certificate. Physicians tend to become defensive in such situations. If they hand out death-certificates hurriedly (usually when they have attended the deceased during a serious illness or as in a not-so-amusing case where his 'pals' electrocuted a student and told the doctor he was known to have a weak heart!), they may find themselves saying 'If I certify a man to be dead he *is* dead', which is as ridiculous as it sounds: it must be regarded as an occupational hazard.

A person hanging on a cross and giving signs of loss of consciousness (e.g. the behaviour of the pudenda) may very well appear to be dead, but until further tests are done he may at best be dying.

It is well known that if the blood-supply to the brain is interrupted for too long (as distinct from slowed) brain damage may ensue when the circulation is restored, as it often has to be on the operating table. Relatives are in litigation with our medical service on this topic while I write. It is impossible to predict which parts of the brain will be affected, or whether the damage will be permanent. If a short survival intervenes between incohate death and brain-death, hopes of recovery of the nervous system will, of course, hardly have time to be aroused.

It is in cases of hypoxia and anoxia that spontaneous revival is interesting. As every nurse knows, respiration and pulse are co-ordinated by the brain. An imperceptible pulse rate will be accompanied, if life persists, with an imperceptible respiration. Such cases are likely to be hypoxic. I digress for a moment to point out that a crucified victim will have great breathing difficulties, and may unconsciously control his respiration to a minimum, as in yogic breath-control. This will automatically lower the pulse-rate. On the cross no response is required; a coma will soon ensue.

Under normal conditions comas due to disease will produce hypoxia or anoxia. Artificial respiration is resorted to, the patient continues in life for a period, though brain damage might well preclude resumption of full capacity and independence of action. Yet hypoxic and even anoxic cases have been known to resume spontaneous respiration some time after artificial respiration is applied or even without it. There are people who have lived in a deep coma for years, with natural respiration, though obviously very faint. There are, as we have seen, a proportion of hypoxic comas from which partial recovery, and even full recovery is actually documented. Modern information, promulgated by the Honorary Secretary of the Conference of Medical Royal Colleges and their Faculties in the United Kingdom,[7] may be extracted for our use:

'. . . (2) Exceptionally, as a result of massive trauma, death occurs instantaneously or near-instantaneously. Far more commonly, death is not an event: it is a process, the various organs and systems supporting the continuation of life failing and eventually ceasing altogether to function, succesively and at different times. (3) Cessation of respiration and cessation of the heart beat are examples of organic failure occurring during the process of dying, and since the moment that the heart beat ceases is usually detectable with simplicity by no more than clinical means, it has for many centuries been accepted as the moment of death itself, without any serious attempt being made to assess the validity of this assumption. (4) It is now universally accepted, by the lay public as well as by the medical profession, that it is not possible to equate death itself with cessation of the heart beat . . . (5) In the majority of cases in which a dying patient passes through the processes leading to the irretrievable state we call death, successive organic failures eventually reach a point at which brain death occurs and this is the point of no return . . .'

The opinion is conjectured that the spirit departs from the body at irreversible brain death. Though this will not be contested, one will do well to remember that primitive and ancient peoples would understand that the spirit left the body at what I have called 'incohate death', and, in a case of spontaneous revival, has *returned* to its old home. A civilisation in which (as with orthodox Jews and Muslims) every event occurs within God's will, will be bound to construe revival as for God's purpose, not the subject's.

The great advance in medical care and clarity of thinking on this subject has, within the last few years, brought us to the point at which we can say that, whereas in former times death seemed to occur in the circulation, detectable by respiration ceasing and the indetectability of the heart beat or pulse, now death cannot be established unless it is brain-death.[8] Death occurs in the

42

brain. Now, from the point of view of the Anastasis, it is obvious that if one looks to the absence of pulse (as shown in the cessation of bleeding!) and failure of response to stimuli as conclusive proofs of death, one has proved only incohate death, not brain-death. What used to be called clinical death is reversible in some cases. Between October 1980 and February 1981 the interest in this question suddenly increased. Transplant-surgery (which earns substantial fees) had made great advances and healthy organs from young victims of accidents were in great demand. Life-support machines, by artificially continuing the circulation and respiration, kept, as they still keep, comatose patients alive—but their kidneys, for example, are wanted! It is a common-place experience for doctors to diagnose brain-death, if the circulation is not reaching the brain and the normal reflexes are absent; and the next-of-kin are shown the patient breathing and are invited to authorise the switching off of the machines (I have seen the mechanical indicator of the pulse stop as the surgeon cuts out the required organ, and heard the comment 'Now he *is* dead!'). No sooner had the question of tests for brain-death as opposed to clinical death been ventilated than a crop of persons came forward to testify that they were certified dead and had recovered, to the disappointment of surgeons.

One testified before television cameras in the company of a child he had begotten subsequent to his revival (thus exactly paralleling a well-known ancient Jewish incident: see p.31 above). As this is a good entertainment very careful research was done, and the standard American tests were shown to be (so far as the layman could observe) more satisfactory than those in use in Britain. The celebrated BBC television programme caused innumerable otherwise charitable persons to ask their spouses to hand them down their 'donor-cards'. The British medical world, ill advised at first, refused to answer questions; but since this would ultimately affect the availability of organs for transplants other counsels eventually prevailed. As a by-product of this the public became much better informed about clinical death and brain-death.[8a] Until brain-death is proved by internationally accepted tests, involving sophisticated mechanical equipment, death is now presumed reversible . . . When various people have a financial and other interest in your being dead it is a distinction in which you can be expected to take a lively interest.

Yet as between lesions, even severe lesions, and clinical death there are stages and degrees, let alone the distinction between clinical death and brain-death; and possibilities of partial or total recovery are various.

Excellent physical recovery from cardio-vascular lesions, with damage to the brain, are now quite commonplace, with the population reaching a higher average life-span than the ancient world knew. The immense will-power of patients is shown by their expressions of frustration. But the traumas are dramatic in their partial character. My mother suffered a 'stroke', made an impressive physical recovery, and conversation appeared to be brisk; but she summoned to her bedside my grandfather who had been dead for more than twenty years and my father who had died some five years before. Memory is obviously an easy casualty in such cases.

There is no evidence that any persons of whose *anastasis* we know, including those rescued from drowning, were, or are, the better for their experience, or made any use of their ordeal. A recent publication of reminiscences of persons who believed they had died and revived has not obtained credence, since the experiences ('I simply put myself into this great hand of light . . . until my mother drew me up by the hair ...') can be explained as losses of consciousness (though the editor of a collection claims he suffered 'clinical death' himself). In a work entitled *Before Death Comes* another writer (M. Rawlings) deals with the reported experiences of persons passing through clinical death, in order to prepare doctors and nurses to accept, and encourage belief in an after-life. Such publications may understandably be castigated as irresponsible and even fraudulent.[9] The miracle of Jesus's Anastasis may lie precisely in his making significant use of what was a genuine revival from reversible death.

We have not yet considered a catalepsy induced by the subject himself. There is at least one which is documented, and in a moment we shall bring it into confrontation with our problem. There is a technical difficulty with the curious word *exepneusen* ('he out-breathed') which Mark takes the trouble to use twice (Mk. 15:37,39). Luke used it once, taking it from Mark and exploiting the poetic-dramatic implications of the term ('Father, into thy hands I commit my spirit: so saying he out-breathed' [literally, 'expired', a commonplace in Latin but not suitable to this level of Greek prose] (Lk. 23:46). On the surface Mark, followed by Luke, insinuates that Jesus determined when he should die. But we must look at that *exepneusen* more closely.

Apart from an instance apiece in Josephus and Plutarch, the verb *ekpneō* ('to out-breathe') from which *exepneusen* comes, is extremely rare without a direct object (as in 'he breathed out his soul') and is exclusively poetical. The instances of Josephus and Plutarch are mannered and stylish[9a] and are not precedents for Mark's level of Greek. We must therefore suppose that Mark (or his predecessor) was utilising a possible Greek equivalent of a semitic term. There is an obvious one immediately to hand. The biblical term for 'to give up the ghost' as a preliminary to dying is the root GWʿ, rendered in Gen. 25:8, 25:17, 35:29, 49:33 and Job. 13:19 by the LXX with the normal Greek verb *ekleipō*, 'to faint', and in some other places by ordinary verbs meaning 'to die'. In Aramaic, the daily language of Jesus's world, evidenced by the Targumic translations of the biblical passages I have mentioned and elsewhere and by rabbinical (Talmudic) literature, the equivalent is the root NGD. Where our older versions have 'he gave up the ghost' the Targums render *gawʿ* with *'itnᵉgîd*. This is the exact equivalent of *exepneusen*, and means 'he fainted'. It often, but by no means necessarily, implied an ensuing death. A glance at the standard dictionary[9b] reveals instances where a person *'itnᵉgîd*, and came to later and had something to say! Mark's *exepneusen* is an artful term leaving open the question why, and at whose option, Jesus *lost consciousness*. We must render it not 'he died', but 'he fainted'.

Jagadananda, a great Hindu preacher, a charismatic personality and head ascetic of an important monastery in Orissa, said,

Samādhi (religous trance) can neither be induced nor resisted [there are some who would question in any case the first of these propositions]. It is involuntary . . . I began to chant *Om.* Then I had an experience. I felt as if I was no longer a man of flesh and blood, but was present everywhere [a typical ecstatic experience] . . . I lost all consciousness. I was in *samādhi* for three days and three nights. When I returned to my senses, I was uttering the sound *ma* [suggesting 'mother'] . . . She said that people had been crowding around me for three days to obtain blessings from my feet, and that the doctor had declared me dead.

He had many such experiences. He was practised in extended trances. He claimed that if a man did not get his senses back for fifteen days and his body started to decay he attained release from rebirth. If the body did not decay his senses would probably return. This discussion shows that revivals from apparent death were a topic of local discussion.[10] *Samādhi* looks similar to death, and *yogis* have often had themselves buried in airless places and emerged alive: in *samādhi* the need for oxygen is minimalised. They risk hypoxia, but not, apparently, anoxia.

It seems we should, on this showing, leave the door open for Jesus to have entered into a self-induced trance after the crucifixion. Subsequently signs of dying appeared which convinced bystanders that he was dead. Otherwise he would not have been allowed off the cross. Mk. 15:39 is intended to confirm this, an aspect of the verse ignored at Mt. 27:54 and Lk. 23:47. Mk. 15:44, which relates how astonished Pilate was and how he ascertained the fact of death from the centurion, is a piece of apologetic, inserted possibly in the second edition of Mark, probably not bearing Mark's own imprimatur. I am not admitting that incohate death did not supervene upon this trance, if indeed the latter occurred, which is a conjecture in any case. However, a sham-death reflex resulting from fear-provoking stimuli coupled with physical or psychological restraints, a disaster-syndrome, is known to science.[11]

To sum up: the advance in clinical medicine raises the presumption on the basis of the Passion story in its outlines (which we have no reason to reject), that Jesus's death could have been reversible for a significant time after burial. If his clinical death was due to suffocation (which was most probable with crucifixion-victims), experience suggests that a rapid diagnosis of death by persons not perfectly qualified, under the influence of a desire to obtain rapid access to the body, could mislead. If he had not been rescued after burial brain-death could well have supervened on account of his untreated injuries. If this may be presumed, the other presumption, almost universally made amongst theologians, that *if Christ revived in the tomb,* it must have been a miracle in the sense of a *fact outside the course of nature,* is unfounded and we should do well to proceed without it.

NOTES

1. *Laws* II.12,531 = 12.958-9.
2. J. A. Montgomery and H. S. Gehmann, *Kings* (Edin., 1951), 296.

3. P. Forestus, *Observ. et curat. medicin.* (Frank., 1634, 1660), XVII, obs.9,p.112, col.1.
4. Ibid.,XXVII obs.27.
5. Ibid., XVII,obs.9: *locum mutavere, atque ita miserrime mortuæ inventæ.*
6. (1946) Law Reports, 73 Ind.App.246; (1942) 47 Calcutta W.N.13,26-7, and S. C. Mitter at *Indian Law Rev.* 1/4 (1947), 343-50.
6a. S. Jellinek, *Dying, Apparent Death and Resuscitation* (London, 1947), 143-4, 147-8.
6b. See T. D. Kirttingen and A. Naess (1963) *British Medical Journal,* i, 1315; H. Siebke et al. (1975) *The Lancet,* i, 1275; M. J. Nemiroff et al (1977) *Paper presented to the Annual Meeting of the American Thoracic Society, San Francisco;* D. Theilade (1977) *Anæsthesia* 32, 339; J. Pearn (1977) *The Lancet,* i, 7; F.St.C. Golden (1980) *Brit. Journ. of Hospital Medicine,* 23, 371. See also C. Doyle, *The Observer,* 21 Aug. 1977.
6*. G. Brown, *Melanesians and Polynesians* (London, 1910), 391-2.
6†. G. M. Lamsa, *Gospel Light* (Philadelphia, 1939), 71.
6‡. B. Cellini, *Autobiography,* trans. J. A. Symonds (London, 1949), 158-9.
7. (1979) *British Medical Journal,* i, 332 (3 Feb. 1979).
8. D. J. Woods and T. Royder (1978). On intense concern over premature burial see Albano (1969) and Arnold et al. (1968).
8a. *Radio Times* 11-17 Oct. 1980 gave publicity to Bill Matthews, Polly Scott and Dave Churchill, who were certified dead *at the degree of brain death* and made a total recovery. See *The Observer,* 15 Feb. 1981, p.15 on transplants.
9. Vaisrub (1977). J. C. Hampe, *To Die is Gain. The Experience of one's Own Death* (London, 1979) deals with reports of people resuscitated from dying, able to tell what they experienced between life and death.
9a. *Ant.*12.357; Plut., *Mor.* 597F. A proper picture of the scope of *ekpneō* may be obtained from Liddell-Scott-Jones's *Lexicon* rather than that of Bauer-Arndt-Gingrich (too optimistic).
9b. Jastrow. *Dictionary of Talmud Babli,* etc., 872, col.i.
10. D. M. Miller & D. C. Wertz, *Hindu Monastic Life* (Montreal & London, 1976), 90-1.
11. I. Oswald, *Sleep,* 3rd edn. (Harmondsworth, 1974), 116-18.

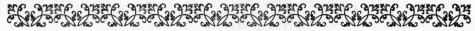

CHAPTER VI

Could Jesus have Revived in the Tomb?

Venturini[1] and other ingenious minds[2] have long since suspected that Jesus was taken away from the tomb after a spontaneous revival. The well-known and ingenious historical novel by Schonfield[3] gave all possible prominence to the notion that Jesus organized a plot to have himself taken down from the cross, feigning death, and then to be conveyed privily away. These conjectures were inevitable. The last was only a version of the oldest explanation given by Jews, that it was the work of 'that impostor' (Mt. 27:63).[3a] There were aspects in the New Testament sources which practically asked for such conjectures, at least from students unwilling or unable to recognise, and give due weight to, other aspects of the same sources, not to speak of archæological finds.

1. THE CRUCIFIXION AND BURIAL.

All admit that crucifixion, whatever its earlier history, was a Roman penalty, known and practised previously to the time of Jesus, and had become in some curious way a method of torture and execution forcibly harmonised with the Old Testament law by way of Deut. 21:22-3. That very text, needless to say, excluded, on the face of it, the notion that a Messiah might be crucified (Hengel 1977, 85). Crucifixion is the ultimate expression of the inhumanity dormant within man (ibid., 87). The Pharisees did not recognize impalement (the Jewish equivalent to crucifixion) as a penalty, but only as a very temporary means of exposing dead criminals who had been lawfully executed by stoning. But other ideas also obtained at the time. We are very fortunate to have a contemporary commentary on the biblical text, which shows what an influential body of self-consciously pious Jews (the Qumran sect are now identified with the Essenes) thought the legal text meant, and we have also sidelights upon it from the historian Josephus.

Deut. 21:22-3 in the MT means, 'And if a man have committed a sin worthy of death and he be put to death, and thou hang him on a tree; his body shall not remain all night upon the tree, but thou shalt surely bury him the same day; for he that is hanged is accursed of God; that thou defile not thy land which the Lord giveth thee for an inheritance.' In the time of Jesus it was believed that a *blasphemer* should be stoned and impaled, and, political crimes apart, it is not clear whether, if the Jewish authorities had a free hand, they would have impaled any other type of offender.[4]

The Qumran folk however, in their special commentary on Deuteronomy to be found in the Temple Scroll,[5] say, 'If a man slanders his people, and delivers his people to a foreign nation, and does evil to his people, you shall hang him on a tree and he shall die. On the testimony of two witnesses, and on the testimony of three witnesses he shall be put to death, and they shall hang him (on) the tree.

If a man is guilty of a capital crime and he flees to the Gentiles, and curses his people, and the sons of Israel, you shall hang him also on the tree, and he shall die. But their bodies shall not stay overnight on the tree (cf. Jn. 19:31). Indeed, you shall bury him on the same day for he who is hanged on the tree is accursed of God and men, and you shall not pollute the ground which I give you to possess.' Max Wilcox, in a brilliant article,[6] explains that at this rate the notion of death upon a tree being a geniune part of Jewish penal law, and thus referable to Jesus, former scepticism about the prophecies of the Passion must be reviewed. Jesus, as it seems to me, fully harmonised the crucifixion with his own native culture's concept of sacrifice. The Roman penalty was thus, in an entirely unexpected way, naturalised, not by Christians in retrospect, but by Christ himself. We shall come back to the bizarre notion of the crucifixion party as 'slaughterer' (p.49). The cross too, as we shall see, early became a symbol of the faith.

Returning to the events in which we are interested, one must remember the salient items reported: (a) Jesus's death was premature by normal standards: crucified persons usually suffer much longer; (b) the legs were not broken, as was usual, because he was already dead when the action would have been taken to accelerate death in view of the onset of the Feast; (c) the side was jabbed or stabbed to confirm death; (d) the body was taken down hastily and buried in a cloth as a temporary expedient; (e) a stone was rolled to, i.e. rolled into the mouth of the tomb. The whole process took place in the last hour of daylight before the three stars of the Sabbath evening had appeared. On each of these five points much could be said (free rein having been given to scepticism) but I shall be brief.

(a) One person is known to have been taken down from a cross in fact (as opposed to romance) and to have survived; but he had had every care, and others expired in similar circumstances.[7] Jesus had none: his revival must be very remarkable. That Jesus's death was obviously premature was regarded as a loophole left by Mark, and gave rise to the apologetic Mk. 15:44 (which we have seen is secondary, p.45). The story, however, demands this, as John indicates at length with his leg-breaking episode (Jn. 19:33). Nevertheless Jesus's scourging,[8] which seems to have prevented him from carrying his cross, will have left him in very poor shape. Medical conjectures as to the cause of clinical death in this case are numerous and tend to cancel each other out.[9] We are in no position to decide. Suffocation would be the normal cause of death on the cross, hastened by collapse, itself normally hastened by shin-breaking (throwing the full weight of the body onto the wrists).

We now know how crucifixion was done in the First Roman War because of the Giv'at ha-Mivtar ossuary.[10] It is conceivable that some had the ankles pinned with the knees to their right instead of their left, but variations on the efficient and expeditious method which is proved by that invaluable skeleton would be difficult to conceive. The anatomically correct position for the upper nails was used — between the radius and ulna[10a] — and the two heels were pinned simultaneously through the centre of the *os calcis,* the nail being well clinched over on the far side of the olive-trunk which served as the 'tree'. If the crucified recovered (which was of course never expected!) his walking again could *not* be despaired of, despite the severe wrenching which would be needed to disengage the feet without chopping off the ankles (as happened in the case at Giv'at ha-Mivtar). He might be no worse placed than the far-famed Œdipus, who, legend insists, became a warrior and a sage, though his heels were pinned together in babyhood (I assume *diatoroi podoin akmai* [Soph., Œd.T., 1034] means 'pierced extremities of (both) feet').

It is absolutely clear that Christians accepted the crucifixion of Christ, though carried out at the orders of a Roman official and by means of a Roman crucifixion party, as a *scripturally* significant and relevant event, to be interpreted in the light of Deut. 21:22-3, however eccentric such an evaluation might appear to be to us. In other words Christians made a virtue of necessity. Paul says, 'Christ redeemed us from the curse of the Law, having become a curse for us, for it is written, "Cursed is every one that hangs on a tree", in order that upon the Gentiles might come the blessing of Abraham in Christ Jesus, so that we might receive the promise of the Spirit through faith.' (Gal. 3:13-14 see below, p.118). There is not the slightest suggestion that the action of the Romans is to be resented, or the unfortunate victim pitied! On the contrary, recurring to the Redemption, Paul says 'God sent forth his son, born of a woman, born under the Law, that he might redeem them which were under the Law, that we might receive the adoption of sons . . .' (Gal. 4:5). If the naturalization of crucifixion as a penalty is remarkable, the calm way in which the whole affair has been assimiliated is even more so. Unless, that is to say, Jesus himself took the thing in his stride, as it were, had internalized it and projected it in a wholly positive manner: which is surely unique, if it is true.

(b) As for the abstention from breaking Jesus's legs (Jn. 19:31-33) the dramatic Johannine information is no doubt partly[11] in answer to the question, 'If he survived and revived how can he have walked about as represented in Matthew and Luke? But since we know for a fact that shins were usually broken[12] — the Giv'at ha-Mivtar skeleton proves it[13] — not only is the question a proper one, but the scene represented by John (which has been doubted) is plausible. I do not doubt but that the basic information existed: for a reason highly typical of the author and of the story as a whole. From Mk. 14:22 (explained at Lk. 22:15) and 1 Cor. 5:7-8 ('For our Passover has been sacrificed, namely Christ . . .') it is plain that Jesus was conceived as offering himself as a substitute for the paschal lamb which should have been eaten by his company had it been a Passover meal.[14] John himself, by quoting Exod. 12:46, shows[15] that if the parallel with the paschal lamb was to be sustained no bone must have been broken, for the lamb's bones were not to be broken (so Num. 9:12). Ps. 34:20 tells us that the righteous 'keeps all his bones: not one of them is broken' (so that the resurrection may find him fit and ready for it). Now all this would be superfluous if Jesus's legs had been smashed, or his ankles chopped off to disengage the feet. Perhaps a blacksmith's pincers were available to disengage the broad-headed hand-made nail, or one nail could drive out the other (as the saying went: Lucian, *Philops.* 9).

Pious persons, especially Pharisees, will have made a point of urging crucifixion parties not to break the shins, even if that would expedite death, since availablity for the resurrection was more important than a few hours' pain.

(c) The side was stabbed or jabbed to confirm death. Failure to respond to stimuli would then have been regarded as a fair suggestion of death, though now, of course, total unresponsiveness is no evidence without the use of machinery to attest brain-death.[15a] Jabbing was indeed a Roman practice,[16] and John is again our sole authority for Jesus's undergoing it. He says further (19:34, cf. 1 Jn. 5:6) that blood and water came out of the wound, and insists on the verity of the testimony to this. One wonders how much of this is imaginary. When the pulse has become imperceptible of course bleeding practically stops; and Jews who had opportunities of watching crucifixions reported how the blood often spurted out (from arteries accidentally or deliberately pierced).

Could a man whose side is poked or stabbed with a lance revive? It is a fact that of all wounds a surgeon has to handle the puncture wound is amongst the easiest to deal with (depending on the depth): but that is a generalization and we have no surgeon here. The answer may be that all is imaginary save the tradition that the side was jabbed to satisfy the soldiers that, being dead, Jesus's corpse could reasonably be given to his friends. The practice is normal to this day of poking (or kicking) the severely wounded who make no spontaneous movement, before calling stretcher-bearers. Soldiers do not have time to 'mess about'. It is also a fact, taken abstractly, that if the part of the body to take the jab was the pleural cavity and the heart and the lungs were not penetrated (which is quite possible if no bone of the thoracic cage was broken) revival would not be precluded. Blood and water could indeed escape since the scourging will have brought lymphatic fluid to the area. But John's reason for appearing to satisfy our curiosity in this elaborate way is partly expressed, and, as usual with him, partly concealed.

Jn. 19:37 cites words from Zech. 12:10, 'And I will pour upon the house of David, and upon the inhabitants of Jerusalem, the spirit of grace and of supplication; *and they shall look unto Me whom they have pierced;* and they shall mourn for him, as one mourns for his only son, and shall be in bitterness for him, as one that is in bitterness for his firstborn.' Mark, incidentally, develops the *mourning* touch, without quoting Zechariah, at 15:38, when he speaks of the veil of the Temple being torn from above to below, as if God (above) tore his garment in mourning (the proper Jewish practice). Matthew's mind is shown by the change he makes in Mark's story: at 27:61 the two (Matthæan) women *sit* (a typical gesture of mourning) opposite the tomb. But more important, theologically, than the Zechariah passage, is Num. 20:10-11 (cf. Is. 48:21) with its *haggadic* development. Moses smote the rock in the wilderness *twice,* and the first time blood flowed out and only the second time water.[17] By John's time it was accepted in some quarters that the Rock of the Wilderness foreshadowed Christ, who was that Rock (1 Cor. 10:4), a character he thus shared with God himself (Ps. 78:35, 89:26, 94:22, 95:1, Is. 51:1). God was certainly the Rock of the Qumran sect (1QH xi. 15)

(d) The body was hurriedly buried in a cloth (a *sindon,* an all-purpose fine linen cloth) as a temporary expedient. The earlier sources assure us that no embalming was done, and this is confirmed by the extremely elaborate story of the Anointing at Bethany.[18] The early church was severely embarrassed that none of the entourage of Jesus ever embalmed him at any stage between his crucifixion and his removal from them. It worried them very much more than it would worry us (cf. Is. 14:19, Jer. 22:19, 1 Sam. 31:11, 2 Sam. 2:5ff.): evidently questions of finance and prestige were involved. The cloth used was a simple sheet (Mk. 15:46) not the regular winding-strips used in a proper embalming. Matthew insists that it was a pure sheet, which is interesting.

He is not telling us that Joseph eschewed a second-hand shroud (was there a market for such?), or one kept by gentile merchants or non-observant Jews in a 'state of uncleanness', for either notion is rather absurd. He is happy to observe (Mt. 27:59) that Jesus, so soon to be risen and 'exalted', was not contaminated (at a time when total immersion in an immersion-pool was beyond him) by a ritually unclean garment. For Jesus *not remaining a corpse*[19] was capable of contracting ritual defilement (p.113), or so the earliest Jewish Christians rather hastily supposed.

John's story is totally different. We know that John's gospel presupposes knowledge of one or more of his predecessors, perhaps in forms which we have. His technique is to supplement, to explain, and occasionally to correct the perspective. His reasons for totally contradicting Mark here may reflect independent information. But we cannot rule out the possibility that he had none; and his motives may be more arcane. According to him Nicodemus, a second disciple of Jesus (Jn. 3:1, 7:50) joined Joseph, bringing a hundred litres of myrrh and aloes — a massive amount. They swaddled[20] the body of Jesus in strips of linen soaked in the spices according to a Jewish method of embalming for interment. The process can easily be visualised if you have seen a broken limb being set in plaster of Paris. One starts with clean bandages and these are continuously impregnated with the wet plaster. It is quite unnecessary to suppose from the story that Jesus was buried in a trough grave, which would have its own ledger stone to cover the entire surface. This grotesque idea was thought of to accompany the notion that the oils alleged to have been brought by Nicodemus were poured in the grave to top it up, as ossuaries are topped up. But, as I have explained, the idea was that the *othonia*, the bandages, were dipped in the vessels, or rather soused in them. Mark tells how the ladies bought the *aromata* (spices), corresponding to Nicodemus's costly materials, and omits to mention the bandages, which they must also have carried. There is a dramatic *and* a literary reason for concentrating on the vessels (and an intriguing one: p.104), but of course the bandages could be taken for granted, as their cost was minimal compared with the spices, which were really expensive.

Early hearers of Mark, knowing how valuable the tomb and its contents were to Joseph, must have been puzzled why it was that Joseph played no further rôle in the story. The first puzzle was why he or his agents did not forestall those women at the tomb? They must have been aware that the women were literary prototypes of festival visitors to the Sepulchre and that the young man figured more as an angel than in his proper person — but they will have known that women (named) were the first to know the truth and that a human encounter brought the young man into the story. Not realising that the Young Man very probably *was* an employee of Joseph, or at least could easily have been in touch with him, they applied their minds to the central question on the surface of Mark's text. Why did Joseph not visit the tomb? Well, because he had done the task of burying Jesus properly on the previous Friday itself: though the story suggests an incomplete interment, which St. John redescribes as if it were temporary. And the belief that Jesus *had* been properly prepared for burial even without the *aromata* (which is rather silly), has left a sediment in Luke's assertion that *othonia* (bandages) were found in the tomb (Lk. 24:12), whereas a few verses earlier he says that the body was only wrapped in a *sindon*. The unnecessary puzzle he has set us merely reflects a much more ancient puzzlement, incompletely resolved.

We know that corpses in Egypt treated in much the same way as is suggested in Jesus's case by John, soon become brittle, and the strips of cloth and the limbs they bind, not to speak of the coffin (in Egypt), become a solid impermeable mass. The unguents eventually have a desiccating and slightly caustic effect. In the Jerusalem area earth is scarce and since land cannot be taken out of use to enable worms to gnaw corpses, some other method of wasting the flesh on the bones had to be adopted. Hence the mode of rock-tomb burial. If John is to be believed Jesus could have risen and moved only in the same sense and manner as Lazarus did (Jn. 11:44). There is more than sufficient reason for believing that the raising of Lazarus was originally an *anastasis* which has been reconsidered by John and rendered by him as a preface to all Christian doctrine on Resurrection. Eliezer (Lazarus) is, after all, an appropriate name for one who goes and comes between the two worlds.[21] However that may be, the Johannine story of a thorough embalming, done more or less leisurely, requires a period of time which was not available according to the synoptic chronology, or, alternatively, a contempt for the Sabbath, which is unthinkable in the righteous Joseph and Nicodemus, and which John himself denies (19:42). The synoptic timetable fits so well and is so essential to the material on which John himself is meditating that I cannot bring myself to suppose he had another source of equal authority which set it aside.

Rather, I take it as certain that what John wants to tell us is that in spite of the fact that wealthy strangers took pains to put Jesus solemnly and firmly *away*, with the burial of a king,[22] he first appeared to his poor follower, Mary of Magdala, whose concern for his body (Jn. 20:15) was as real and as confident as theirs had been, and it was to her that his essential personal messages are given. To John Jesus's Anastasis *is not less symbolic than actual*. It can safely be symbolic because no one had, then, the smallest doubt but that it had occurred. Mark, on the contrary, had opted, for reasons some of which we have seen (while others await us), to make the *annunciation* of the Anastasis symbolic, not the Anastasis itself. For him the annual pilgrimage to the Sepulchre (not *necessarily* the present Holy Sepulchre) was still the high point of the Church's year.

I envisage a sheet being placed partly under and then over the body stretched out on a bench cut in the wall of the tomb,[22a] in which no one had been laid (as both Luke and John are careful to say: Lk. 23:53, Jn. 19:41), which was free from the defilement of death (about which, true to the place and time, the original participants were concerned when Jesus regained life). Originally the tomb was fit to accommodate other interments. The sheet would operate as lint, and would adhere to the open wounds. If there was a flow of blood it would be held to some extent by this cloth. I am not interested in the Turin grave-cloth, which enters the news at intervals as a journalistic exercise. This is an ancient painted representation, intended, long ago, to stimulate piety. It has no similarity to a cloth draped over a body, since this cannot produce a one-dimensional image (as anyone can verify by observing the behaviour of his own bed-sheet!).

(e) The stone was rolled to. We do not know whether it was held with a wedge. The description distinctly suggests a rolling, stopper-type stone, not a rectangular block which is hard to move without a crow-bar. It would be held in place by its own weight (Prov. 26:27) Since a great fuss is made about this stone, the absence of mention of the normal wedge may be significant. A stone rolled downwards to stop the hole needs no wedge, as a matter of fact. Someone has suggested that there was no stone placed over the mouth of the grave![23] This is nonsense, for reasons which will appear. Mark says Joseph *prosekulisen lithon* (Mk. 15:46), rolled a stone against or into the entrance of the tomb. The tomb was cut (i.e. excavated) out of living rock: *lelatomēmenon* means precisely 'quarried' or 'mined'. It could not have been entered from the rear by wall- or tomb-breakers. It was an underground chamber to which one went down, possibly by rough steps (see Sukenik, 1947). The entrance was probably very small and was closed either by a stone that rolled in a channel across its face, as in lavish tombs still extant[23a], or, as Mark's *prosekulisen* suggests, down into the hole from above, like a stopper. To move it away would therefore be a movement upwards, as the correct reading of our text confirms.[24] Such stones are indeed difficult to shift, but of course their object is to protect the corpse or corpses from wild animals and unauthorised entry from without, *not to prevent egress from within!* It is assumed that once tomb-visiting is over and the entrance has been sealed the occupants will bide quiet.

As the importance of this stone is enormous we must postpone further consideration of it to the appropriate place, but note how *lithos* (stone) occurs twice, in Mk. 16:3 and 4 and at the end of the syllabic lines (p.138), and this confirms not only that everyone knew there *was* a stone but that its importance was crucial to understand the story.

2. JOSEPH OF ARIMATHÆA.

Broer, after the most elaborate scepticism of Joseph (Broer, 1972) concludes that his name is genuine (pp. 290-3) as well as significant (284) though he cannot tell why. Joseph's name is remembered for four independent reasons: (a) the Patriarch Joseph was extremely interested in burials (Gen. 50:14), and indeed Joseph's own burial was a known item on the agenda at the First Redemption, viz. from Egypt, the Exodus (Gen. 50:25-26, Exod. 13:19, Josh. 24:32, Sir. 49:15, Heb. 11:22, Acts 7:15-16). Secondly (b) the reading sometimes printed in current texts, Harimathæa, is false and we must dismiss it; Arimathæa is a known village in Judæa, otherwise called Armatha, Ramatha. *'arimā*, *'arîm*, *'ārûm*, mean 'prudent', *'armûtā* means 'premeditation', 'subtlety', and the Aramaic *'arimûtā'* means 'wisdom'. Joseph certainly showed himself shrewd on this occasion, though, as fate would have it, not quite shrewd enough. He did not bargain on his guest's reviving and being disposed of elsewhere.

Even more important (c) is a point visible to Eusebius but forgotten since. The place which is repeatedly spelt *Armathaim* in the LXX (1 Sam. 1:1 etc.) is the home of Elkanah ('God has possessed'), father of the divinely-promised (and the pious populace would believe, divinely-begotten) prophet of the Kingdom, Samuel. Armathaim/Ramathaim was the birth-place, residence, and burial-place of Samuel, therefore the place of pilgrimage to Samuel's tomb. Eusebius says (*Onom.* 225, 11ff.), 'thence came Joseph said in the gospels to be from "Arima-thæa"'. It was highly proper that a man from thence should play kinsman to the prophet of the New Kingdom, the New Covenant, who also was born, as Luke made clear, by the promise of God (the *Magnificat*, Lk. 1:46ff., should be compared with 1 Sam. 1-2). Lastly (d) the name of the owner of the tomb will have been registered in the books of his family's bone-packers.

John (19:38) makes out that Joseph was a secret disciple of Jesus: here he is following Matthew who (27:57) says that he too 'was recruited as a disciple of Jesus's', which implies that he was (like Matthew's contemporaries) recruited at long range, as it were, though it does not absolutely rule out personal contact. We could usefully compare the Lucan story of Zacchæus, who could claim to be Jesus's pupil—a claim not likely to be denied by the disciples, who profited from him. I may be excused for conjecturing that both Matthew and John are adding afterthoughts, in an attempt to whitewash the disciples, whose reputations suffered in Mark more disastrously from the burial story than from their whole deplorable journey from Galilee to Jerusalem.

But Joseph is described by Mark as a respectable (*euschemōn*)[25] coun-cillor (*bouleutēs*), as befits one whose place of origin suggests 'subtlety'. It follows that he was rich (Mt. 27:57 alluding to Is. 53:9),[26] for that is the case with councillors.[27] Mark goes on to say in an arresting phrase (15:43) that he too was one who expected the Kingdom of God,[28] in other words a pious Jew of whom Jesus, if he had had the chance, might have approved. For him at any rate the Kingdom has not yet come, so his alleged discipleship of Jesus was not of the closest. Luke's description of him as good and righteous is almost superfluous in view of what he did. He was not a true disciple of Jesus, for the point of the story is that he, a stranger, undertook a duty, out of the well-known Jewish piety, to bury the dead whose own people could not or would not do that duty for him. What John the Baptist, with or without his head, could expect as a matter of course was denied to his successor.

The duty to bury the dead was an established 'good work', an aspect of Jewish morality.[29] The *halakhah* (Jewish law) says distinctly that a neglected corpse has a right to burial where it falls, as near as may be to where it is slain. One might wonder, though, whether the gentiles involved in the crucifixion of Jesus would ridicule Jewish superstitions in respect of (a) rapid burial, and

(b) burial near the place of death? We know that Romans were capable of showing gross disrespect to Jewish feelings and beliefs. It is of interest that knowing Jews could take advantage of a heathen superstition which insisted that unburied dead (especially innocent victims) were a real danger to the living, and that the crucified dead in particular had a nasty habit of going about as ghosts.[29a] The Romans interested in despatching the three crucified victims on this occasion would be familiar with being offered bribes by pious Jews, and would be more than ready to consider accepting them. It is nice to be bribed to do what, in your own view, is a proper thing to do.

One might imagine that John relied on common knowledge of this when he drew up 19:41 ('And in the place where he was crucified there was a garden, and in the garden a new tomb . .'). Burial in a garden suggests the burial of a King: and indeed a garden may well have materialised by John's time. But it seems to me to be at least likely that John, accepting the Marcan picture of the women's figuring (as we shall see) as brides of Christ (Mary stands for all), was simply relying on Cant. 4:16-5:1, where the garden (mentioned twice) is the place of bridal myrrh and spices (*arōmata*). Mark however is content to let us suppose that Joseph had, or acquired, a tomb very close in to Jerusalem, a prestige-worthy situation, and therefore very expensive. It may have been near the place of crucifixion: indeed that is highly likely. Josephus the historian actually tells us that pious people undertook the task of burying crucified victims[30] who otherwise would have been buried in a common grave for malefactors. Jesus's relatives were nowhere to be seen. His disciples, even Peter, were keeping their heads down. Peter afterwards alleged that even if he opened his mouth he was in danger of arrest, and Mark, with ironical kindness, preserves his excuse for us (Mk. 14:70, 'You certainly are one of them, for you are a Galilean . . .')!

Jesus's relations[30a] had found his trances and lectures to religious enthusiasts embarrassing: they even thought of putting him under restraint. There is no reason for thinking that Mark's solitary comment on the family of Jesus at Mk. 3:21 is a slander ('when his people heard [of his goings-on] they went out to catch hold of him, under the alleged impression that he was "beside himself" '), with its significant silence as to why his mother and brothers called to fetch him (Mk. 3:31-33). The relish with which the story is told (ibid.), implying that Jesus and his real companions frustrated such schemes, underlines, for me at any rate, the real meaning of the episode.

The malice of John's reference to Jesus's brothers at Jn. 7:2-5 is quite open ('Even his [hypocrite] brothers did not believe in him!'), yet it does not follow that the imputations were undeserved. The women who watched the crucifixion (the verb *theōrein* used at Mk. 15:40, 47, 16:4 certainly suggests attendance at some [holy] performance!) did so from afar off: and those who visited the tomb did not include relatives of Jesus. Indeed he seems to have emphasised in his lifetime that blood was *not* thicker than co-membership of the religious community—and the inevitable seems to have happened. Indeed Luke makes out that Jesus's friends *distanced themselves* as prophecy predicted (cf. Lk. 23:49 with Ps. 38:12, 88:9).

One may argue that John is particular to show Mary the mother of Jesus and the Beloved Disciple standing beneath the cross (Jn. 19:26-27), and every Rood reinforces this image. But the literary artificiality of it is fairly clear. The passage has nothing to do with Mary's being without a son, nor the Disciple (who is imaginary) being without a mother (neither notion is corroborated elsewhere); its function is to show that Jesus's command makes any 'beloved disciple' free of the house of any female Christian qualifying as 'widow' who can identify herself with Jesus's mother. The Christian community has developed, by John's time, a sociology of its own. At any rate if they were so close to the Cross as to converse on their futures with the Crucified, what were they about when his burial arrived on the agenda? Their negligence, lasting, according to all accounts, all the three days, seems even more preposterous. Of course they were not there. They were in hiding, which is what the story elsewhere confirms without hesitation. Jesus himself was alone on the Cross, meditating on Ps. 22, He had occasion to (p.48); 'all they that see me laugh me to scorn (v.7)'; 'I am poured out like water, and all my bones are out of joint (v.14)'; 'they pierced my hands and my feet. I may count all my bones (vv.16-17); 'For the kingdom is the Lord's . . . all they that go down to the dust shall bow before him, even he that cannot keep his soul alive. A seed shall serve him (vv. 28-30)'!

The fact of the matter is that Joseph of Arimathæa laid out good money for the *sindon,* for tips to the soldiers and the procurator's officers (Pilate kindly *gave* the body as a gift: Mk. 15:45, if genuine, is still ironical), and perhaps even for the tomb itself—for we do not know when he bought it—all in order to accommodate an honoured guest. There need not be the smallest doubt but that both he and the women, independently, *bought* grave materials (Mk. 16:1), and they were certain in their own minds not only that Jesus was dead but that he would stay so. Jews have frugal minds. They part with cash reluctantly, and avoid obvious risks.

Joseph's motive is clear. To bury the dead is virtuous. To offer shelter to a corpse that has no 'fathers' with whom it can be buried,[31] is surely a charitable act. Reciprocity operates. The principle is hammered home very emphatically at Mt. 25, which comes immediately before the Passion narrative: *v.*35, 'I was a stranger and you took me in . . .', the reward being that the hospitable inherit nothing less than a kingdom, which the one who was charitably treated then has at his disposal now (v.34). The burdens of hospitality can be considerable (Gen. 19:8!), but the obligation of reciprocity is sacred. Merit is transferable, and can be shared. The family have solidarity in virtue and vice (Lk. 4:23).[32] And no solidarity was so firmly present to the contemporary Jewish mind as the right to be buried, and, as was often necessary, to be re-buried, in the so-called 'secondary burial' (p.58), in the closest proximity with one's near and dear ones: the skulls of many *en route* for re-burial in ossuaries (when the family could afford them) can be found *in situ* in baskets in underground tombs, the remainder of the skeletons neatly piled in 'family' heaps. Joseph and his children's children would, at the Last Day, have the merit of sheltering a martyr in their family tomb.[33] In the ordinary way no stranger dare stand within the barrier of the (exalted) dead martyred by the state (b. Pes. 50a). At the resurrection Jesus would rise in their company and sanctify them all![34]

The skeleton at Giv'at ha-Mivtar in which we have taken an interest, a young man done to death by the Romans and therefore a martyr,[35] not necessarily a member of the family in whose grave his ossuary was packed, would, at the End of Time, testify that they found the oils with which his broken limbs were embalmed, topped up his ossuary, and gave him shelter until the spirit rejoined the bones. Their charity would cover many sins. Apart from anything else, the Giv'at ha-Mivtar case proves that crucified persons could be rescued (no doubt by the persistent, or the charitable) from being thrown into a common grave.[36] Joseph's tomb was known, of course, to his family, and to the bone-packers who had his family down on their list.

But this was not the end of the matter. If Jesus was a prophet (Mk. 6: 4,15, Mt. 21:11, 23:37, Lk. 7:26, 28), and it was a fair risk that he was (indeed his death is depicted by Mark, by Luke and by Paul as typical not merely of the suffering of the just but even of the fate of prophets [Gubler, 1977]), to be buried with his bones implied even a chance of revival and, if not, then a certainty of resurrection! See what the author of 2 Kngs. 13:21 says, 'And it came to pass that as they were burying a man . . . they cast the man into the sepulchre of Elisha; and as soon as the man touched the bones of Elisha he revived and *stood up on his feet*'. No wonder Ben Sirach says, 'As in his life he did wonders, so in death were his works marvellous' (Sir. 48:14)! There was a fair chance Joseph or his family might profit from this too.

Since the Mishnah contemplates that criminals executed by the state should not be mourned, and should be cast into appropriate graves far from the city, so that the unrighteous should not be buried near the righteous, nor the relatively less righteous with the relatively more righteous, it has occurred to many that one reason why we never hear of the finding of Jesus's body, even by a Jewish Sanhedrin eager to ridicule the tale of the Anastasis, is that Jesus was really taken down and cast into a communal pit, and perhaps there so mingled with others and perhaps even caused to decompose by lime that recovery of the body was impossible. If, as seems certain, Jesus was understood to have suffered death like many former prophets of the Lord (Lk. 13:33) a burial in the common burial ground of the poor would not be an unfitting insult. Just that fate had awaited the prophet Uriah the son of Shemaiah, as told at Jer. 26:20-24. A burial in a common pit would be even worse (Jer. 33:23 LXX actually suggests that happened to Uriah's corpse).

However, quite apart from considerations upon which I place the greatest weight below, the garbled and unreliable stories of the communal graves of criminals leave it open that relatives could collect the bones even of convicts executed by Jewish courts. Furthermore Pharisees would have been anxious to preserve the skeleton of one whose bodily sufferings had atoned for his guilt. They therefore would not have appreciated any additional insult to a corpse. Moreover communal graves are appropriate for victims whose relatives dare not come forward. This indeed would be the case where the crime was virtually treason.

Our case was a peculiar one and one aspect deserves to be thought over. Jesus was condemned by the Romans, and could certainly be taken for a martyr: it is constantly stated that his true supporters were the pious populace. Therefore all his disciples and those who believed in him could safely, in conscience, mourn for him, and would be justified in acquiring and burying his body. Those who took the point of view of the Chief Priests and Scribes plainly would regard Jesus as rightly convicted (indeed the conviction, on religious grounds, justified the m^esîrâ to Pilate), and they would do all they could to discourage public mourning and honourable burial—if they had time and opportunity, and had nothing better to do. There is thus no reason to assume that the story of Joseph is a complete fabrication; and, as I have said, both reminiscence as its nucleus, and its elaboration as faith-history make perfect sense. Blinzler, who gave the closest attention to the theory that Jesus might have been cast into a pit (Dhanis (1974), 93-6) rightly saw that if such a disgrace *had* occurred the church, expert at making scriptural capital out of any banal reminiscence, could certainly have coped with it (cf. Is. 53:9!) and (in its way) made a virtue of necessity. He was therefore not cast into a pit.

3. BONE-PACKERS.

As I write these words I can imagine the question, 'Where in the New Testament or in the literature of the first century do we hear of "bone-packers"?' The process is well known,[37] but one has to see the point. Admittedly the pious collected the bones of their dear ones (except, usually, parents)[37a] personally; and close relatives could certainly snap the desiccated corpses and make the neat piles of bones we can still see (under archæological supervision!). But packing in ossuaries was a highly specialised task.

The embalmed bodies lay in their tombs until they were sufficiently dry. Space, especially near Jerusalem, was very scarce, excavation of tombs and grave-niches very expensive, and economical methods were imperative. The bone-packers, who presumably had difficulties in recruiting, were probably, like our undertakers, organised in family businesses. Their dismal task was to snap the skeletons into manageable lengths and pack the bones into ossuaries. The ossuaries cost money, their lids had to be fitted neatly, and the larger were the more expensive, we may be sure. Therefore the exact space the bones would occupy, if correctly packed (like a Chinese puzzle), was known, no doubt a professional secret. Amulets and valuables were sometimes packed with the bones[38] hence the fear of tomb-robbers.[39]

The size of the ossuaries (some of them bore the names of their occupants and their claim to fame)[40] was as relevant as the need for them. Family graves were needed for generations of occupants. This was possible only if the drier skeletons were promptly packed in ossuaries and piled at the back of the tomb (as at Giv'at ha-Mivtar), or in ossuary chambers, which might contain scores of them in heaps. If one attempted to pack a skeleton prematurely one had a more than ordinarily unpleasant task on one's hands. These bone-packers will have had an acute sense of smell, and will have known, without a prolonged inspection, which corpses were ripe for treatment. This is highly specialised knowledge, for the drying out of a skeleton depends on many factors including the climate and the physical state of the corpses at burial.

Their clients' tombs will have been listed, and even mapped, and interments dated: that is obvious. A corpse buried straight into soil would decompose sufficiently for exhumation, *ossilegium* ('bone-gathering'), transporting (in the characteristic matting) and packing, in between eight months and one year.[40a] If placed on a cool bench in a underground rock tomb the process could not be commenced until a virtual mummification was completed, for the tendons must have severed of themselves (so says the traditional learning).[40b] Joseph was looking forward to being packed along with Jesus in some twenty to thirty years' time, depending on the quality of the unguents used. One cannot help feeling sad: his efforts were frustrated. His mention in the gospel is his compensation (I leave over the question of the sepulchre having been bought from him). The suggestion that he was an entirely imaginary character[40c] is ridiculous and illustrates how deep is ignorance on this subject.

4. THE TOMB MUST HAVE BEEN GUARDED.

Irrespective of the custom of tomb-visiting (cf. Jn. 11:31), it was an ancient Hebrew usage to keep a watch on a grave for a period (Job 21:32). Such was the value of the corpse to Joseph that it is inconceivable that it could have been left unguarded. During the Passover, when Jerusalem and its environs were crowded, there was more than ever a need to be watchful. The crucifixion made Jesus a martyr. The so-called Maccabean martyrs were translated to a tomb under a synagogue at Antiochia (Syria). The remains of martyrs could well be squabbled over, not because relics as such were worshipped—that came later. The famous case of Gotama the Buddha illustrates how devotees will quarrel over the minutest bone.

A martyr has a distinctly higher status than an itinerant holy man, an unproductive vagrant, and not least in his own family's eyes. He whose relations with the family were hardly of the most cordial and at times could be abrupt (as depicted at Jn. 2:4) could, when safely dead, be valuable, if only as the former companion of the family, to membership of which his title might be none of the most obvious (his antecededents were already open to discussion). The family might well send for the body notwithstanding Joseph's outlay, and take it without compensating him. Or the disciples or some of them might consider setting up a lucrative business in necromancy (pp.74-5) for which his body would be invaluable. Amulets could even be made from the iron used in a crucifixion (Lucian, *Philops.* 17). Or Jesus's enemies, the Sanhedrin, might anticipate any of these fanciful developments and have notions of their own. The least Joseph would do would be to see that the tomb was guarded until the sealing on the third day, after the routine inspection which we can be sure he intended to carry out, or have carried out, by, or for, himself.

The comical story at Mt. 27:62-66 is sometimes believed to be part of Matthew's independent information. 'So they (the chief priests and Pharisees!) went and made the tomb secure, sealing the stone in the company of the guard' (*v.*66). The nucleus of this may well be reminiscence that the place *was* guarded. However Josh. 10:18 (where a cave is sealed to keep people in) and Dan. 6:17 (where a den is sealed to keep a prophet in) are biblical 'precedents' which Matthew seems to have exploited in his usual way.[40d]

A scholar (Kratz, 1973) has the credit of investigating all biblical and some pagan instances of escape-stories. To him it is clear that Mt. 27:62-66 is an example of escape, and indicates that Matthew saw the resurrection of Jesus as an escape-miracle, a pattern of eschatological freedom. It is perfectly true that the presence of guards is a substantial common feature of miraculous escape stories, their behaviour heightening the miracle. Unfortunately the examples chosen are all distinguishable from ours. Either the guards were not asleep, or some or all of them died, were terrified or fainted. Indeed there is an ancient folk-tale, apparently widespread, of comical and quick-witted behaviour by guards who are cheated of the thing they were guarding, for example a treasure or a condemned criminal's corpse.[40e] This does have a bearing on the absurd aspects of the tale to which we shall come, from another angle, but it does nothing to prove that *no* guard was set upon the tomb when *pious followers would be certain to set as high a value upon the supposed corpse as Joseph.*

There is one aspect no one has noticed. Matthew and Luke are quite certain, as they were with the daughter of Jairus (cf. Mk. 5:23 with Mt. 9:18, Lk. 8:42) that the subject of the story is dead: when Joseph takes down the body of Jesus it is *it* which is buried (Mt. 27:58 *sōma* means a corpse, 59 *auto* ('it'), 60 [the same in a good manuscript tradition]; Lk. similarly at 23:52, *auto* at 53, repeated later in the same verse according to an important manuscript tradition, which, in part, actually has three *auto*'s in the same verse). Mark however intriguingly says that Joseph boldly asked Pilate for the *sōma*, but taking *him* (*auton*) down buried *him* in a tomb . . . This is not to be dismissed (as by some) as evidence of Mark's incompetence as an editor. To Mark's mind the tomb as Joseph left it had the Lord in person within it, the Lord being the chief character of the drama. Such a slight yet significant hint lies in the masculine, rather than the neuter noun. Pilate gives a lifeless corpse; but Joseph receives and buries the Lord: the value of the treasure within that little cave is emphatic. It could not have been left unguarded. And of course the stone will have been in place.[40f]

5. THE YOUNG MAN.

It is no doubt a valuable discovery that Mark's last verses (16:1-8) are not a historical source themselves.[40g] They are evidence of a formula for recitation at the Sepulchre, pre-Marcan, perhaps long pre-Marcan. The high point in his gospel, they contain theological implications. The words 'see where they laid him' betray the purpose of the section. There are a number of features in the story, however, which (i) serve as the hook upon which the story holds, and without which (as reminiscence) the story cannot be envisaged at all, and (ii) are unnecessary to the story at any stage of its composition and inclusion in Mark, and therefore go back to the tradition upon which the story was based. If we find elements in Mk. 16:1-8 which are fugitive or unstable in the post-Marcan development of the tale these, surely, are of such a description. Of the first class surely the most important is the women's visit *obviously to mourn the righteous dead.* We must never forget that ritual mourning was *de rigueur* as a practice (Mk. 5:38-40) and had high 'entertainment' value (Mt. 11:17/Lk. 7:32) (cf. the spurious Mk. 16:10), particularly for the corporate relief of sensations of guilt and fear. That they carried vessels of embalming oils for the purpose of embalming him can be taken as certain since the Marcan text specifically says *aleipsōsin,* '(that) they might anoint (him)'. Taking the text as a recitation at the Sepulchre at the Feast of the Resurrection, any other term of adequate[40h] ambiguity, e.g. 'honour' (him), would have been preferable. The women who would have priority at the annual pilgrimage in this case might well carry *arōmata* (in censers this time), but their object would not be to *anoint*. Of the second class we may well pick out 'the Nazarene'. Jesus was a very common name, and about the time of the Anastasis that identification (*v.*6) was reasonable, but it would be pointless a few years later. The phrase *mē ekthambeisthe,* 'Don't dither', fits well enough after *exethambēthēsan* (*v.*5), which has a theological background—it was appropriate to persons receiving a vision of the divine; but it is a bathetic response from the Young Man whom Mark depicts as an angel, and therefore goes back to the story as reminiscence.

The Young Man is indeed a key figure in our reconstruction.[41] A popular study insists that there *was* a young man, and that he was the first witness of the Anastasis.[42] It is plausible. The author of the popular book is ridiculed by scholars[42a] on the basis that he has no idea of source- or redaction-criticism, takes the story, which is faith-history, as if it were secular history, and treats the Young Man as if he were real. However, the function of the Young Man is not simply to operate a theophany, or to do duty for an appearance-story, or to make the women dither: they must have dithered prior to any vision of a Young Man. Mark shows us the women already gripped by the doubts and insights which arose from the stone's having been moved and the tomb's being empty except for the Young Man. (By the way how much greater their surprise would have been if the stone had been still to, and the body gone!) The Young Man and his white garment relate, as we shall see, back to (?) another Young Man with a white garment who figures earlier in the story; and it is an actual reminiscence of an actual messenger which gave rise to the story of the Young Man. The theologian's doubt whether there was a white garment, because there was no real young man, and there was no real young man because of the white garment, is typical of a sceptical mind in a circular spin. Another instance of class (ii) of the story's features (see above) is the message about Galilee (*v.*7). This had absolutely no point while the passage was recited at the Feast (save to remind participants that Jesus operated in that mission field and that the original women were Galilean, not Judæan). It was, in some form, part of reminiscence of a message, and the Young Man was the means whereby that message was received.

If he was not the first witness of the Anastasis he could have been deputed by some other witness, to wait for the inspecting party. I am content to view him either as the original finder of Jesus or his companion.

The Young Man, like the Women at the Tomb, made earliest Christian's minds reel. Dithering was quite in point. The symbolic potential of the Young Man is immense. If Jesus, after the Anastasis, was established as a manifestation in flesh of the deity, then any intermediary of his between himself and his disciples was no mere person. In that world angels were expected to be seen as phantasms in the form of a *young man* (Jos. *Ant.* 5.213). We may ask ourselves what stages there must be in the story? Jesus's words we may assume come first, the lad's understanding of them, the women's memory, tradition of what they remembered, and then the recitation-text, before at last Mark incorporates it. The first Christians asked, why a young man, why like that, why after all did he say what he did, why to women, why *those* women, and so on. The first gospel story teems with scriptural allusions and ironical commentary. Let us get to the texts themselves.

The Women peered into the tomb and according to Mark (16:5) they saw a young man sitting on the right (obviously *their* right), cast-about (swathed) in a white garment, and they were 'stupefied'. As well they might be. The watchers' right is the auspicious and more honourable side of the tomb, and that is where Jesus will have been laid.[43] The young man was sitting where what would have been corpse blood[44] would have defiled any clean person overshadowing it, sitting on it, sharing its roof, and yet the young man was dressed in the style typical of one who had just immersed himself in an immersion-pool, a tank of living water. Had he immersed himself as priests do before presenting themselves before the deity in the Temple, and as the laymen who slaughtered their companies' paschal lambs had done on the previous Friday? But of course the said laymen did not dress themselves in a *sindon* apiece, a priestly attire long afterwards affected by rabbinical students.

I do not say for a moment that the women were put in mind of the Young Man who ran away when Jesus was taken in the Garden. But we are intended to recollect him, and for several reasons. Mk. 14:51-2 runs,[45] 'And a certain young man accompanied him, cast-about with a sheet (*sindon*) on his bare body, and they caught hold of him, but he left his sheet behind and escaped bare.' No doubt the hearer of our present passage is expected to think that after his shameful flight (Gourges, 1981) he has got his sheet back, and is dressed once again! There is no proof that it was the same Young Man, and we are not for a moment to think that in any realistic terms he was. But there is a symbolic connection. The one who fled leaving his garment (cf. Gen. 39:12, Joseph in Egypt) is easily identifiable in realistic terms. He was evidently a religious enthusiast who had immersed himself so as to be purified and properly dressed for the Redemption.[46] Jesus's own *sindon* seems to have held some such symbolic meaning. No wonder police might think the youngster worth catching! One who is to face the Power of God in person does not allow his nudity to appear (Jn. 21:7 alluding to Exod. 20:26, 28:42!), and the one who immerses himself must not allow anything whatever to come between the water and his body.[47] Ancient man thought that sin, like sweat, adhered to garments, and after ritual immersion the penitent must put on a pure, fresh garment.[47a] There are many symbols which the church read into that young man's escape without his *sindon*. It was the garment of the proselytes immersed by way of baptism. 'Baptism' was, in Jesus's vocabulary a pseudonym for suffering, martyrdom—the young man who lived to tell the tale was not up to being a martyr! And escape from a *sindon* is also escape alive from a shroud.[48] But most important for us is a further illustration of Mark's methods. Amos 2:11-16 is interesting as it speaks of young men as prophets on the Last Day, or at any rate on the Day of destiny: 'And I took of your sons for prophets, and of your young men for consecration. Are not these things so, you sons of Israel? . . . Therefore I roll under you, as a waggon full of straw is rolled. And flight shall perish from the runner . . . and the warrior shall not save his life . . . and he that is swift of foot shall not escape . . . And the strong shall find no confidence in power: the naked shall flee away in that day, saith the Lord' (following the LXX version). I suspect that Am. 3:3 ('Shall two walk together unless they have come to an agreement?') may have helped Luke in his construction of the Emmaus story (p.110), for the text applies to that same Day. The Amos passage therefore *was* in evangelists' minds apropos of the Anastasis.

We have worked in the presumption of Marcan priority to the other evangelists. The story of the young man who escaped (Mk. 14:51-52) did not appeal to them, and Mark alone records his adventure. We have seen that there are inferences to be drawn from the tradition, and they justified its being preserved for posterity. The desire simply to give an impression of the report of an eye-witness is hardly to be attributed to so artful a writer as Mark. Nor need we waste our time trying to guess what the lad's name was! There have been conjectures, probably futile. One of the traps, however, awaiting the unwary New Testament reader is the desire to relax after having discovered a hidden meaning. It is only too likely that the text worked hard for its position in the gospel, and was selected and placed where we find it for more than one reason. 'Fulfilment' of the Amos passage may not suffice.

In this case note the following also: Jesus kept his garment and did not escape; he lost it at the end. The lad saved his body by sacrificing his garment (as recommended at Lk. 13:16!). The garment was worth less than the body. Did he lose his soul (which was worth more than his body: Mk. 8:36-37) whilst saving his body and abandoning Jesus? It seems so.[48a] And yet that was not what happened . . Ironically, Jesus's capture and consequent sufferings, constituted the young man's deliverance. His true 'escape' arose not from Jesus's triumph (as he had expected) but from his capture! The others 'all fled' (*v.*50), without having been seized by the arm of the law. He sacrificed his garment in the moment of crisis. How much greater the salvation procured by Him who sacrificed the garment of the soul, the body itself, sternly repressing (Mk. 14:36,41) the natural instinct which even would-be heroes have to save themselves at the very last moment! That young man has not hitherto been recognised as a symbol of a paradoxical Redemption; but it is far from improbable that that is one of the tasks which its author, Mark, expected Mk. 14:51-52 to perform.

Returning to our own Young Man, his white clothing *excluded mourning*. White suggests sanctity (so the Dura frescoes).[49] Though Mark uses no angels in his narratives, being dressed in a white sheet suggests an angel.[50] Angels are not subject to impurity and so can sit on any part of a grave, occupied or not. The women had a severe shock—an angel was awaiting them, they thought. And so he was, in a manner of speaking,[51] since he was Jesus's messenger.[52] His message is curious, and Mark seems to have to some extent doctored his previous verses to prepare, in some measure, for it.

After telling them in a very unangelic idiom[53] 'not to dither',[54] he satisfies himself that they are visiting Jesus the Nazarene 'the crucified one' (*zēteite* means 'you are paying a call on?').[55] I imagine the majestic words that follow must often have been recited at the Sepulchre, with the guide's left hand pointing down at the words. 'He is not here' and his right forefinger upwards at 'He has been raised!' (p.138 below). 'He has been raised, he is not here—observe the place where he was laid! Go, tell his pupils and Peter (i.e. not excluding Peter) that he leads you (all) into Galilee. There you shall see him, as he told you.' Then they left the tomb and fled. They trembled and were overcome, out of themselves, appropriate to those who have had a vision.[55a] They *did* obey him to this extent: *they pretermitted the dramatic mourning which all the pious would have expected of them.* Instead of doing his actual bidding they told no one. They were afraid, as well they might be. This development did not bode well for anyone. His hearers, Mark knew, realise the truth, which the silly women suspected. They had bought their *aromata* in vain.

I do not doubt that their fear was genuine. Where it stands at the end of the gospel it suggests that they recognised the hand of God at work, and his unseen presence. But the tradition that they were afraid was read by Mark in another sense also. At Mk. 10:32, immediately before Jesus's final prediction of the Passion to the Twelve, we are told 'They were on the road going up to Jerusalem, and Jesus was *leading them,* and they were *amazed,* and those who accompanied (him) were *afraid.*' Thus three words from our ending of Mark figure already before the final prediction. Mark's intention, evidently, is to link a genuine, historical, fear with the whole process of this special revelation.

Let us now examine the message they failed to deliver. First it does not call the disciples to the tomb or even to the vicinity. It presupposes that Galilee is the place to which they must go, under his guidance, the region in which they had been led by him before (Mk. 1:28, 39. 3:7, Lk. 23:49). The tomb was not the place around which their activity should turn: the cult of the dead was *not* to be pursued, a message calmly ignored by Mark who incorporates it! But we are not aware how far the Young Man interpreted the message he was given to pass on. That he was a mere intermediary is clear from his directing the women to tell the the disciples and Peter as if Peter was not a disciple. No doubt Mark understood all this to mean that Jesus indirectly reinstated Peter after his bragging, so soon followed by cowardice. As for Jesus's leading them into Galilee, like sheep, it was futile to attempt to pretend that there was a 'Galilee' for example on the Mount of Olives, a place where Galileans assembled,[56] and it is equally unnecessary to assert that Galilee was a focus of divine expectation for which Judæa must be abandoned.[56a]

But we are not done with the Marcan 'message'. We must take yet another step backwards. The text which Mark has incorporated was probably originally in Greek but was written by a bilingual person who knew that the original message was in Aramaic or, if a pronouncement, in Mishnaic Hebrew (p.93). The Greek original of the English 'Galilee' is a vocalisation of a Hebrew or Aramaic cluster which would then have been written GLYL, but pronounced, according to context, *galīl* or *golēl*. It can be taken as certain that in the original it was preceded by the definite article, 'the GLYL'. 'He goes before you to the GLYL, and there you will see him'. For in the original the tense will almost certainly have been present (for future), forcing the translator to opt for the Greek future tense, obscuring an ambiguity. What this amounts to is that the disciples' meeting-place with their Lord, the trysting-place, as it were, is 'GLYL' Imagination must now get to work to establish what GLYL means. What implications were legitimate, and what not? Fancy could do wonders with that word (p.93), and the fact that there was such concentration upon it suggests powerfully that Jesus himself gave them practically no help. If so *we can easily guess why*. The authentic message of the Risen One must be squeezed dry of every drop of meaning, because there was so little else to which they could apply their minds. About that 'GLYL's' relevance to the disciples there was no doubt but it was as *cryptic* as the Last Words (Mk. 15 par.).

The same story in Matthew shows our Young Man, the first link in the chain of interpretation of that GLYL-message, firmly established as a real angel (Mt. 28:2-4) who himself rolled away the stone: *v.*2! Someone's guess, the last may well be true. Jesus could easily have made his presence known, alive in the tomb, during the Saturday night, and the watchers (quite possibly including the Young Man) placed there by Joseph (who had no idea where the disciples were) could have helped him out. Matthew refers to Jesus having predicted that he would be raised — in fact so far as we know he predicted that he would rise, which we know is not quite the same thing. The message now contains a new element, that he has been *raised from among the dead* (*v.*7). In Mark such a message could be said at best to be implied, if the 'leading' in 'he goes before you into Galilee' is supposed to be a physical process, which is by no means necessary.

In Luke the angel has become two angels (Lk. 24:4), who sarcastically ask why the women seek the living among the dead (p.137). They should remember (as they evidently did not) that when he was still *in* Galilee he told them that he would rise on the third day. No message to the disciples is included in this; yet here they do report to the Eleven, as in Matthew they had run to give their report. Public dissatisfaction with those Women since Mark is here very clearly evidenced.

It is obvious what is primary here and what is secondary.[57] The earliest account was that the women kept quiet for a significant time. Jesus did *not* call his disciples (no wonder) and was content to be with friends who were really concerned about him. He directed the disciples' attention to 'GLYL', through the women who anyone could know must be bound to visit the tomb at the earliest practicable moment. *It was therefore specifically a message to women.* And he let that sink in. We can almost hear the first Christians pondering on what that message meant: GLYL. The Young Man perhaps thought it meant that Jesus would expect to see his disciples at home, having invisibly led them, like lost sheep, back to the place where they all belonged, away from Jerusalem, the scene of their débâcle. So far as he was concerned, Jesus might eventually make a complete recovery and join them there. The likelihood of his being done to death again could be ignored. Judas was out of the way (we do not know for sure how), and the Romans had done their worst. The hierarchy were satisfied that the 'hero' had been sufficiently pilloried, and *that* Passover was over. I do not imagine the Young Man had a long time to ponder over this, but others followed it up later. 'GLYL' implied so many things!

A better explanation found its way to Luke. It was not that they would, or ought to, return to Galilee, as if to complete the cycle. In his estimate the headquarters of Christianity had shifted from Galilee to Jerusalem, where Jesus's 'appearances' are to be localised, thence to shift (in a manner of speaking) finally to Rome. A circle (GLYL means circle) has a centre, and Luke was metropolis-minded, not rural-minded. Therefore the reference to Galilee must have been to remind them of the past, and one might use GLYL, somewhat unconvincingly, as a catch-phrase for predictions of the Anastasis.

But Mark himself saw another meaning in the word, and there were yet other possibilities. *Rolling* is the semantic basis of words from the root *gal* (p.94) and its duplications. Cant. 4:12, 15 give us the word as a fountain, a well of living water (cf. *gulôt mayîm* Josh. 15:19); waters roll (Am. 5:24); *gulgolet* is a skull. GL means a well, etc., GYL means joy. One's mind boggles. One thing is clear, that GLYL, *golēl*, also means a *stone*. Jesus perhaps deliberately, perhaps accidentally, pointed to the stone. And what fantastic possibilities this opens up (p.103)! No wonder it was to *women* that the message was given (ibid.). By his Anastasis he draws them to him in a way that postpones male disciples to female disciples. There is this secret meeting with the women, through an intermediary (a 'go-between'), as the culmination of a story in which the Twelve have supinely let their master be denounced to the enemy by one of their own number.

John's account of this moment wastes no time with the Young Man. Everyone knows of him, and he can be dropped. Mary goes to the tomb while it is still dark, sees the stone removed and communicates her fears. Only after Peter and the Beloved Disciple have made their own inspections and returned (again supinely) without her does she have her vision of the two angels inside the tomb. The emphasis in the story lies in the refrain at 20:2, and 13: ἦραν τὸν κύριον . . . καὶ οὐκ οἴδαμεν/ οἶδα ποῦ ἔθηκαν αὐτόν, 'They have taken the Lord/my Lord/my 'husband' . . .and I do not know where they have put him!' Neither the angels (i.e. subjective inspiration) nor the foolish male disciples can help her. The "they" does duty not merely for hypothetical servants of Joseph, but, in a literary sense, for the angels of God who buried Moses! The Jesus whom she does not recognise in his new garb as Adam the gardener, is just behind her and she says εἰπέ μοι ποῦ ἔθηκας αὐτὸν κἀγὼ αὐτὸν ἀρῶ, 'Tell me where *you* have put him (again 'put'), and I shall take him (*note* 'him') up.' Indeed his body *was* valuable. Then he calls her by her personal name as he may never have done in life. She is the first one to *see* the Lord (20:18). Does the point need to be spelt out? The 'husband' of the first 'bride of Christ' is revealed neither by angels nor by male disciples; and what 'they' have done with the body is immaterial. The function of all intermediaries and messengers is swallowed up. Christ stands and shows himself spontaneously without intermediaries, as he always will. That is John's message.

NOTES

1. C. H. G. Venturini, *Natürliche Geschichte des grossen Prophet von Nazareth* (1800) Charlesworth (1972-3). Theologians, except Evans (1954), 130 n.133, scout the idea: Lampe, 102; O'Collins, 10; Brown, 73.
2. Eça de Queiroz, *The Relic* (London, 1954), a reference owed to Dr. Mário da Cunha Gonçalves.
3. H. J. Schonfield, *The Passover Plot* (London, 1967).
3a. The Greek word *planos,* which, on the surface, certainly means 'impostor, deceiver', actually began life meaning 'wandering, roaming'. It is perfectly appropriate for a bogus medicine-man; but, with the gospel irony I have mentioned, it is especially appropriate for Jesus in the other, older, sense. Enemies of Jesus say of him what is true, but not in the sense they have in mind. Jesus, whom the tomb could *not* hold, was indeed a 'wanderer', for after the Anastasis he was not bound to space or time. And indeed he did 'wander' out of the tomb, the one thing the Jews aimed to prevent!
4. *Ant.,* 4.202, also Targums on Deut. 21:23 (*LNT,* 454).
5. Temple Scroll, Col. 64. 6-13 (text Yadin, *Megilat ha-Miqdash II,* 1977, 269, comm. at pp. 202-4; trans. Vermes, 1977, 251).
6. *J.B.L.* 96 (1977), 85-99.
7. *Vita,* 420-1. Cf. Polyb., *Hist.i.*86.
8. Sava (1957). The Passover lamb is flayed.
9. Valuable but discordant studies at C. H. Dodd (1968), 429n. A vast array: Blinzler (1960), 274-7 and nn; Sava (1957). See also *Ex.T.*83 (1972), 104-7, 248 (*bis*).
10. Haas (1970), 38ff: tomb 1, ossuary no.4, skeleton 'A' (Jehohanan). Charlesworth (1972-3). A luxurious and exhaustive study appears at Kuhn (1979). Marginal revision is now required to Moore (1974). Tzaferis (1970).
10a. *I.E.J.*20 (1970) 57-8, pl.24.
11. Kennard (1955) wrongly urges that Jesus's legs were broken.
12. A Roman practice: Mommsen, *Römisches Strafrecht* (1899), 920 n.6. Petrusevang. 4:14. Blinzler, 287.
13. *I.E.J.* 20 (1970), 57.
14. P. Borgen, *N.T.S.*5 (1958-9), 246-9.
15. O'Rourke, 'John fulfilment texts,' *Sc.ecclés.*19 (1967), 433ff., 439 urges caution.
15a. Korein (1978), 6-10.
16. Plut., *Cleom.*XXXVII.7. Note also the apocryphal story about R. Johanan ben Zakkai, which, if it proves anything, proves that people believed the Romans tested alleged corpses in that way: b.Gitt.56a, Midr.R., Lam.I.5, 31 used by J. Neusner, *Development of a Legend* (Leiden, 1970), 229-34.
17. Targ. ps. Jon. Num. 20:11. I have not seen G. Richter, *Münch. Theol. Zeits* 21 (1970), 1-21.
18. *LNT,* ch.12 .
19. Ibid., 270-1.
20. Is John referring to the story of Jesus in the manger? The manger was a stone niche resembled a bench grave in a tomb.
21. *LNT,* 87-8.
22. Plut. *Cato Jun.* XI.2-3, *Ant.* 17.199; Test. Abr. 20.
22a. For plans and photographs of a contemporary tomb see Sukenik (1947).
23. Lockton (1924), p.30-1, 37-8.

23a. An excellent illustration of such a stone *in situ* will be seen at Bibl. Arch. **35** (1972), 93.
24. *Anakekulistai* is the correct reading (*lect.diff.*) at Mk. 16:4. Task of Sisyphus(!), a heroic task even in Hades: Hom.,*Od.*11.593ff (*megas*); Luc., *Luct.* 8; Dionys. Hal., *Comp.*, 20.
25. *Euschēmōn = illustris/nobilis/honestus.* Acts 13:50. *Vita,* 32.
26. Broer (1972), 195-6.
27. Midr.R., Gen.LXXVI.6 (Sperber, *R.I.D.A.* 19,1972,21).
28. Schreiber (1969), 59-60. Cf.Lk. 2:25, 38. Brown (1973), 114.
29. Basic text: Tob. 1:17, etc. Jeremias (1971), 148. *Studies* II, 107-10.
29a. Lucian, *Philops.* 29.
30. *BJ* 4.317.
30a. Crossan, *N.T.* 15 (1973), 81-112; J. Lambrecht, ibid., 16 (1974), 241-58.
31. Cf. 1 Kngs. 1:21, 14:31, 15:24, 22:50, etc., Acts 13:36. A scholar has most interestingly discovered that when the Jews said of a man 'he slept with his fathers' they implied he died leaving legitimate (male) issue.
32. *JA,* 44, also *Studies* II, 68ff.
33. Keller (1954), 19-20; Blinzler (1960), 295 n.66.
34. Mt. 25:31ff.
35. Plut., *C.Gracc.* XVIII.2.
36. Holtzmann (1931), 311; Baldensperger (1932-3). Rejected by Benoit (1969), 229. Of value: Cousin (1974); Charlesworth (1972-3), 150 n.28.
37. Meyers (1971) also his *Jewish Ossuaries* (Rome 1971) (reviewed *I.E.J.* 23, 1973, 121-6; *J.B.L.* 83, 1974, 462-4). *Bibl.Arch.* 33 (1970). 1-29. L. Y. Rahmani, 'Ancient Jerusalem's Funerary Customs and Tombs, Pt. 1', *Bibl. Arch.* 44 (1981), 171ff. 175-6.
37a. See traditions at *Tractate 'Mourning' (Semaḥot)* XII.8-9 (trans. Zlotnick, 1966, pp. 81-2).
38. Ossuary from the Kedron valley: Fitzmyer, *J.B.L.*78 (1959), 60-5; Z.W.Falk, *H.T.R.*59 (1966), 311-12; *Studies* I, 115.
39. A.D.Nock, *Essays* II (1972), ch.31, p.528. M.Hengel, *Z.N.W.*57 (1966), 151-8.
40. One Givat ha-Mivtar skeleton is packed and labelled, claiming to have been a builder of the Temple Klausner. *From Jesus to Paul* (London, 1943) 290 n.13 mentions an ossuary labelled 'Sapheira'.
40a. 2 Sam. 2:10ff. The practice at St. Catherine's monastery at Sinai.
40b. *Tractate 'Mourning'* xii. 6. One did not actually *disjoint* a corpse using force.
40c. Geering (1971). See Broer (1972).
40d. My study of the use of Daniel in the Passion narrative is *Downside Review.* Jan. 1982, 62-8.
40e. See below, p.87, n.3f.
40f. It did not occur to me immediately that the most famous martyr of the ancient Greek world, Socrates, made a point of telling his disciples that they should *not* concern themselves unduly about his *sōma* (his corpse) after the poison had taken effect, since *he* would not be there! The contrast between the person and his corpse (emphasised at Plato, *Phædo* 115c-e) was entirely appropriate in a high culture which strove to limit superstitions about burials.
40g. Schenke (1968), 86ff., 94.
40h. The word *aleipsōsin* (from *aleiphein,* to anoint) seems to belong to pre-Marcan material, since it does not serve to cover the activity of pilgrims to the Sepulchre, which a more vague word would have done (the verb *sebesthai* is possible, since so one 'honours' the dead or the gods). But it remains a problem whether *aleipsōsin* ('they might anoint') is there by chance; whether the marvellous irony which it contains (see below) is pre-Marcan; or it is retained, *or invented,* by Mark himself. Since *aleiphein is possible* for the anointing of a Jewish corpse, whereas *myrisai* (to 'myrrhify', as at Mk. 14:8) would have been far more appropriate (see Cant. 5:1b), it does possess situational plausibility. But who, if not Mark, could have chosen *aleiphein* for 16:1, while every Greek-knowing hearer would have been aware of the other meanings of the verb, so much more obviously intelligible than the Jewish practice, and yet so amazingly

inappropriate to the women's ostensible object with reference to one who needed neither priestly (Ex. 40:15, cf. 13, Num. 3:3 LXX) nor any other anointing? As Liddell-Scott-Jones' *Lexicon* shows, but better the old *Thesaurus Eccles.* of J.C. Suicerus, I (Amsterdam, 1728), 185-7 (less well R. C. Trench, *Synonyms* 9th ed. [London, 1880], 136-7; Schlier in G. Kittel *Theol. Wört.z.N.T.*I, 230-2), *aleiphein* meant to anoint (i) as an honour to a living person (Lk. 7:38); (ii) as a demonstration that the anointed was joyful (Ruth 3:3, Judt. 16:6, Mt. 6:17); (iii) as a treatment for broken skin (Lk. 10:34) (did he still need it?); (iv) as a magical-therapeutic treatment for the very sick (Mk. 6:13, Jas. 5:14) (was he not past it?); (v) as part of the preparation and 'rubbing-down' for athletes: all martyrs are 'athletes', but in his case one 'contest' was over and, as for the next, he was 'in the field' already(!); and lastly (vi) as a well-known metaphor for *incitement* to vigorous effort, i.e. to 'get him out into the field' (but he needed no inciting from them!). The use of the word *aleipsōsin* is one of the miracles of poetry, but I am uncertain whether Mark invented or observed it, and I prefer (at present) the latter.

41. Whitaker; Trompf (1973); Bode (1970), 170.
42. F.Morison, *Who Moved the Stone?* (London, 1958). I do not find this work much used.
42a. Bode (1970), 26 n.1.
43. 'Right' means there could have been a left (bench). *En tois dexiois* is like *ek dexiōn* (Sir. 12:12).
44. A quarter *log* of corpse-blood or mixed blood from one who dies *in* the structure conveys uncleanness by being in a structure which overshadows the person thus rendered unclean: Mishnah, Ohol.II.2,III.5. The blood of a crucified man placed indoors is especially considered: III.5 (see Blackman, *Mishnayoth Taharoth*, VI (London, 1955), 214; Danby, 653).
45. Farrer (1948), 143-5; (1951), 141, 174, 334. More recently the young man has been studied by Knox (1951), Vanhoye (1971), Neirynck (1979), Gourges (1981).
46. Procedure incidentally conveyed in a caricature at P.Oxy.V.840.24-28 Jeremias, *Unknown Sayings*, 1957, 36-49i. Cf. Dupont-Sommer, *Semitica* 15 (1965), 61-70. We are *not* considering Christian baptism (Gourges).
47. Mishnah, *Miq*.IX.
47a. Pettazoni. *Harv.Theol.Rev.* 30 (1937), 6. Rev. 3:4, 16:15.
48. Mk. 15:46 (*bis*), Mt. 27:59, Lk. 23:53. P.Par.18 *bis*; P.Lond.1.46, 206. All these are not trivial details as uninformed persons have suspected.
48a. St. Thomas More, *Expositio Passionis* in T. Morus, *Opera* (Frankfurt/Leipzig, 1689), 177-8 (trans. M. Basset in *The Workes of Sir Thomas More* [London, 1557], 1402-3), conveniently reproduced by G. Marc'hadour, *The Bible in the Works of St. Thomas More, IV* (B. De Graaf, Nieukoop, 1971), 85-8.
49. Garte, 11-12. Cf. Dan. 7:9, Eccl. 9:8, Mk. 9:33.
50. Ezk. 9-10, Dan. 10:5, 12:6-7. Test.Levi 8:1 Acts 1:10, 6:15, Rev. 3:4-5,18, 6:11, 7:14 15:6, 19:8. 2 Esd. 1:39-40. Or celestial glorification (Gourges, 1981).
51. Apart from his diction: see n.53 below.
52. Cf. Mk. 1:13, Mt. 13:41, 16:27, 26:53.
53. The correct form of reassurance is at Mk. 5:36, 6:50. Cf. Old Testament usage. *Fest.Th. Klauser* (1964), 250. Missed by Grass, 183. No wonder they remained 'afraid'.
54. Literally, 'don't be stupefied', the verb is very rare in the LXX, but *ekthambeisthai* does occur in Mark prior to a revelation. 'Troubled' (Trompf, 320 n.3) is inadequate. Sir. 30:9. Galen 16.493.
55. Rosen, *Anc.Soc.*3 (1972), 236. Men., *Dysk.*978 (Gomme-Sandbach, *Menander*, 1973, 152). Preisigke, *Wört.*, s.v.2,4 (add P.Masp.68.3,11).
55a. Horbury & McNeil (1981), 94-5.
56. The point was wrongly taken by Bornhäuser from R. Hofman (1825-1917), *Galilaea auf dem Oelberg . . .* (Leipzig, 1896) (53pp.); A. Resch (1835-1912), *Das Galiläa bei Jerusalem* (Leipzig, 1910) (53pp.): *Der Auferstandene in Galiläa bei Jerusalem* (Gütersloh, 1911) (40pp.). All three works go back to Suarez (d.1580) who relies on patristic sources,

themselves indebted to the *Acta Pilati* 13-14, an entirely apocryphal work intending, here, to effect a harmonisation of the gospels and Acts, a misguided object, leading to a mistaken result.

56a. van Cangh (1972).

57. Luke did not blatantly alter Mark, as is usually supposed: Evans (1970), 92; Hooke (1967), 44. Brown, 107-8 wonders whether Jesus communicated verbally at all.

CHAPTER VII
The Disposal of the Body.

Any theory that the women visiting the tomb had a *spontaneous* vision (the last thing they would have expected), that there never was a Young Man in it, and that the only fact to which these ladies could have testified was simply that the body was missing—a theory that has understandably captured many minds from very early times, comes up against the question, 'Well, what happened to the body?' It is known that women *can* have simultaneous ecstatic visions, but these have to be induced by long periods in preparation and no one allows them to interfere with history, verifiable matters. As for the body itself, nobody, Jew, Christian or gentile, ever produced a corpse or parts of one claiming that it belonged to Jesus. It is certain that any rumour that the body survived will have produced a quite different set of circumstances from those we know. This is why Matthew and his successors could afford to follow up the hint given by Mark that the Young Man was an angel, to all intents and purposes, and reduplicated him making him/them an angel/angels. Until John the notion that Jesus's body could become *insubstantial on earth* did not find a voice. There was neither need, nor use, for any such notion. The stone was rolled away so that he might emerge.

We have seen that there is nothing in the gospel stories to hinder our supposing that Jesus revived in the tomb by a natural process. He survived, at that rate, an incohate or clinical death masked, perhaps, by a self-induced trance. Possibly helped by the latter he will then have recovered in the cold tomb. The process of dying had been interrupted. He survived long enough to attract the attention of at least one independent witness, quite possibly the Young Man or some companion of his, or the pair of them, and then insisted on sending a message that amounted merely to this, that his disciples should apply their minds to 'GLYL' (p.66 above, p.92 below).

If he emerged from the tomb on his elbows and knees or was carried out and later was actually able to stand (as I envisage it) whatever can have happened to his body? Gangrene must soon have set in. He will hardly have been fit to be seen, in the ordinary way, at any point, and the inevitable high fever, collapse and a continuation of the interrupted process of death, up to brain-death, will have supervened. The loud silence of the gospels and epistles warns us that the post-Anastasis life was short, and uncommunicative. Yet it was not devoid of incident. If three or more views persisted about GLYL, just as different views persisted about the Last Words on the Cross (Mk. 15:34-36 par.), there was practical unanimity as to the intent of what he *did*. He bent his energies to one end and achieved it. Never mind about 'GLYL' as a *word!* By all means let the imaginative ponder over it! But he achieved 'GLYL' as a thing, through the most unpromising material, his wretched students. The message goes that he is still doing it: but I anticipate. The disposal of the body now preoccupies the would-be detective. The possibility of a lime-pit has already been discussed (p.58 above).

1. A NEGATIVE ANSWER.

Let us examine first the so-called explanations which lead nowhere.

(a) Jesus appeared and disappeared. Mt. 28:9 has the word 'met'; 28:15 has 'seeing'; Luke 24:15 has 'approached and accompanied', 24:36 'stood in the midst'; and then there are the spurious Mk. 16:12 and 14 (p.135). And he disappeared: there is Lk. 4:30 and Jn. 8:59, and 10:39. In Lk. 24:31 we have 'invisible', and 51 'departed . . . and was carried up'. It is remarkable and I think significant, that John, who lists four 'appearances' of Jesus after the Anastasis, nowhere states that he *disappeared* as, in another sense, he apparently did at some critical points in his ministry (Jn. 7:30-36, 8:59, 10:39, cf. Lk. 4:29-30)! By contrast (yet is it a contrast?) at Lk. 24:34 the verb 'appear' has the sense rather of 'vision' than 'observation' (cf. Acts 9:17, 16:9). and it is of interest that the 'appearance' to Mary Magdalene at Jn. 20:14 is confidently phrased quite differently: 'she saw Jesus standing', so at *v.*19 'Jesus came . . .and stood . . . and said . . . ', so at *v.*26, 'Jesus came . . . and stood', whereas the 'suspect' chapter 21 of John seems to revert to an earlier literary device: 'he appeared in this way . . . '

The fact is that just as 'appearance' implies a subjective vision, dependent on the psychic and mental state of the recipient, who is the focus of the vision, so 'disappearance' is the cessation of this symptom. Therefore a plain statement that Jesus disappeared tells us nothing about his body, rather something about the state of the visionary. And the Johannine passages have quite another object, as I have already explained.

(b) Was the body stolen? This fear not only must have existed from the beginning, it is the obvious reflection to occur to the women, whom we can assume to be entirely historical, the one absolutely certain fragment of secular history in this connection. In 1970 it was suggested that tomb-robbers stole the body, folding the clothes(!).[1] We know about first-century tomb-robbers (Sukenik, 1947): they are not interested in corpses in the ordinary way. They could in fact use grave-clothes,[2] but, for reasons we must explore in detail, Jesus's body could be turned immediately into cash. Like the Arabs who found the Qumran scrolls, the robbers would have been sorely tempted to cut the body into bits and sell them off separately. Indeed the number of bits circulating would, unlike the Qumran documents, have exceeded the total corpus with which they started. Mt. 27:64 contains two glimpses of truth: the disciples *would* be intensely interested in the body, and both they and the authorities, aware of the possibility of thieving, will have seen the point, in principle, of the tomb's being guarded for its owner. This being so the rescued Jesus, though actually moribund, would have no difficulty in convincing the watcher(s) that God had indeed raised him up. Klausner suggests that Joseph removed the body (since John hints that the site was a temporary one), having had second thoughts—but it was much more useful to him where it was. If his tomb was as yet incomplete (like the Talpioth tomb which became silted up

72

whilst chambers were still unfinished) he could improve it, specialist labour being plentiful in that vicinity, then, as now, a centre for underground tombs. Had Joseph indeed had second thoughts (about which we have absolutely no information) and buried the body in another tomb, his family would have discovered the intrusion and their silence could by no means be counted upon. Not only are a miracle-worker's relics worth a great deal (I shall explain precisely how), but the family would be so proud of his company that all the world would know about it.

Now the notion that 'they' might take away the body and rebury it somewhere, with all the possible implications, is very old. Not only does the little drama in Matthew testify to it but John does also in the words he puts into the mouth of Mary of Magdala. In a symbolic sense 'they' *have indeed* buried Jesus in a cult location, and John protests against this, as indeed does Luke: Jesus is not to be sought for in pilgrimage, nor among the dead. It is amusing that Mark, who includes a pilgrimage- or festival-recitation at the very climax of his gospel, unintentionally connives at the anchoring of Jesus in a tangible place. He would no doubt defend himself, if we challenged him, by saying that to his mind the sending of the 'flock' to 'Galilee' was quite adequate to make the point—the women after all *fled* from the tomb, and *were afraid:* they did not gloat over it!

In the times of Luke and John no whisper can have been heard of any grave of Jesus's existing anywhere. Was there one before Luke and John, say about A.D. 70? We must look again at Matthew's comical story. No one now treats it seriously.[3] It is in two parts. At Mt. 27:62-66 we learn that the chief priests and Pharisees, who might have had other things to do, went to Pilate, even on the Sabbath, and asked for a guard to watch the tomb, because 'the impostor said "after three days I shall rise again".' The guard would be needed lest his disciples steal him and tell the people 'he was raised from the dead', and, they pathetically add (in typical gospel irony), 'the last error be worse than the first'. The only credible parts in the story are these: (i) disciples would be intensely interested in their rabbi's body; (ii) Matthew could not believe the tomb was unwatched, and (iii) the Jews between A.D. 30 and 70, hearing of the Anastasis, did indeed conclude that the last error was worse than the first: it was catastrophic. A dead martyr is bad enough, a live one is really frightful.

Now we must apply our minds to the Jewish expectation that disciples might want to steal their master's body surreptitiously. It was not so absurd in itself. Holy rabbis, *irrespective of miracle-working powers,* had numinous qualities, and their bodies retained them. Disciples wished to be buried near their masters. This is a quite commonplace Jewish notion. Meir ben Baruch of Rothenburg died in 1293 in the fortress of Ensisheim. His body was kept for fourteen years. A wealthy Jew of Frankfurt redeemed it from gentile custody asking only in return that his body should be buried next to the scholar, and his wish was carried out. There is a legend which goes back to about A.D. 150 or not so long afterwards, it reveals the mentality of Palestinian Jewry. The men of Meron were tomb collectors, in the sense that when one holy person is buried in a spot others tend to accumulate around him and the process is continuous. The famous Simeon bar

Yohai, a pupil of R. Aqiva and repository of *halakhah,* was buried in Meron, and, to cut the legendary story short, his son's body was stolen, in response to a vision of Simeon, by the Meronites from the men of Giscala. These were so keen to defend the tomb of R. Eleazar, a scholar in his own right, that blows were exchanged. In the end the Meronites increased their stock of famous tombs.[3a]

The interest which localities have in tombs of numinous persons is quite easy to explain. Pilgrimage has social, cultural, and, above all, financial implications. A locality may grow up round a tomb, indeed may owe its livelihood to the presence of a shrine, the authenticity of which has really very little to do with it. Every reader will call some example to his mind.[3b] It is quite certain that at least as early as the so-called Maccabean martyrs tombs were embellished and venerated and were objects of pilgrimage (the ancient counterpart of tourism) (see 4 Macc. 17:8-10). From early times two kinds of tombs have attracted attention in the Holy Land *and still do.*[3c] The supposedly improper use of tombs in precisely the ways I shall detail is castigated by a Karaite scholar in the tenth century.[3d] Castigated or not, the Kabbalists of Safed (Galilee) made a practice of finding unknown graves so that such practices could be developed. The two types of tombs are (i) the cenotaph, which looks like a tomb and can be presumed once to have been occupied by a known person, but is venerated for the extreme holiness of its alleged former occupant, and (ii) the tomb still inhabited by its occupant. Both are sites of pilgrimage. The best examples of type (i) are of course the tombs of the patriarchs, which certainly figure in our story. But at the moment of the Anastasis the analogy which would be in everyone's minds would be the second type. Both in the Jewish and the Muslim worlds tomb-visiting is a well-recognised activity. The occupant of the tomb is supposed to receive some benefit by the visit(!), and is begged to provide (a) guidance, (b) relief, e.g. from sickness, (c), the answer to practical problems. According to Jewish legend even the *unburied* dead saint may settle law suits: b. B.M.84b (Sonc. 483-4)! Offerings are made at the tomb, and lamps are lit. The tomb provides therefore an income for the people of the vicinity and especially an unearned income for the custodians of the tombs. Though each offering may be slight, the total is enormous. Temples and shrines, and where tombs are cult objects, tombs, accumulate great wealth; and where the protection of the holy place is the state's responsibility the state naturally has a finger in the pie, regulates admission, and levies fees from the custodians.

Black-magic is associated with tombs. The famous curse-tablets of the pagan world were often 'posted' in tombs![3dd] The misuse of tombs for incubation (p.78), and other hardly 'religious' practices was perfectly well known to contemporaries of the disciples. Jeremias, whose work in this field is of very great interest (though he has not precisely recognised the distinction between ancient tomb-cults and the subsequent cult of relics (*leipsana*)) very suitably informs us[3e] of ancient Jewish teachings about the burial of significant heroes of biblical legend. One of the reasons why the grave of Moses is unknown (or if knowable is not available for visits) is so that the Israelites might not build a sanctuary and there make offerings, burn incense, etc., and the nations might not profane it with icons, etc. Adam was buried deep so that no idolatry could be practised with his bones.

Jacob's bones were protected from burial in foreign hands lest necromancy should be practised with them (Midr.R.Gen., XCVI.6 to Gen. 47:29).

To sum up: to suspect the disciples of stealing the body from Joseph's custody is not at all unreasonable. Whether to supplement his attempts at a hasty burial, or to prevent his accumulating merit at their expense, or to make sure that they were buried near him, or to start—and of course to control—a cult: any or all of such reasons would be adequate. But all the evidence negatives the disciples' being able to do any such thing.

The second part of Matthew's invention is prepared for by the first. At Mt. 28:11-15 we have one of the amusing parts of the gospels. The guard, having (as apocryphal works elaborate and explain) been set and been deceived, must of course report the empty tomb. What they had reason to expect was a punishment (Kratz, 1973, 70-72). The chief priests and elders held a conference (thus increasing the likelihood of a leak) to decide what to do about it. They hit on the egregious notion of bribing the soldiers to say they slept while the disciples stole Jesus, *and if this should come to the procurator's ears* (as if it might not!) they would square matters for them. They did as they had been told to do, and spread the rumours which continued into Matthew's own time.

The notion that guards, whose admission that they had been asleep on guard-duty would entail very serious consequences, possibly a death-sentence or at the very least the ruin of their careers, should go and spread the story that a dead body was stolen from a tomb while they were asleep (we bear in mind the ancient novels having this theme as a component),[3f] is a tale which one would not dare to tell even to the Marines. Matthew means to say that the current Jewish 'explanation' of the Anastasis about A.D. 70 was that the body was stolen! Everyone knew it was a ridiculous explanation. For of course whatever happened to the body (which no Jews ever pretended to produce, granted that crucified corpses *were* available) no disciples made pilgrimage to its tomb, its total disappearance remained unaccounted for, and the Anastasis itself is not disposed of, certainly not disproved, by any such theory. Instead of pilgrimages to Jesus's *body* (which have never happened, so far as we know) evidence of pilgrimages to the empty tomb well before Mark lies in Mk. 16:1-8 as we have repeatedly observed.

What is conclusive against the body having been stolen is its great financial value. This had increased with time and by stages. Had he died a natural death prior to the arrest (i.e. had the Passion been obviated) his body would have been of great value since he was notoriously a miracle-worker. Unlike the pious dead of Judaism, knowers of *halakhah*, patriarchs and others, whose miracle-working in their lifetimes was slight or doubtful, Jesus performed charismatic cures wherever he went, even amongst the sceptical. Prayers for cure from diseases were offered at the tombs of the pious on the basis that the merits of the latter would secure God's aid; how much more could be expected from God when the merits of Jesus were in issue, he for whose sake even persons at death's door were recalled to life! Even on the cross his body had value; as a martyr for (his variety of) Judaism it would (as we have seen) be even more precious. A martyr merits much more from God than a mere pious person. To call upon a martyr to pledge his merit with God is obviously much more efficacious than to ask for the intercession of one of the pious men of times past. To have a miracle-worker's body was a financial investment; to have a martyr's was doubly so. This was no small matter and we do well to take careful account of it.

Mark himself is most particular to tell us that in Jesus's lifetime suppliants could obtain miraculous healing *without his knowledge* from touching any part of his clothing *from behind* (Mk. 5:28); and 'wherever he went, to farms, villages or towns, they laid out the sick in the market-places and begged him (Jesus) to let them simply touch the hem of his garment; and all who touched it (not 'him') were made well' (Mk. 6:56). This must be read with significant passages in Acts. Quite subordinate persons, the ambiguous Peter, and the no less complicated Paul, had practices of an even more striking character. 'Believers . . . both men and women . . . even carried out the sick into the streets, and laid them on beds and couches (stretchers?), that, as Peter came by, at least his *shadow* might over-shadow one of them' (see Acts 5:14-15). Paul's clients wanted something more substantial. 'God performed special miracles by the hands of Paul; inasmuch as that to the sick were carried from his body handkerchiefs or aprons, and the diseases departed from them, and the evil spirits went out' (Acts 19:11-12). The belief that an inanimate object emanating from a charismatic could carry his charismatic power without his personal participation was not confined to the Jews, but it figures in their scriptures at 2 Kgs. 4:29 (Elisha sends his staff to the aid of the Shunammite woman). Since the demand must have exceeded the supply I am sure few of us will doubt that Paul would have given preference to those whose faith enabled them to make contributions to his favourite charity. No one suggests that he supplied handkerchiefs and aprons *gratis*. Thank offerings to *living* saints were substantial enough: 2 Kgs. 5:15, 23; b.B.M.84b (Sonc. 482). It seems to me that Mark is preparing us for the idea that to obtain miraculous healing from Jesus contact with his conscious and living body was not necessary; and the author of Acts sees his vicarious body, viz. certain members of the apostolate, endowed with the same indirect powers. Without their teacher neither Peter nor Paul would have been able to establish any reputation as healers. He worked indirectly through them.

As if this were not enough the former wonder-worker was now said to have risen from the dead! Whether he did so is not so important from this point of view. If it was widely believed, the disciples could take advantage of it and they would have in their possession a means of income beyond all other pilgrimage-places. The women's report would be quite enough to set off a cult amongst women if not others. If Jesus's family's attitude towards him had been indifferent before, it could have changed overnight. Provided they could protect themselves from detection, thieves would discover rapidly that their booty had increased in value. The rumour which has caused it to appreciate could not be disproved. We have evidence that Peter feared to lose face with James, the Lord's brother, some years after this (Gal. 2:12). It is said now that Peter and Mary Magdalene were competing sources of information about the Anastasis and its cult.[3g] There were three substantial potential bidders in the market for those relics *not counting Joseph himself who had made the initial outlay.* Even an impecunious claimant (and the women who had looked after Jesus and his disciples (Lk. 8:3) were not impecunious) could easily find backers.

Whichever party might have got hold of Jesus' remains and re-buried him, the location would not be a secret. Secrecy would be no-one's object. Even a *supposed* tomb would draw visitors to the embarrassment of the authorities, since —healing miracles apart—it is human nature to venerate as a martyr anyone whom authority has destroyed in questionable circumstances (as recent events in that archaic world, Iran, have proved). If a rumour were circulated (we have no trace of one) that Jesus's body was cast to jackals by irate priests, specimens of his bones would immediately be 'found' which would serve to found shrine after shrine. And no such thing happened.

The body was never stolen, whether by disciples or impresarios of pilgrimage. No miracles have ever been worked with it! In case someone should object that if Jesus *dematerialised* there would have been no body to work miracles, and that a bogus relic would fail, the objection is wrong. Miracles are done by God in the vicinity of relics, bogus or not, since it is the subject's own faith in the possibility of their being genuine which operates, not the 'genuineness' of the relics. As a matter of fact the cult of relics as such is of known origin in point of time, and to some extent in point of provenance. Relics derive from hero-cults in Greece, and from the cult of gladiators who succeeded to the mythical power of heroes; the early Christian martyrs were consciously (and indeed self-consciously) assimilated to gladiators *and* the victors in the international Games, and their relics were worshipped, perhaps a century after the Crucifixion (at any rate not sooner), outside the main stream of Jewish piety, the tendency of which I have described above.[3h]

(c) Why was the body not reburied, then? We are proceeding on the hypothesis of an *anastasis*. After the Anastasis of Jesus the question of ultimate disposal certainly must have arisen. Apart from the fact that there is no rumour of a tomb of Jesus (just as there is no traditional grave of Moses), what would deter the disciples from burying him elsewhere, as Mary of Magdala suspected, and perhaps not only she? Those who were so concerned to provide the glorified one with a canopy in his lifetime (Mk. 9:5) will have given some thought, now at last, to a sufficient burial.

There are excellent reasons, if we remind ourselves of the Jewish concept of burial, why they should reject that idea. The bones await the Spirit at the resurrection.[4] As the body decays the deceased atones for his sins.[5] The righteous decay less, and the wicked more. The holy one will not see corruption.[6] The early Christians understood Ps. 16:8-11 as a prophecy that the Christ should not decay in death and was 'raised' by God to that end (Acts 2:25-32, 13:34-37)! When Isaiah was disenterred (prior to A.D. 70), so Sozomenos (c. A.D. 450) (ix.17.3-5) assures us from a Jewish pseudepigraphal source, his corpse was found uncorrupted. If no atonement is made in life the wicked suffer in their bodies as well as their souls. The body that lies in the tomb is called *nefesh, psyche:* it is the person's deputy.[7] It suffers on his behalf. To bury Jesus again would be possible *if he had not undergone resurrection.*

In view of the myth of Isaac, Jesus could classify his Anastasis as resurrection (p.35). This theological interpretation of an event would be in keeping with Jesus's autonomous handlings of theological data. Now he was perfectly familiar with *anastasis*, for he was credited with working some, and I have no doubt he did do so. This is irrespective of the Jewish popular tradition that when the Messiah comes he will awaken some of our well-known dead. Those whom Jesus revived were not sinless people, nor was life restored to them by God in token of their obedience to him. For them, as with the beneficiaries of the ancient prophets' powers, *anastasis* was a token, a shadow, of resurrection (so Jn. 5:20). They could be buried again. Their *anastasis* was not a means whereby, through solidarity, *their* friends could achieve resurrection. Jesus's case was quite different from theirs, apart from the fact that no charismatic revived him.

Therefore to rebury Jesus would imply that his disciples believed he still awaited the resurrection. If they had buried him they would be taken to have redefined the prediction of the Passion (p.79), giving it, once again, its original meaning. After the Anastasis the impression was gained (cf. Jn. 2:22) that he had repeatedly predicted that after crucifixion he would rise, after three days, from the dead, whereas what he originally intended, as we shall see, was that, despite his humiliation, he would 'overcome', in the sense that word has obtained in recent years. If he were to be buried again the virtue of the Anastasis, with the re-interpretation it offered to so much of Jesus's life, would be lost. One whose Anastasis is authoritatively depicted as resurrection can hardly submit to being reburied. There is evidence (p.127) that it *was* so depicted.

Another, and more obvious reason for not reburying Jesus would be the fear that the custodians of the tomb would claim to be conclusive custodians also of the Word (cf. Jn. 2:22). *Encoemesis*, the practice of sleeping in temples, caves, or the vicinity of tombs to obtain visions, prophecies, or dreams, was ubiquitous in the Hellenistic and Jewish world.[8] For a small fee the custodians could make available 'authoritative' solutions to the many problems, social, political, and economic which Jesus deliberately left unsolved. That is not to speak of questions which would arise much more frequently, e.g. where treasures were hidden, how to find lost sheep or coins, or to win a contest for someone's love. Since none of the disciples could be sure who would be custodians, even if the body fell into the hands of the family, the obvious alternative to burial (see below) would be most inviting.

(d) The predictions of the Passion had a dual rôle. There was their original sense, which we have outlined, i.e. that he would 'overcome'; and there was their eventual rôle, namely that Jesus predicted the Anastasis and what would emerge from it. In the light of the second rôle a reburial would be highly incongruous. The predictions are summarised at Jn. 20:9: 'they (Peter and the other disciple) did not yet know the scripture (cf. 2:22), that he should rise from the dead'. Here the authority is thrown back behind Jesus himself to the sources that Jesus is said to have quoted and interpreted (see below). Jesus's own predictions, as we have them, are actually cumulative in effect, and are best set out in parallel columns.

Mk. 8:31-33	Mk. 9:31(-32)	Mk. 10:32-34
And he began to teach them that it was necessary that the Son of Man should *suffer many things* and be *rejected* by the elders and the chief priests and the scribes	He taught . . .and said to them that the Son of Man	He began to tell them what would befall him . . . **The** Son of Man
	was denounced into the hands of men and	will be denounced to the chief priests and the scribes, and they will condemn him to death and denounce him to the Gentiles (lit. 'Nations') and they will mock him and spit upon him and
and be killed, and after three days rise up.	after being killed after three days he will rise up.	scourge him and kill him, and after three days he will rise up.

Each prediction reveals more. The conventional use of the passive in 'was denounced' and 'will be denounced' implies *God's* activity. Peter objects (Mk. 9:32) but the disciples leave it at that, coming up with a misunderstanding of what they think they have grasped (Mk. 10:35ff). Mark dispels the idea that they were in some conspiracy with Jesus to hoax their contemporaries. The words 'be killed and after three days rise up' imply a death, a burial, and, when he is conclusively dead, rising again. No one would understand this as referring to an *anastasis,* a voluntarily leaving the grave. The 'third day' implies ultimate and final justification: indeed at Lk. 13:32 we have a saying of Jesus, where he divides his stages of life into three 'days': in two days he performs exorcisms and healings, and on the third he 'will be perfected'. Certainly the days are not to be taken, without more, as referring to a strict chronology.

If they were puzzled by what they were told, how much more must they have been puzzled by what they were not told! I do not doubt the genuineness of the words *anastēnai* (rise up) or *anastēsetai* (will rise up). They evidence a time when it was not established that Jesus was 'raised up' by God. In context the expression means neither an *anastasis* in the tomb, nor resurrection. It means Jesus will be vindicated as God's Suffering Servant, to whose Song he refers (p.120). One might think that Jesus claimed he would be vindicated at the Resurrection of the Just. He is, after all, the Just One, and his condemnation by the opposition is their own condemnation.

These predictions neither prevented Joseph from buying the *sindon* nor the ladies from buying the *aromata* nor Nicodemus (if he existed) from playing his part. But they would stand in the way of Jesus's being reburied. It is ridiculous to contend that such predictions correctly anticipated an *anastasis* from the tomb (they did not), only to rebury him. There would be nothing to prevent the scribes' and elders' taking a periodical walk around the graveyard and reminiscing about their success in dealing with that young enthusiast. From an early period, well before Mark, the church had an emotional investment in Jesus's *not* having been reburied.

Let the disciples of John the Baptist by all means bury *their* teacher. Though many a Christian would clearly have liked to have 'taken up' the body of the Master (Jn. 20:15), it was a matter of satisfaction to think that that is *not* what happened.

2. A POSITIVE ANSWER.

(a) An inescapable fact is that even the aroma of a bone of Jesus would have given occasion for a monument, a shrine, a cult, and, what is much more important, an unearned income for ever. Tomb-building was quite a cult (Mt. 23:29, Lk. 11:47-8, Acts 2:29). Tombs of saints well known in the Jewish world in the time of Christ,[9] as since, have been places of pilgrimage. The custodians of such places are typically idle, greedy, grasping, quarrelsome, litigious, and disliked. The Holy Sepulchre itself under the Ottomans is a perfect illustration of this, but the Muslim and Hindu worlds, in which such shrines abound, supply us with endless unedifying spectacles, and have done so through the ages.[10].

To make matters worse, the Lord's Supper (Mk. 14:22-26, 1 Cor. 11:23-25) contains an invitation from Jesus himself to his 'family' to eat his flesh and drink his blood 'of the Covenant'. Now as it happens invitations to feasts (*klinē*) used to be issued by devotees of a pagan deity on their own parts, or actually in their god's name, to small groups participating in this cult, and these invitations implied that there would be a sacrifice to the god in question, followed by a modest banquet (cf. 1 Cor. 10:27-28). Such letters of invitation, beautifully written,[10a] survive from Greek-speaking Egypt. The practice was well known. There was another practice called *perideipnon* (funeral, or rather memorial feast), widespread around the Mediterranean amongst both Greeks and Romans and apparently known long before in various forms to the ancient inhabitants of Palestine.[10b] If Jesus authorised his peculiar ritual to be repeated periodically as a memorial feast (cf. the wording of Lk. 22:19 and 1 Cor. 11:24-25) one suspects it could easily be taken as the institution of a Christian substitute for the well-known pagan custom of death-feasts. It is not entirely out of the way to say that the practice of funeral masses may, in its origins, owe something to a survival of such notions. Now if one wanted a *location,* nothing could be better than a known tomb. For their *perideipna* the ancients carved out tables and chairs (*sic*) in tombs themselves, which sometimes had kitchens attached! The heirs or representatives of the deceased organised commemorative feasts at the tomb, and the deceased symbolically participated in the comestibles, sometimes poured down to him through a funnel! If Jesus had been buried in a recognisable tomb his pagan converts, and perhaps some Palestinian Jews also, would have instituted memorial banquets and death-feasts, and could even have adopted the Eucharist as a vehicle for the purpose. Functionaries would compete to organise the invitations and celebrations, and to collect the necessary 'funding'.[10c] If feasts in honour of the new deity were *de rigueur* it would have been only a matter of time before Jesus's cult became assimiliated to that of the god Serapis, for example.

Now how could this be tolerated by those that saw in Jesus after his Anastasis no less than the invisible YHWH, who could not countenance death-feasts (Deut. 26:14, Bar. 6:26(27), Sir. 30:18; cf. Tob. 4:17)? Jesus, in a symbolic and dramatic gesture (Mk. 11:15-17) 'cleansed' even the Temple from scandalous abuse of a corrupt sacrificial system. Far outstripping that celebrated anti-desecrationist, Nehemiah (see Neh. 13:4-13), Jesus saw the Temple merely as *a* house of prayer (cf. Josh. 22:26-34) as indeed he says (quoting Is. 56:7) at Mk. 11:17. He would, in due course, become himself a substitute for the Temple, a house 'not built with hands' (Mk. 14:58, Jn. 2:19, 2 Cor. 5:1, Heb. 9:11), a proposal quite incompatible with the localisation of any cult of his—as is said emphatically at Acts 7:48, 17:24. As a martyr Jesus would have attracted the world to his tomb, but to those who believed God to have spoken through his mouth after the Anastasis the possibility of a burial would be nothing less than alarming.

If a rumour got about that even a fragment of Jesus's body survived not one but many shrines would have appeared. The want of authentic relics has never been a problem.[11] It is said that enough pieces of the True Cross once existed to launch a ship. The fact that there has never been the remotest suggestion that a fragment of Jesus survived is utterly conclusive. It was incontestably known by family and by sect, whom the Anastasis had reconciled for the while and after a fashion, that Jesus's body (in the literal sense) was irrecoverable. Indeed one must not look for him among the dead.

(b) The case for the unexpected alternative, cremation, is strong.[11a] The objections to burying the body were mainly twofold: *for some* it would have admitted that the Anastasis had not been resurrection; and that it would have given undesirable opportunities to the custodians and their nominees with unforeseeable consequences. Mere omission to bury would not serve, since secrets amongst as many as six persons are not secrets, let alone eleven. Imposture and hoax 'findings' and 'reburials' would ensue. There is only one alternative which meets all requirements. The one objection to it is that it would be repugnant to Pharisees, who remained a field for recruitment into the church for some time. Cremation is unacceptable to Jews,[12] though it did occur in ancient times.[12a] The reason is basically that those who cause themselves to be cremated—as some Hellenising and apostatising Jews must have done—deny the Resurrection, which the bones must await.[13] The idea of Jewish religious students cremating the body of their teacher, even in the days when wood was relatively cheap in Palestine, is scandalous. Yet . . . In the case of Jesus there were two excellent positive reasons why he both could be cremated and should be. And the very pious community of the Essenes, certainly well known to Jesus and his disciples, regarded concern for the mortal remains of the dead as superstitious, when what mattered was the 'immortality' of the soul.[13a] So there existed a body of respectable opinion which ignored the ordinary people's anxiety to bury, or re-bury, their dead 'with their fathers'. A cremation would not offend them at least.

Firstly the ram that stood in[14] for Isaac was burnt as a holocaust[15] (a whole offering) and its ashes were continuous, so the rabbis said, with the ashes on the Altar of Burnt Sacrifice in the Temple at Jerusalem. For the sacrifice of

Isaac took place just there (at the Dome of the Rock).[16] The ram *was* Isaac,[17] and Isaac himself was burnt and he requested his father to burn him to fine ashes. The ashes of the ram *were* the ashes of Isaac.[18] He was the first holocaust,[19] and this is why the deaths of many innocent Jews at the hands of Gentiles and in *ovens* are collectively described to this day as 'holocaust'. Isaac was a sin-offering,[20] and was, in his quality as holocaust, accepted by God as propitiation for the sins of his people Isaac was sinless.[21] *All* martyrs are a *whole burnt offering* (Wis. 3:6).[21a]

The iconography of the '*Aqêdâ* (p.34) shows the fire of the altar burning[22] The Isaac-ram was burnt to ashes on the fire, kindled on the wood which Isaac himself bore on his shoulders to the place of sacrifice, *as a man condemned to be crucified carries his stake.*[23] God provided the ram, but *haggadah* tells us that not the ram, not Isaac, but both of them in the one form were burnt to ashes.[23a]

The '*Aqêdâ* took place on the Day of Atonement, some say, others during Nisan (the month of Passover).[24] It is to be observed that Mark makes out that the eve of the Passion was also (for Christians) the Eve of the Day of Atonement.[25] John shows Jesus carrying his cross, though the synoptic story reduces this to vanishing point. The ram caught in the thicket (visualised at Beth Alpha as an animal tied to a tree) is the type of Christ nailed to the Cross. Isaac, but *not* the ram, experienced resurrection, though his body was reduced to ashes. Cremation was therefore *authorised* by the only relevant precedent, that of Isaac, and (obviously) *pro tanto* only.

But there was also a biblical requirement that the paschal lamb (1 Cor. 5:7) should be cremated. Exod. 12:10, 'And you shall let nothing of it remain until the morning; but that which remains of it until morning you shall burn with fire.' There is good reason for this. The remains, i.e. basically the bones, would otherwise be gnawed by dogs, etc. Just as the offerings in the Temple were burnt, so the residue of the lamb must also be burnt.

A biblical scholar will pause. To burn the corpses of men was, at any rate in historical times, a dreadful revenge (2 Kngs. 23:16); how could any consideration induce religious students to *burn* the body of their master, with whom any of them might have given much to be *buried*? But the bible has yet another precedent, of which almost no one would dare to avail himself. Let us forget the botany of the Sinai peninsula. On Mt. Horeb Moses saw a *bush* in which there appeared to him the angel of the Lord, nay the Lord himself (Exod. 3:2-4) —indeed the Lord *dwelled* in the bush (Deut. 33:16). The Lord spoke *first* to Moses from that bush; though of course he spoke to him often at other places and times. That bush, though it burned with fire, was never consumed: to Moses that was a miracle (Exod. 3:2-3), for the bush remained fresh though it was perpetually on fire. The text does not tell us why the bush was not consumed. Only a prophet could answer that question. The Word of the Lord may well be consigned to the flames (as at Jer. 36:27), but it can never be consumed. The flames may appear to consume it, but they do not. The bush (a kind of 'tree') carried the Word in its communication with Moses; but the Word finished speaking between Jesus's *anastasis* and his ascension. Crowned with *thorns* (Mk. 15:17) in a mocking imitation of the royal radiate crown, Jesus re-entered (as it were) the

82

Bush and brought the story to its close (cf. Clement of Alexandria [second century], *Pæd.* I.8). The Redemption promised at the Bush (Exod. 3.7-10) was now at last completed. The Word will outlast heaven and earth (Mk. 13:31).

(d)   Did Jesus authorise it? Fathers of the church later saw the crucifixion as foreshadowed by the sacrifice of Isaac.[26] As early as the Talpioth ossuaries a cross of faggots implied the resurrection (p.127). In Jn. 1:29 we find the Ram as the Lamb of God prefiguring Jesus's sacrifice.[27] Unexpected as it may seem, the concept of 'Lamb of God' is certainly to be traced in the *Testaments of the XII Patriarchs,* a significant document of the thought-world of Jesus and his disciples.[27a] If Jesus did not authorise or require his cremation one wonders who would initiate so brilliant a notion, which solves so many problems at a stroke. Pharisees would certainly question such proceedings, but we can see the answer that would at once be offered. The Ascension is certainly a euphemism (p.112). Resurrection and Ascension were united in the early churches' notions of what happened . . . To the author of the Talpioth inscriptions (p.126) it must have been clear that Jesus, upon whom he called, was in Heaven, able to employ the divine power of reviving the dead. He had therefore ascended . . . This implies a certain death, and, as we shall see, the disappearance for practical purposes of the body.

Jesus's audacious treatments of scripture and *haggadah* in reference to himself go back to the earliest gospel tradition. He was willing to compare himself favourably with such characters as Moses and Elijah, and it has been suggested by a responsible scholar that he did identify himself with Elijah. He uttered prognostications about the Temple, and behaved, within it, in a manner that would astound even the enemies of Judaism. There is one passage in Mark which definitely provides a parallel between his Passion and the Isaac story. Satan tried to spoil the sacrifice of Isaac by throwing a stone;[28] Mark 8:33 shows Jesus rebuking Peter,[29] whose objection to the Passion-programme was understandable, in language appropriate to such a parallel, 'Get behind me, Satan . . .' Peter's mind was too practical. Further, Luke approves of the analogy, and at 22:41 seems to be alluding to the stone-throwing. Further Isaac was sacrificed by his own father, and Jesus's obedience to the Passion was explicitly attributed to his Father's will and pleasure (Mk. 14:36), in spite of rational objections. Further there is a possible connection between the *haggadah* on Gen. 22:2-14 and the Passion in Mk. 14:32 *kathisate* (the disciples must sit), for at Gen. 22:5 LXX *kathisate* the young men must sit until Abraham and Isaac come back to them (Isaac does not, at least at that time!). In the disposal of his own body Jesus would, of course, after his Anastasis, have full authority. Jesus did not call his disciples to him, he went to them, preserving his initiative to the last. Did he tell them to do with him 'as with Isaac'? That was all that was necessary.

(d)   Whatever may be said of Ascension, resurrection does not in reality require the corpse to be in any particular place despite the Pharisees' superstition, and the disciples would not have been deterred by such a consideration. The Matthaean, Lucan and Johannine appearance-stories have given rise to the almost universal notion that resurrection must remove the body from the earth. It is perfectly true that the Jewish myth of the resurrection includes the raising of the skeleton, but it did not necessarily have to leave the earth. And if we examine all the instances of life after death in the gospels (our nearest and most obvious information on the subject) they will be found to agree that the removal of the corpse from the tomb in no way hinders, just as the presence of the corpse in the tomb in no way prevents, the reality of life after death as Christ himself taught it.

The thief might enjoy Paradise with Christ (Lk. 23:43)[30] though the bodies of both men were still in their places of interment. Lazarus the Poor Man was in bliss though the location of his corpse was obscure, just as the Rich Man was in hell though his body was richly (we may presume) interred.

In the famous discussion of resurrection itself (Mk. 12:23-27)[31] there is not the slightest suggestion that the resurrected were different from Abraham, Isaac and Jacob, all of whose bodies, though they were buried, were supposed never to have seen corruption.[32] Corruption means being eaten by worms; the dead will be alive (Is. 26:19) but this does not require any particular event for the body. Their merits are available for their kindred. Even when Paul speaks (1 Cor. 15:35-54) of the body with which resurrected Christians will eventually meet Christ 'in the air', a body which is not visualised as incorporeal or immaterial, he does not envisage either the leaving of the earthly body or the keeping of it: it is the 'meeting' which is the topic of discussion.[33]

Therefore the cremation of Jesus's body would have no bearing whatsoever on his existence with God or his capacity to return at the Second Coming. John indeed, as we have seen, boldly asserts as Jesus's own opinion that there was no resurrection apart from him. This must include his own experience. He could enable his friends (e.g. Lazarus) to share his Anastasis. He possessed a theological formula which, on the one hand, made his individual experience effectively collective, and on the other cancelled out, so far as his friends were concerned, the popular and Pharisaic doctrines of resurrection.

The metaphor of the wheat-germ, which has to 'die' in order to provide the next year's harvest, a metaphor known to both Paul and John, fits very well when one remembers that the disciples already possessed Jesus's body in the form of bread,[34] so that, in view of the resurrection-potential of that bread (as explained in Jn. 6-7), nothing that happened to Jesus's corpse could possibly be relevant. Furthermore the gospels concentrate on Jesus's preaching of the kingdom almost to the exclusion of resurrection, and his exaltation has more value than the Anastasis, which is an intermediate stage in the process.[35] The disposal of his corpse would have no credal value. St. John rightly says (Jn. 6:63) that it is the spirit which gives life and Jesus's words are spirit and life—the flesh avails nothing.

To summarise, neither the general outlook of the gospels, nor the special references to resurrection as a doctrine that occur here and there, have any connection with the disposal of Jesus's earthly body. On the contrary the Eucharist, the means of making his disciples one body with him, has taken attention entirely away from the question of that disposal. If my conjecture is right this was entirely reasonable.

And yet the question did arise at least once. Abraham makes a caustic remark to the Rich Man at Lk. 16:31. No one's *anastasis* from the dead (the exact phraseology after the Transfiguration, at Mk. 9:9, which Luke himself does not reproduce) will persuade those who have not listened to Moses and the prophets. As elsewhere towards the end of his gospel, so here Luke, alluding to Jesus's own acts of raising the dead (7:14,22), emphasises that Jesus's life, and the church, must be seen against the background of scripture. Few persons who are revived from clinical death have learned anything from their experience, or have passed on anything useful. The *Testament of Abraham,* an apocryphal work roughly contemporary with the gospels, tells how Abraham had leave to go to heaven, to learn the secrets of the other world (p.108), and return for a short space before he died: but he communicated nothing to anyone!

No new injunctions, no sensational discoveries, no lurid warnings came from Jesus's Anastasis:[35a] neither instructions nor guidance emerged beyond what he had already given them in his ministry. The scriptural pattern alone validated and explained Jesus's endeavour and his sacrifice. The physical disappearance of Jesus as a person only emphasised the importance of scripture, for being risen from the dead is no title to interfere with the work Jesus did in his lifetime. Resurrection did not imply that persons inhabiting or appearing to inhabit their lifetime bodies would or could pontificate for the enlightenment of those still alive. Their lifetime bodies were not needed even for hypothetical purposes.

(e)   The final conjecture in this chapter relates to the disciples and the disposal of the ashes. The men of Galilee, as I imagine them, took upon themselves the extraordinary task of cremating their Master. Perhaps one or more of them might have observed a Roman or Greek cremation—they would have been common in Galilee. There was no question of their placing the ashes in an urn, Gentile fashion, since the same objections would apply to the location of the urn as to the burial of the body. If the cremation took place in the daytime it would have attracted unwelcome attention. Granted that religious sects had bizarre theories and quaint rules, this nearly exceeded the average person's power of imagination.

Allowing for its not being beyond the wit of men to achieve a private cremation, the no less important problem must have arisen what to do with the ashes. Unless they were disposed of, inconveniences I have dilated on would persist. The Roman Catholic authorities responsible for burning protestant dissenters or heretics condemned after their deaths often took care that the ashes were cast into the river to prevent trade in relics. Fortunately there was an obvious solution.

The offerings presented in the Temple were of several kinds. Some were burnt whole upon the altar; of others only parts were burnt (as at Lev. 7:17) and parts were taken by the priests, the remainder of them and the larger part of other offerings being burnt not on the Altar but in the Place of Burning.[36] Exod. 23:18, which connects the blood of sacrifice (according to the Targums this is the Passover) with unleavened bread and is therefore part of the scriptural 'dossier' behind the Eucharist, requires in effect that the remnants of sacrifices be burnt overnight, since the 'fat' is not to remain until morning. It is by no means ultra-fanciful to apply the verse to Jesus. If he was to hand over his body in the form of unleavened bread and to define his blood as like the blood of the Passover, his 'fat' could very well be burnt at night after Passover. In any event there were three Places of Burning in the vicinity of Jerusalem,[37] chiefly I suppose to accommodate visitors at Passover and any inhabitants who were entitled to consume limbs of offerings in their homes or lodgings. The Place that concerns us is that in the Kedron valley[38] right against the Temple wall which was also the City wall. Down that Valley came periodically torrents of rainwater. Into the Valley went a flow of blood and ash from the Altar and its platform.[39] The resulting mixture accumulated and was sold to gardeners and smallholders.[40] The law of sacrilege did not apply to the ashes.[41] Nearby was a perpetual bonfire on which meat of various offerings burnt day and night, and a stream of priests, in garments kept specially for the lugubrious purpose,[42] moved like ants from the Temple to the Place of Burning and back, during the hours of daylight (see Exod. 29:14, Lev. 4:12, 21, 6:11, 16:27).[43]

During Passover when the offerings private and public were unusually numerous the heap will have grown. Further the number of pilgrims at Passover was very large. Ancient calculations are not nowadays relied on: they put the number of lambs slaughtered at 255,000 or 256,000.[44] A modern calculation puts the number of lambs slaughtered at Passover at 12,000. We cannot imagine even 12,000 little bonfires to burn the remnants of so many lambs. Some wards of the City will have used other fires, but many 'companies' must have used the Place of Burning in the Kedron valley. The Passover lamb is also a sacrifice, and is therefore appropriately disposed of there. Any ashes deposited by a priest, or, in the case of the day after Passover, by a lay Israelite, on the heap at the principal Place of Burning will have gone absolutely unnoticed and no embarrassment would be caused to anyone.

If it were known to the family and to the disciples, that his ashes, especially the occiput, parts of the pelvis, and femoral condyles, which seldom yield to the flames alone, had been deposited there, where innumerable bones were burned, and where the torrential rains which fall between November and March would wash large quantities of ash away, it would be utterly and conclusively established that no trace of Jesus's body could ever be located anywhere. Ignatius, expecting martyrdom, wanted no portion of his body to remain—that he should be, as it were, a sacrifice, and physically disappear like Christ (Ign., Rom. 4:2).

Now it happens that sin-offerings may be burnt outside the Temple if we follow Exod. 29:14. In another context the author of Hebrews comments

'Our altar is one from which the priests of the sacred tent have no right to eat [a whole offering, like the Red Heifer]. As you know, those animals whose blood is brought as a sin offering by the high priest into the sanctuary have their bodies burnt outside the camp. Therefore Jesus also suffered outside the gate, to consecrate the people by his own blood. Let us go then to him outside the camp, bearing the stigma that he bore.'

(Heb. 13:10-13).

The idiosyncratic writer is speaking of a form of worship independent of the Temple and its cult, but his simile would be more forceful if in fact Jesus, who suffered outside the city wall, was known to have been burnt there too.

1. Whitaker (1969-70) referring to the Nazareth inscription.
2. Euseb., *ad Mar.* supp. ii, Migne P.G.22, 985D adds 'no thief would risk being caught by unwinding them'. O'Rahilly (1942).
3. Danielou (1968); Campenhausen (1968); Evans (1970), 57, 86, 149; Wilckens (1977), 45; Kratz (1973). The escape by a *Theios anēr* (divine person) by supernatural means is an ancient motif attaching itself to our story: cf. Acts 5:17-25, 12:3-11, 16:23-32 with our Mt. 27:62-66, 28:11-15. Walter (1973). Giblin (1975) denies the need to presume Matthew had an independent source.
3a. For a picture see *Enc.Jud.*8 (1971), 926 fig.6. The sources are Midr. R., Eccl.XI.3 (Sonc. 290-1) and b.B.M.84b (Sonc.484), also Pesiqta 93b,11-94d,3. Jeremias does well to make a feature of this (*Heiligengräber*, 1958,140). Horbury and McNeil (1981), 155.
3b. V. Turner and E. Turner, *Image and Pilgrimage in Christian Culture* (Oxford, 1978). Feasts = fairs (p.36-7).
3c. E. Marmorstein, *Heaven at Bay* (London, 1968), 185. The 'Guardians of the City', alert to every discovery of ancient tombs, protest against gardening or archaeology near the tombs of teachers of the Mishnah or mediaeval luminaries. The concept of 'grave with the wicked' figures at p.186.
3d. Sahl b.Mazli'aḥ (*Enc. Jud.* 8, 1971, 922(b)).
3dd. Jews too used curse tablets: U. Schmoll, *ZDMG* 113 (1963), 512.
3e. Jeremias (1958), esp. 142.
3f. Herod., *Hist.* 2.121 W. Aly, *Volksmärchen* . . . (Göttingen, 1969), 67-8. J. A. K. Thomson, *The Art of the Logos* (London, 1935), 102-109. Pausanias 9.37.3.
3g. Pesch (1980).
3h. Through vengeance martyrdom may hasten the Kingdom of God: *Ass.Mos.* 9:7 (cf. Lk. 19:11) (the work is dated after A.D.3 but certainly before A.D.70 and possibly pre-A.D.30: A. M. Denis, *Introduction aux Preudépigraphes Grecs d'Ancien Testament* Leiden, 1970), 135). Joseph is shown as a martyr in the *Test.Jos.*, and as to the effects of the merits of Joseph there is no question. Martyr cults certainly preceded Christianity On the efficacy of martyrdom see Grayston at *NTS* 27 (1981), 649-50, 652-3. On the subject at large A. Schlatter, *Der Märtyrer in den Anfängen der Kirche* (Güterslch, 1915); H.v.Campenhausen, *Die Idee des Martyriums in der alten Kirche* (Göttingen, 1936). The first example of cult of relics is in the *Martyrdom of Polykarp.* W. Reuning, *Zur Erklärung des Polykarpmartyriums* (Diss., Giessen, 1917). Crucifixion and martyrdom were early associated: Jos., *Ant.*12.256. Martyrdom is sacrifice: 2 Tim 7:6. Gladiators were known at Berytus under Agrippa (so Josephus). Ignatius sees himself as a gladiator: Ign. Eph. 3:1, Tral 10:1, Rom. 5:1. On the verb *thēriomacheō*, which is in this area, much remains to be said. F. J. Dölger, 'Gladiatorenblut und Märtyrerblut . . .', *Vorträge der Bibliothek Warburg* 1923-4 (Leipzig & Berlin, 1926), 196-214.
4. Ezk. 37:4-10, 12-13. Jn. 5:25, 28-9.
5. Mishnah, Kil.XIV.3, b. Ket.111a, Ber.18b, Sanh.46b, 47b.
6. Lindars, 38ff, studies Ps. 16:8-11 especially apropos of Acts 2:24-32. Jesus's flesh did not rot: this does not exclude cremation. To *him* bones implied corruption: Mt. 23:27?
7. Lifshitz at *Z.D.P.V.*76 (1960), 159-60. *Corp.Ins.Jud.*2 (1952), 1009, 1024, etc. Lev. 19:28, Num. 5:2, 9:6, Ezk. 44:25 (LXX). Kaibel, *Ep.Gr.* (1878), 815.4. Soph., *El.*1126-8. Cf. *psychikos anthropos* at 1 Cor. 2:14, 15:44, cf. Jas. 3:15.
8. Epict.II.16,17; Plut., *Mor.*109B-D. Is. 65:4. Sir. 46:20, 48:13. b.B.M. 107b, Ber.18b, Sanh.65b, Nid.17a, Hag.3b. Billerbeck, *Komm.* IV/I, 511-17. An instance of an attempt to consult the dead *including Jesus*: b.Giṭṭ. 56b-57a.
9. Jeremias (1958), 49, etc.; (1961). Schenke (1968). Surgy (1969). *Ant.*16.179-83,188;13.210-12; 1 Macc. 13:25-31.
10. Shib Chunder Bose, *The Hindoos as they are*, 2nd edn. (Calcutta, 1883), 143. My *Rel. Law and the State in India* (1968), 477-8, 489ff. *Durga* v. *Syed.* A.I.R. 1961 S.C.1302.

Kedarnath v. *State* A.I.R. 1974 Or. 75. Smith and Derrett at *J.Am.Or.Soc.*95 (1975), 417ff. *Ketkar* v. *Mohammad* (1968) 2 Supreme Court Journal 934.

10a. *Pap.Köln 57* provides an example. Koenen, *Zeits.Pap.Epigr.* 1967, 126. *New Documents Illustrating Early Christianity* 1 (1981).

10b. On sacrifices 'to' the dead see Jub. 22:17 with Charles, *Apoc.* & *Pseud.* II (Oxford, 1913/1968), 46. They *continued* within Christianity: *Apolostic Constitutions* 8.44,1 (trans. J. Donaldson in the *Ante-Nicene Christian Library,* vol. 17, Edin., 1870, pt. 2, p.253).

10c. Th. Klauser, *Die Cathedra im Totenkult der heidischen und christlichen Antike* (Münster/W., 1927), 54, 70; with *Nachtrag* (ib., 1971), 201. J. M. C. Toynbee (1971), 37, 41, 50-2 61-4,136. On *profusio* see C. P. Oeconomus, *De profusionum recept. sepul.* (Athens, 1921), Klauser, *Ges. Arbeiten* (*J.A.C. Ergänzungsband* 3) (Münster/W., 1974), 118. Participants at death-feasts *sat,* they did not recline (hence also the Textus Receptus, read in Huck-Greeven, *Synopse,* 13th edn. [1981], at Mk. 5:40 *anakeimenon* [a potential diner] is correct).

11. Chaucer, *Cant. Tales,* Prol.691-701. Boccaccio *Dec.* VI. 10. Migne, P.G. 46, 913D.

11a. By coincidence Desmond Stewart whose work was on quite other lines (D. Stewart *The Foreigner: A Search for the First Century Jesus,* London, 1981), concluded that the body must have been cremated.

12. b.Giṭṭ. 56b-57a. Am. 2:1. Is. 33:12, 1 Kngs. 13:2, 2 Kngs. 23:20. 'Besttatung', *R.A.C.* 2 (1954), 198, col.2. Frey (1932), 154.

12a. Archæologists are not of one mind. Many take Am. 6:10, 1 Sam. 31:12 (cf. 1 Chr. 10:12) seriously and are not moved by Ezek. 21:32, Josh 7:15,25 Is. 30:33, Am. 2:1. See R. d eVaux, *Ancient Israel,* 2nd. edn. (London, 1965), 57; *Enc. Jud.* 5(1971), 1073.

13. Ezk. 37:1-7 (cf. Eph. 4:16!). Riesenfeld (1948); Evans (1970), 108.

13a. Josephus gives this impression at *BJ* 2.154. On the other hand some secondary burials have been found in or near the Qumran graveyard: but that does not mean that the deceased were actual mmbers of that community; they may have wished to share their charisma by proximity and could have died far from that monastic retreat.

14. Cf. Jer. 19:5, 2 Kngs. 3:27. Spiegel (1967), 79-81 and n.13.

15. Neofiti Targ., Gen. 22:8 Isaac=the ram, the lamb of the holocaust. Le Déaut (1965), 31. Ps.Philo, *L.A.B.*XVIII.5, XXXII.2, XL.2. Pseudo-Philo is a work of Essene origin contemporary with the gospels.

16. Gen. 22:2. Cf. the Jubilees version of the story.

17. Neofiti Targ. on Gen. 22:8.

18. Sefer Hayyashar. Ginzberg, *Leg.J.*5 (1928), 254-5, 303. Beer (1859)67, 183 n.788 (ref. Heb. 11:19!). Vermes (1961), 205 n.2. Schoeps (1946), 399. Midr.R., Gen. LXIV.3, Tanḥuma and Rashi on Gen. 22:14 and Lev. 26:42. j.Taan.II.1 with Rashi. b.Taan. 16a, Zeb 62a. TanḥWay.XXIII. Sifre and Midr.R., Lev. 26:4. Midr. R.Lev.XXXVI.5. Spiegel, ch.4, esp.37 n., 41-2,44 ('the haggadah . . . is ancient indeed').

19. Levi (1912), Schoeps (1946), Daniélou (1947), (1950), Lerch (1950), Vermes (1961), Spiegel (1967), Dahl (1969).

20. The lamb as a sin-offering: Lev. 4:32. Mishnah, Ker.VI.9 (cf. Rom. 8:3, Heb. 13:11).

21. b.B.B.17a. He enjoyed the World to Come whilst alive.

21a. Applied to Christ himself by Clement of Alexandria, *Strom.* V.11.

22. At Dura (c.A.D.245). Garte (1973). Above, p.37, n.28. The Beth Alpha mosaic. Illustration of Dura: *Enc.Jud.*6 (1971), 285, fig.15; Beth Alpha: E. R. Goodenough, *Jewish Symbols in the Greco-Roman Period* 1 (1953), 241-53; *Enc.Jud.*4 (1971), 711-12. A 15th-cent. French Book of Hours (*ad terciam*) shows the fire well alight and the ram, as a lamb, tied to the bush or tree (C. Bermant, *The Walled Garden,* New York, 1974, p.12).

23. Jn. 19:17 *kā zeh she tô'ēn selûvô biktēfô:* Midr.R., Gen. LVI.3 Schoeps (1946), 387. Lerch (1950), 19-20, 29f. Palestinian experience of crucifixion: Mishnah, Yev. XVI.3, Ohol.III. 5,IV.11, Shab.VI.10, Tos., GiṭṭVII(v),1 j GiṭṭVII.48c Liberman (1944), 36-7. Pes.Rabb.XXXI.2. Spiegel, 77 and n.1, 84. Romanos 41 *v.*23.

23a. See Spiegel, also Yose ben Yose at Horbury & McNeil (1981), 170.

24. P. d.R.El.XXXI. Midr.R., Lev.XXIX.9f. Isaac an atonement for Israel: Midr.R.,Cant. I.14,1. Midr.R.,Exod.XV.7.
25. *LNT*, 410-11.
26. Barn.VII.3. Hanson, 287 n.27. Tert., *ad.Marc*.III.18.Greg Nys., ho. Res. 1 Jo. Chrys. ho.Gen.XLVII.3. Theodoret, quæst. in Gen.74 Ephrem (d.373), *Hymns for the Epiphany* ii,29. Romanos (ed. 1963), 41 (6th cent.). Gen. 22:1-18 is a lection for Holy Saturday Prophetologion, 1970, 467). Le Déaut, *La nuit pascale* (*Rome*, 1963), 133ff. Smith (1932). Speyart van Woerden (1961). *Lexicon der christlichen Iconographie* I (Rome (1968), 23-30.
27. Hanson (1974), 50, 65, 74, 79-86 tends to underplay the rôle of the 'Aqêdâ.
27a. J. C. O'Neill. 'The Lamb of God in the Testaments of the Twelve Patriarchs,' *JSNT* 2(1979), 2-30 (*Test*. Jos. 19, *Test*. Benj. 3:7ff., see p.27).
28. Sefer Hayyashar XXIII.38. b. Sanh.89*b*. Wünsche I (1907), 49ff., 53-7, Zech. 3:2. b. Qidd.81*b*. Tanḥ Gen.46. Midr.R., Gen.CVI.5. Spiegel, 104-7. Jub. 18:2-19. Midr.R.Lam., introd.24. TanḥToldot 7, fol.46a (Rabb.Anthol., 303). Ginzberg, *Leg.J*.i, 277-8.
29. Dinkler (1964), ignoring the 'Aqêdâ haggadah, shows this as a post-Easter reworking of a tradition.
30. S. Ben Chorin, *Bruder Jesus* (1970), 221 suggests a new translation which cannot be substantiated.
31. Evans (1970), 32. Exod. 3:6 implies that they are dead. Wellhausen cited Ps. 6:5. Nineham, *Mark,* 322.
32. b.B.B. 17*a*.
33. 1 Thes. 4:15ff., 2 Thes. 1:7f, 1 Cor. 15:35-53. Resurrection of the body (Rom. 8:23) requires a body but its 'total transformation' is nowhere methodically envisaged. Sider (1975).
34. On the resurrection potential of the church irrespective of bones see 1 Cor. 6:14, 2 Cor. 4:14, 1 Thes. 4:14, 17.
35. 1 Pe. 1:21, Phil. 2:9,11, Heb. 9:24, 1 Tim. 3:16. Branton (1961), 45. Evans (1970), 76, 136, 142. Delling, 90. Marxsen (1970), 145. Geering (1971). O'Collins (1973).
35a. Cf. Socrates at Plato, *Phædo* 113a-115a.
36. Mishnah, Zeb.V.2, XII.5, Meil.II.3, 4-5,8 (Danby, 575-6). *J.E.* XII, 84 col.1.
37. b.Zeb.104*b*, 105*b*-106*a*.
38. Cf.2 Kngs. 23:6. Maim., *Code V*III,III,ix,8;VI.ii10-15. b.Yom.23*b*, Pes 26*a*.
39. Mishnah, Tam.II.2, b.Tam.29*a*.
40. Mishnah, Midd.III.2, Meil.III.3, Yom.V.6, b.Yom.43*b*.
41. b.Meil.9*a-b*.
42. Mishnah, Tam. I.4, II.3, III.6,9, VI.1, b.Tam.28*a*.
43. Above, n.37.
44. *BJ* 6.422ff. Scouted by Jeremias, *Jerusalem in the Time of Jesus* (London, 1969), 78, 83.

CHAPTER VIII

Between Anastasis & Brain Death.

The great obstacle to believing that Jesus revived in the tomb has been, understandably, the problem what became of the body. As we have seen, re-burial was out of the question and surreptitious disposal equally improbable for similar reasons. A compromise solution, which was both authorised by analogy with Isaac, and required if one took seriously Jesus's comparing himself with the Paschal lamb, namely cremation, has recommended itself to us as a conjecture worthy of notice. The Ascension is a euphemism, filling a vacuum on the analogy of the few great pious men of Israel who were supposed to have gone to heaven alive, e.g. the Patriarchs, Elijah (2 Kngs. 2:1, 11-12) and, as we shall see, Moses. No one can seriously contend that it excludes a physical cremation. Luke, the only known creator of the (chronologically discrepant) Ascension stories alluded to feebly but significantly by John (Jn. 6:62), is to be praised for his literary gifts. There is no more reason to suppose that he intended his text to be taken literally here than in the Nativity stories of his gospel, which are obviously symbolic. To be found amongst those stories is the insinuation that Mary bore Jesus painlessly as Sarah bore Isaac,[1] a piece of *haggadah* that survived in the church for quite some time.[2] And Isaac was the first Jewish baby, not to be *swaddled* but to be placed in a cradle!

Jesus having, as I take it, emerged from the tomb, the question remains what did he do in the short period of life which must have remained? In trying to recover this we must keep apart in our minds the theological *value* of what he did (which is incalculable), and what he simply *did*.

Time was short. Even the most expert medical help could not retrieve one whose injuries had not been treated for as long as twelve hours. The loss of blood would have had a dehydrating effect making chances of recovery very slim. Shock, untreated (except by refrigeration), would suspend the healing process. I surmise, as I have said, that eventually gangrene would finish what the torture had begun.

The Johannine stories, and the Lucan, conflict fantastically with this. The Johannine 'appearances' give him less than a week's survival; but John appears to be stretching matters to enable perhaps two specific Sundays in the church's year to be hallowed, to emphasise the effect of gradual submission to the Master's approval. The dates are not historically verifiable, and John may have had no more information on Jesus's survival than we have. When he wrote his gospel Luke himself subscribed to the early notion that crucifixion, *anastasis*, and ascension were part of a single process, a notion reflected (as we shall see) in John also (see Lk. 24, to be read as a continuous drama). The period of forty days figuring at Acts 1:3 is incredible, and need not be taken seriously since he is repeating

90

the period during which Moses was under instruction from God on Mt. Sinai (Exod. 24:18). Though Jesus might have survived (unknown to Luke) for two days or even three, the period was, *in effect,* identical with Moses's forty—and indeed the effect of the Anastasis was such that the point is well taken. By the time Luke wrote Acts it was desirable to provide a Christian scenario leading up to Pentecost.[2a]

It could be argued that there is a known case of a man who was flogged repeatedly, and to the bone, in Jerusalem itself, and survived for years to be a nuisance to everybody.[3] It is clear, therefore, that expert medical attention was available (from charitable people) at the place in that period, even for very severe lacerations of the precise type Jesus underwent. But the man concerned was an alarming case of spirit-possession, which affects susceptibility to pain; and Jesus underwent severe injuries beyond laceration.

What, then, did he do in the necessarily short time available to him? Three things, it seems—all of them very significant if one looks at them in the light of what can be inferred from our sources, if we leave aside for the present what these actually have to say.

1. THE MESSAGE TO THE DISCIPLES.

All our sources are agreed that Jesus did not summon his nearest and dearest, namely the disciples, one of whom is alleged to have been his favourite—though what credence we can give to this (Jn. 13:23) is not clear. Any ordinary person in such circumstances (if they can be imagined) would have summoned help from such a quarter. Through the ladies whom the circumstances themselves had selected as persons to care for him he appears to have sent a somewhat curt message, which the Young Man thinks fit to couch in the brusque terms 'Don't dither', or, as we should say 'Take a grip on yourselves', and 'Off with you, now . .'. The women are not asked for medical aid or food, both well within their province, nor even for their prayers(!), also within their expertise. As if Peter and the (other) disciples might be hiding in different localities, they are told to take a message to them separately, the Young Man surmising (rightly) that only they could find them in that crowded and chaotic city. This assumes rightly that the bare bones of Mark's story are reliable despite his ultimate motive, which we already know. Had the traditional text included a command *not to mourn* or to *summon all believers* it would have been perfectly fit for its ultimate purpose, but it did not.

The curiosity of this position, which no one doubts, struck early hearers of Mark. Why did the male disciples not come at once? Perhaps they did and checked what the ladies had told them? Why not? But the ladies were too shocked or too discreet to pass on the message of their own initiative? Or they supposed the disciples must have been privy to the removal? The implications of the empty tomb were multiply embarrassing, to the family, to the disciples, and to themselves. They saw where Jesus was laid (Mk. 15:47) but left it to a stranger, even one remoter from Jesus than they were, to provide a watchman. Like many women of their race and time they lacked personal initiative, and here was a case where it proved to be a serious handicap.

At that rate how did the disciples eventually come to know the facts, for the word, or rather the silence, of the women alone is small testimony (*Acta Pilati* 7)? So the vacuum is gradually filled. The disciples 'came' but in good time Jesus had taken the initiative and come to them! Even before John invents Peter's and 'the other disciple's' abortive visit to the tomb it remained clear to everyone that Jesus had known *when* he wanted to communicate with them, on what subjects, and in what way.

My guess is that as strangers buried him so strangers took care of him. They soon acquainted themselves, if that was necessary, with what could reasonably be expected of those whose place they had taken. This left Jesus free to communicate in quite a new tone with his former table-companions, whose partner he had constituted himself, according to the insight of John, in the celebrated foot-washing scene.[4] They were his partners, but in the sense of being bagmen: he supplied the capital and they were to go about selling his stock.

The message to the disciples consists in this, which every one of our sources corroborates, that they await his direction not less obediently than they had done up to the débacle, in the course of which their inadequacy had been demonstrated for all time.

It could be argued that they were not quite so hopeless a 'shower' (to use the exactly correct English idiom) as they appear in Mark's gospel. It has been remarked that Mark did not set out to vilify Peter.[4a] It could be argued that Peter, the most probable source of the direction which Mark's narrative takes, had laid it on with a trowel, in order to magnify the scope and degree of forgiveness he personally obtained. But it must be remembered that Mark must have had his inaugural recitation between A.D.55 and 60. The old myth that he worked in Rome has no substance in it. Not only was he a Palestinian but there is no reason why he should not have written in Palestine, probably not too distant from his Galilean homeland. At that time there were still alive not only pupils of the original apostles, but actual members of that band. Moreover Gentile and Jewish Christians were still in Palestine and its adjacent territories fully capable of monitoring the presentation. For my part I cannot conceive a work of this importance obtaining currency without the approval of at least one prominent member of the church's central organisation. The drift of the gospel, so extremely unflattering to the disciples,[4b] can therefore confidently be taken to be, in substance, true. I shall explain later why that is quite probable in any case, and the contrast with the same persons after the Anastasis is no less credible.

And when Jesus sent a message at second hand to the disciples and to Peter separately its content deserves to be scrutinised closely,[5] as indeed it soon was.

2. THE WORD 'GLYL'.

The gurgling sound we have reproduced GLYL cannot be an invention of Mark or his source at 16:1-8, nor are we to understand Galilee as the early church's location of the Second Coming (Acts 1:11), nor are Mark's multiple redactional references to Galilee to be explained in that way.[5a] On the contrary the massive early Christian, and subsequently Marcan, interest in Galilee arises out of Jesus's message, from which every scrap of value was extracted in the same way as they scrutinised, sifted and related reminiscences of his adventures in life.

The Hebrew language is structured on the basis of consonantal roots. Our sensitivity to the difference between *fir* and *fur*, *hear* and *here*, *fit* and *fat*, *mate*, *meat* and *mite* would be unintelligible to Hebrew-speakers. To them not only *fir* and *fur* but also *far* and *fore* must be modifications of one idea. Their vowels indicate the mood of the basic idea. Pronunciation, moreover, differed from place to place. Scripture itself was unpointed, that is to say the vowels were not written. Literate persons visualised all words on a consonantal skeleton, as it were, and mentally heard an array of vocalisations according to context. If a word had no context, or a poor one, or an ambiguous one, delicious fun could be obtained by ringing the changes (called *'al tiqrê*, 'don't read X but read Y'), and indulging in endless puns, most repugnant to European taste.

Hebrew was still spoken for religious law. Pronouncements were to be formulated, as they still are, in Hebrew, not Aramaic, the vulgar language. Cross-punning, however, between Hebrew and Aramaic was quite possible, as it actually occurred between Hebrew and Greek.

Jesus directed the disciples, through the women, concerning GLYL, to which I have reduced the evidence we have. The Young Man understood that Jesus intended to lead or would lead (*proagei*) them into *Galilee*. 'Galīl' could have meant (i) a circle or district (as at Is. 8:23 MT), (ii) the place Gilgal where Joshua ('Iησοῦς) renewed the covenant with the people (cf. Josh. 12:23 MT/LXX, 5:9). (iii) the region called Galilee (where these people came from), (iv) all that Galilee means metaphorically, and (v) what the experience with Jesus in Galilee might mean to (a) the ladies themselves, and (b) to the disciples. All of them had a range of experiences in Galilee and the women had experience of serving him in Galilee, though (as I have indicated) they could hardly be of the inner circle of his friends, etiquette not permitting that. This special *value* for Galilee is certainly true whether or not the possibly doctored Mk. 15:41 ('who, when he was in Galilee, followed him, and ministered to him; and many other women who had come up with him to Jerusalem') is reliable as such.

The message as it stands is ambiguous. Whatever Jesus was actually doing, *proagei* could mean that he had already preceded them, as a spirit, shepherd-like, back to their homeland (cf. Mk. 10:32). Matthew resists all temptation to take it in this way, and understands that Jesus would meet his folk there again for a resumption of business! *Proagei* by no means necessarily means that Jesus had left the area of the tomb or its environs. The actual meaning must have been that when they eventually left Jerusalem (i) it would be for Galilee, and not elsewhere, and (ii) it would be under his guidance and not others', and *still not their own*. In view of the change the Anastasis had operated, this is perfectly intelligible as an instruction.

Galilee is also a technical term, that is to say, in biblical language. It means first the circle of mixed Jewish and gentile populations which ringed northern Jewish territory (where Jewish 'visibility' in sociological terms was understandably high), and secondly the mission-field in which the message of salvation would gather up Jew and Gentile at the End of Days. Is. 9:1-2 (MT 8: 23-9:1): 'In the latter time he has made it glorious, by the way of the Sea, beyond Jordan, Galilee of the Gentiles. The people that walked in darkness have seen a great light; *they that dwelt in the land of the shadow of death,* on them has the light shined.' Ezk. 47:8-10 (LXX) speaks of lifegiving water proceeding *to* Galilee northwards (from Jerusalem) and thereby purifying waters and conferring life on every *psyche* (*nefesh:* soul, whether living or dead), which it touches.

When Jesus originally recruited his first missionaries from amongst the 'princes of Naphtali';[6] he knew that Galilee was the location and Galileans were to be the means for the coming of the Kingdom in power.[7] 'To Galilee' was therefore his message; but not to be implemented until he was ready to despatch them with their instructions.

The word GLYL is a reduplicated root, stemming from GL which means 'round', 'rolling' (above, p.66). *Golēl* means the stone, GL means a well. We shall see what significance all this has shortly. It is secondary, not primary information, but it explains the emphasis on the *lithos* (the stone), and on the ladies (p.103), before there were pilgrimages and festivals at the Sepulchre and before the source of Mk. 16:1-8 was even got together.

3. THE COMMISSIONING OF THE APOSTLES.

Apostolos (apostle) means agent, deputy, envoy, ambassador, and is the equivalent of the Hebrew *shaliah,* one 'sent out'[8] The fishermen of the tribe of Naphtali were the first agents Jesus recruited. Agents must be commissioned by their principals and envoys must be accredited by their monarchs. So Paul starts off his letters, 'Paul, an apostle of Christ Jesus, through the will of God, and Timothy our brother, to the saints and faithful brethren . . .' (Col. 1:1-2); 'Paul, an apostle, not from men, neither by appointment by a man, but by Jesus Christ, and God the Father, who raised him up from the dead, and all the brethren that are with me, to the churches of Galatia . . .' (Gal. 1:1-2).

Jesus commissioned, in the course of his ministry, numerous disciples to act as his deputies for the announcing of the Kingdom. His instructions are indicated verbatim by Mark and for the reasons I have given above they must be taken as substantially true. This is confirmed by the fact that Jesus's financial instructions for his agents are correctly stated in Mark[9] and became watered down rapidly as the missionaries accommodated themselves to prevailing conditions.

In Mk. 6:6-7, Lk. 9:1-3,10,60, Mt. 10:16/Lk.10:3,9,11,17-20 we have this earlier information. The Twelve and the Seventy were sent with considerable precaution, and were promised and obtained (as far as we know) a safe return. Their commission was limited: to subdue demons, and to announce the coming of the Kingdom. The programme at Mk. 6:12-13 adds merely the anointing of sick persons with oil (another exorcists' practice), and their cure. *Now,* the Twelve are to go into the whole world (so says the late Mk. 16:15-18) and announce the gospel to all creation! Though the vocabulary differs, interestingly, from Mt. 28:19, the sense agrees, and the legally-minded Matthew adds (*v.*20) that they shall 'teach them (the baptised persons) to observe all the commandments I gave to you . . .'. It has been argued that Matthew never had a source other than Mark (Neirynck, 1968/9); but Mt. 28:16-20 has been found to contain evidence of a commissioning though unhappily conveyed in scripturally opaque themes.[9a] Luke (24:47) explicitly orders them (as a matter of scriptural obligation) to preach *in Jesus's name* repentance for the remission of sins for all the nations. John differs, again significantly: *any person* who believes will have life in Jesus's name (Jn. 17:2-3,20:31, etc.), and the apostles are given specifically the power to release or to confirm the sins of anyone. The formula hinted at by all these sources, and also by Mt. 16:19 (cf. 18:18), if this is a rewriting of earlier material in the light of the post-Anastasis events, amounts therefore to something altogether grander and more final than anything envisaged during Jesus's ministry, whether in Galilee or elsewhere. Whether the apostles or church-leaders in Jerusalem really lived up to it in the sense required of modern missionaries (e.g. Mormon-style) is quite another matter.

The fact is that *for some time* they began to speak *parrhēsiai* (without restraint),[10] to act as Jesus's deputies, to raise the dead, heal the sick, confront the authorities, whether of church or state, and in all respects behave with a freedom utterly out of character with their pre-Anastasis personæ. The nature of their extraordinary preaching is shown at Acts 2:24. Campenhausen (1968, 88) is wrong to disparage the traditional argument that only a resurrection could so convert them. Jesus had once characterised them as lacking faith (Mk. 4:40). That could not be said now. Some of their friends thought they had seen a ghost (carefully dispelled by Luke at 24:37-43: ghosts and visions do not eat [Tob. 12:19]!). But the subsequent trials and sufferings of many of the apostles proved their faith beyond doubt. Mark himself indirectly testifies to this (Mk. 10:38-39). Mark provides us with the materials to compare the sending of the Twelve and the Seventy on the one hand, and the post-Anastasis commissioning on the other. This he outlines in the cryptic message *via* the women, a message the latter would not have relished repeating to the touchy recipients, to whom status still meant so much (Mk. 9:34, 10:37,42). Those last passages provide sayings which are embedded in settings which may not be historical, but the picture of the disciples discussing who was 'greater', and who would be Jesus's lieutenant and sublieutenant thereafter, is obviously plausible.

The facts and the 'appearance' stories tell virtually the same tale. John is very emphatic and precise: 'Peace be with you! As the Father has sent me (*apestalken me*) (i.e. has made me his emissary) so I also send you. So speaking he breathed on them and said to them, "Receive the Holy Spirit. Whose sins you release, they are released to them; whose you retain, they are retained." ' There could be no greater commission.

It could be argued that the disciples, after mourning for their dead Master woke up to the utility of imagining themselves destined to a like fate (cf. Mk. 10:38-39), and cheerfully and quickly took up the cross from which he had been taken down. Those who had been so inadequate before, suddenly, through visions or subjective impressions, believed that a rôle had devolved upon them for which not one of them had proved himself fit. That would have been a miracle

95

indeed! Had they been impressed with his talk of 'rising again'? Indeed they had not (Mk. 9:9-10, 10:34-35). Such quaint ideas made no more impression on them than had the last words of Socrates on *his* disciples (Plato, *Phædo* 115 c-d)!

But notice Luke's retrospective description of his gospel at Acts 1:1-3: '. . . what Jesus began to do and teach . . . until the day when he gave orders to the apostles (whom he had chosen) through the Holy Spirit, and was taken up, apostles' οἷς καὶ παρέστησεν ἑαυτὸν ζῶντα μετὰ τὸ παθεῖν αὐτόν ἐν πολλοῖς τεκμηρίοις — 'to whom he presented himself alive after his Passion with many proofs (of his survival) . . .' This, I believe, is substantially true.

How did Jesus commission them? Possibly by visiting them in his own time, by some appropriate conveyance, speaking perhaps very little, but placing his hands, whose wrists bore the marks of the nails (Lk. 24:39, Jn. 20:20) on their heads (a method, used later by the disciples themselves, which became traditional: Acts 6:6, 1 Tim. 4:14, 5:22; cf. Acts 9:17 which was not a commissioning). The laying on of hands[10a] conveys the Spirit, without which their morale would have been low, and their efforts vain. Anthropologists are familiar with transfer of charisma by contact.

Earlier in his gospel Mark had outlined the sequence of events to which that 'first day of the week' would conform: raising the dead (5:42) *aneste;* incredulity (6:3-6); and charging with a mission (6:7-13). Jesus was equated with God amazingly soon after the crucifixion (p.132), Jews (strict monotheists) have often deplored Christians' likening Jesus with God, except in so far as he might claim to be his devotee ('son'); they are seldom convinced that the 'stumbling-block' has been removed when it is pointed out, correctly, that Jesus purported and indeed claimed to be God's agent, legate, ambassador, and plenipotentiary. As such, according to Jewish legal ideas, he must be 'like' the one who 'sent' him. This solution, no doubt, makes good sense; but it does not take us the whole way. The persons whose bones were placed in the Talpioth ossuaries (p.126) apparently believed Jesus exercised the divine powers *after his ascension.* This took the metaphor of 'agency' to an extreme. Hymns were sung to Jesus by early Christians as if to God. Could this be accounted for by what Jesus *said,* irrespective of what he *did,* after his Anastasis? We know he said very little indeed. There is the loud silence of our texts, properly understood. As for his actions, the commissioning, possibly by laying on of hands, could have been done without any suggestion that Jesus, risen from the dead, was identical with God. No other person 'risen' from death has been worshipped as God! No precedent, therefore, existed: nor has any other example occurred since! The silence is so loud, it cries out for a conjecture, and one is to hand.

I can well imagine that Jesus said that he was ascending to the Father (as at Jn. 20:17, the idiom and appropriateness of which are perfect). He could well have made succinct remarks that have left echoes in the gospels, which latter were, of course, written up with hindsight. An example would be at Mk. 14:62 ('sitting at the right hand of Power'). But a lecture, an exposition, must have been beyond him, given the condition in which he must have been by the time he met his disciples. There is no evidence that any hostile enquirer approached him out of curiosity or in a spirit of scepticism (as happened in his lifetime: Mk. 12: 13-14, etc.), and obtained any reply. But I feel entitled to tender what follows with all deference as a mere conjecture. The disciples, fearing that his body might have been reanimated by an evil spirit or the spirit of some predeceased, disembodied person (Mk, 6:49, Lk. 24:37; cf. Mk. 6:14: Herod had such a notion of 'reincarnation'), *could* have asked, trembling, 'Lord (a polite form of address), who are you?' (Mt. 14:28, Jn. 21:12, Acts 9:5 par.). He *could* have replied in Hebrew *'eḥeyeh*, etc., 'I AM THAT I AM', or 'I SHALL BE THAT I SHALL BE', and 'I AM', or 'I SHALL BE' (Exod. 3:14; Is. 46:9, 47:8, 48:12 [cf. Is. 44:6, Rev. 1:8]; Zeph.2:15; Rev. 1:4, 4:8). This dual formula was the ineffable Name by which God identified himself for Moses in a passage which only Mark amongst the evangelists takes the trouble to point out to us. Jesus himself (Mk. 12:26) calls attention to the 'passage of the Bush' in connection with the resurrection. There *'eḥeyeh*, in Greek *egō eimi, ho ōn* ('I WHO AM') (LXX) *sent* Moses as his legate (*apostolos*) to the Children of Israel. The simple expression in Greek, *egō eimi*, which can be unthinkingly translated 'Here I am', or 'It is I', is a magic formula, a veritable theophany. Indeed it could be manipulated by impostors, as Mark himself tells us (Mk. 13:6). *Egō eimi is* quoted as from Jesus's own lips significantly (Mk. 6:50c; Jn. 8:24,58, 18:5-6), or is attributed to him (Acts 9:5). If he did utter this formula,[10b] exactly appropriate to one who despatched apostles as messengers from God, it would take care of our problem without residue; and, for those actually present on the occasion, would settle not only their doubts, but also their future.

4. PAUL'S EXPERIENCE.

The greatest obstacle to an intellectual conviction that Jesus did rise bodily from the dead and, in a short time, commission his apostles, is the celebrated passage in 1 Cor. 15:1-8, whereby Paul links the appearances of Jesus to his seniors with that to himself. Since his experience on the road to Damascus (Acts 9:3-6) was a vision, a typical result of prolonged mental confusion, distress, and consequent proneness to cataleptic charismatic experiences,[10c] it has been inevitable that scholars should 'reduce' the 'appearance' of Jesus to Peter, etc., to the level of Paul's own. It must be admitted that the vocabulary of our sources made it all too easy for them to do so. Let us examine the passage upon which some pedantic comments must, in all fairness, be made. It has been studied by others to distraction,[11] and certain words in it beaten threadbare.[12] By some it is suspected he was quoting an early formula.[12a]

'Now I want to remind you, brethren, in what terms I preached to you the gospel, which you received, in which you stand. By it you are saved, if you hold it fast—unless you believed in vain. For I transmitted to you as of first importance what I also received, that Christ died for our sins in accordance with the scriptures, that he was buried, that he was raised on the third day in accordance with the scriptures, and that he appeared to Cephas (Peter), then to the Twelve. Then he appeared to more than five hundred brethren at one time, most of whom are still alive, though some have fallen asleep.[12b] Then he appeared to James, then to all the apostles. Last of all, as to the "abortion", he appeared also to me.'

Let us admit, without recapitulating so much argument or embarking on speculation and cross-speculation as to the meaning(s) of the grouping of persons named or alluded to, that the sequence is intended to emphasise a chronological sequence (whether there was one or not) and to link Paul's own experience with that of the others. Persons not always loyal to Jesus figure in the list. Who are the Twelve, granted that Judas had only recently disappeared? From this passage it has been guessed (wrongly) that there *were* no 'Twelve' before the Anastasis. There appears to be a descending order of prestige, and a leading idea behind the list is the commissioning of the persons involved, the series of Jesus's 'contacts' ending with 'apostles'.

Yet, at the same time, it is not impossible that the appearances are heteroclite. There is some plausible explanation for the position of the apostles in the penultimate position. That the apostles did have a period of self-orientation after Jesus was removed finally from them is extremely likely; and that this is the historical nucleus behind Luke's dramatic presentation of the Pentecost experience is not less likely. At that rate a subjective but collective awareness of Jesus's presence on the part of a group in need of his guidance, after his final departure, would be perfectly possible. It would coincide, historically and rationally, with the penultimate position of the apostles in that list. But this does not exclude other forms of 'appearance' even to the identical persons, prior to that!

The word always translated 'he appeared', *ōphthē*, literally means 'he was seen', but is so regularly used with the dative case in contexts consistent with a supernatural vision,[13] that it would be unrealistic to allow Paul to imply directly that Jesus was physically seen by this series of persons. The verb is wholly ambiguous as shown at Tobit 12:19 (LXX:BA). On the other hand we cannot assume, as it is often assumed, that either Paul raises his experience to the level of Peter's, or reduces Peter's to the level of his. There is a third possibility.

Taking Paul's meaning to be that Jesus personally commissioned, after the Anastasis, a series of persons whom he chose to meet individually except where he wished it otherwise; and that, for that limited purpose, his own experience was comparable with theirs, I find these statements authorising me to believe that Jesus was actually seen by Peter, James and others: for them it was no less an actual seeing-in-the-flesh than a vision of aspects of the divinity. As we shall see, Jesus, emerged from the tomb, was, paradoxically, recognised as the power of God. Peter and James, as the Americans say, could 'use' such an experience. For James, who knew his brother, it was no less a vision of the divinity than it was the ocular recognition of the much changed figure of his sibling. It was no less a vision for being actual sight. I shall return to the idea of Jesus as an aspect of God later (pp. 132-3). Meanwhile I arrive at this conclusion from the curious phrase 'the "abortion"'. Usually translated 'one untimely born' the expression, which renders the Hebrew *nēfel*[14], has thus been forced to lose something of its force.

Conversion to belief in Jesus was traumatic, and amounted to a new birth, signalised by baptism (cf. Jn. 3:5). But for the grace of God, who revealed Christ to Paul, the latter would never have reached that birth, and would have been an 'abortion', the very abortion mentioned in Ps. 58:8(9), doomed to everlasting night and deprived of the Rest which awaits the Just who have laboured in faith. The implication is that even the Pharisee contemporaries of Paul were, unless they heeded his message, on the way to being abortions, never seeing the sun. Now even in his most sarcastic moments Paul is not to be taken as suggesting that Peter and his colleagues were unconverted after their long experience of Jesus's ministry. Mark allows that they saw the sun, as it were, and in one dramatic moment Peter certainly saw it (Mk. 8:29), a moment which Matthew does not hesitate to identify as a supernatural vision enhancing earthly sight (Mt. 16:17). Paul is not suggesting that Peter and the rest were abortions up to the Anastasis. Therefore this passage throws light upon the appearances to Peter, etc. Paul's own vision *was* his conversion, but the others were privileged to have visions which took that for granted. This leaves the door open for them to have had actual sight of Jesus, described by the term incorporating Paul's experience and 'up-grading' it, as it were. All alike had, at various times and in various ways, glimpses of God through their various histories of contact with Jesus. Paul was privileged in a special way: despite his maltreatment of the church (which he dramatises: Acts 9:1-2, 22:4) he (and he alone of the kind) was thought worthy of a specific, apparently unprepared, call to the ministry of the Word.

Notes

1. Lk. 2:7 takes advantage of Haggadah about the Jewish midwives at the time of Pharaonic persecution.
2. *Studies* II, 33ff.
2a. Wilson (1967).
3. Jesus son of Ananias: *BJ* 6.300-309.
4. Jn. 13 as studied at *R.I.D.A.*, 3rd ser., 24 (1977), 3-19. See also "Domine, tu mihi lavas pedes?" reprinted at *Studies* III (1982).
4a. E. Best at *C.B.Q.* 40 (1978), 547ff., 557.
4b. Apart from the Passion narrative cf. Mk. 4:34 with 6:52, 8:17-18,33,9:32,10:32.
5. Evans (1954). But Is. 52:12 must be taken to require an exit from Jerusalem.
5a. As suggested by Van Cangh (1972), following Lohmeyer.
6. Euseb., *dem.ev.*9.9.
7. *N.T.*22 (1980), 1-30.
8. Subject to the remarks of Barrett, 'Shaliaḥ and apostle', at *Donum Gentilicium* (Fest. Daube) (Oxford, 1978), 88ff.
9. *JA*, 181ff. Cf. *BJ*, 2.124-7. They were to live off their hosts and not exploit them.
9a. Meier (1977).
10. It is intriguing that the gospels find the need to attribute open speech (as opposed to rudeness) to Jesus, almost as if (i) the apostles needed this precedent, and (ii) there were those who doubted whether in fact Jesus did so speak. Mk. 9:32, Jn. 7:13,26, 10:24, 11:14,16.
10a. R. Péter, 'L'imposition des mains dans l'Ancien Testament,' *V.T.* 27 (1977), 48-55.
10b. On the formula R. Bultmann, *Das Evangelium des Johannes*, 17th edn. (Göttingen, 1962), 265, takes the view that the predicate-less expression *egō eimi* in John implies that

Jesus is the 'Son of Man'. C. K. Barrett, *The Gospel according to St. John* (London, 1967), 282-3 is helpful, suggesting that *egō eimi* at Is. 43:10, etc. might be an allusion to Exod. 3:14-16. But neither of these writers realises that *egō eimi* in Jesus's mouth, and particularly in St. John, directly relates to Exod. 3:14; nor did C. K. Dodd, *The Interpretation of the Fourth Gospel* (Cambridge, 1968), 350. The absolute *egō eimi* seems correctly evaluated by F. Hahn, *The Titles in Christology* (London, 1969), 303. See Kautzsch at Hastings, *Dict.Bib*.V, (1904), 625.

10c. Questioned by those who would emphasise his clear-headedness!

11. Bammel (1955), Glombitza (1958), Stanley (1961), 118-27, Conzelmann (1965), Fuller (1972), ch.2, O'Collins (1973), 35, (1974).

12. *Etaphē* does indeed not prove that Paul knew of the empty tomb. Delling at Moule (1968), 78-82. Evans (1970), 43-56.

12a. Kearney (1980).

12b. Had this been a Buddhist text we should have recognised '500 disciples' as an absolute cliché. '500' means 'a large number of'.

13. Of Lordship (Evans)? On *ōphthē* Rengstorf (1960), 117-27, Wilckens (1963), 81-3: Kremer (1966), 54-8: Marxsen in Moule (1968), 33, 37: Evans (1970), 63-4: Grass (1970), 186-9; Pelletier (1970), 76-9 (avoidance of *ephanē* noted; Gen. 12:7 referred to in the light of Philo, *Abr*.8); Fuller (1972), 31; Brown (1973), 90 (physical sight not excluded). Plato at *Phaedo* 81d uses *ōphthē* of seeing ghosts near tombs, etc. Vision of God in his glory (Bartsch, 1980).

14. *Nēfel* is a dead thing, the embryo alive is *wālād* or *'ûbār*. For the word and the idea see C. Spicq, *Notes de Lexicographie Néo-testamentaire* (Fribourg & Göttingen, 1978) I, 237.

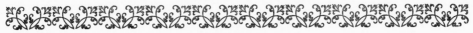

CHAPTER IX
The Sediment of History.

When a mixture is allowed to stand, a sediment may gather at the bottom of the bottle. When imaginative creative narratives of a highly complex and sophisticated type, such as are our gospel accounts, are analysed to determine how much in them is historical, in the sense of reminiscence of actual event (secular history as opposed to faith history), one is faced by disparate phenomena. On the one hand we have the subtle story of Mark, which is steeped in theological presentation, so that the mixture of reminiscence and comment upon that reminiscence leaves us a very small residue which separates itself from the 'fluid'. On the other hand we have the secondary accretions of the other three evangelists who, while they are evidently dissatisfied with Mark, are bound to him invisibly: he, rather than any independent traditions that may have percolated through to them, commands their field and dictates their own creativity. They are compelled by him even when they are, in some measure, rebelling against him. But the sediment in these others is very much less. In Luke's work one can hardly separate tradition from 'redaction' (Wanke, 1973; Dillon, 1978). Luke is in dialogue with Mark (Dillon, 68). It is in this sense true that the gospel accounts reveal more of the authors than they do of any actual events.[1] They tell us more of divergent theologies than of divergent traditions:[2] and yet their tendencies are within a pattern, and manifest a direction.

This is not to suggest that they were not, in the exact sense of 'history', historians: for all historians introduce evaluation and tendency into what they select as relevant facts. What is evident is that the evangelists who followed Mark can be analysed so as to leave very little which, separated from imaginative and creative enlargement, embellishment and distortion, can be called a sediment of history. Nevertheless there *is* a sediment — of secular history, not faith-history.

Of particular interest must be those items which one would not have expected, seeing how the participants were placed. In particular, while each author is emphatic that Jesus was no longer bound to time and place, two, quite independently, insist that his body was palpable and substantial. They are also eager to show that not he, but Another (i.e. the Paraclete, the Holy Spirit) is spirit: he, as the risen one, was not either *a* spirit or *the* spirit. Furthermore as preaching developed the Ascension was separated from the Resurrection (Wilson, 1967). This reveals unresolved contradictions which a factual 'sediment' would accommodate. Thus there are three levels: take for instance Jesus's asking for food in Luke. At the factual level the tradition was that he ate and drank with them; at the apologetic level he eats in order to prove that he is not a ghost; at the literary level he eats in order that he may occupy the place which the three angels who represent God in his visitation of Abraham in Gen. 18 occupy, as a result of which Isaac was born to Sarah. I have chosen this example, because it reveals both the sediment and the progress of ideas in the course of the creative effort.

The proofs of the Anastasis are said to be the so-called empty tomb (which was not necessarily literally empty) and the 'appearances'. The empty tomb is Mark's way of presenting the matter, to please people who already knew Christ had risen. We have no reason to assume that Mark knew of 'appearances' he suppressed.[2a] The 'appearances' are Mark's successors' method: their churches included members who did not yet believe, or had ceased to believe. It is quite unacceptable for us to lump together the empty tomb and the appearances as if they were cumulative, mutually supplementary proofs of the Anastasis.[3] The earliest form of the Christian message was centred on the tomb: the 'appearances' *as written up* result from the resurrection faith, they were never the basis for it.[3a] No doubt this is what Matthew and the rest have done, but it is literally preposterous. But we must say in their defence that they could not make a clean sweep, and have recourse *de novo* to eye-witnesses, as, conceivably, Mark could have done, had it been necessary.

Let us turn to the gospel materials and notice the entirely different nature of the mixtures presented in them. The very substantial thesis of Alsup, which concentrates on the patterns, and disparages previous methods of handling the passages, relieves us from lengthy disquisitions.

1. THE EMPTY TOMB.

Let us suppose ourselves in Mark's original audience. They know of pilgrimages to the Sepulchre and value the traditional account that 'legitimated' it (Schenke, 1968). We hear him explain that the ladies were told that Jesus was not in the tomb. They do not see the tomb empty. Their stupefaction arises from seeing the Young Man there dressed in purity and joyful expectation. Mk. 16:5-8 is quite clear that they visited the tomb and received a prophetic message analogous to, and as good as, an angelic message without actually being one (p.64). We should at once be reminded of the traditional fact, which everyone knew, that Moses, who spoke directly with God (Deut. 5:4) was buried (as *haggadah* relates) somewhere by the angels (cf. Jude 9), and had (and has) no known grave (Deut. 34:5-6).[4] Jesus, it seems, has thus been accorded part at least of the fate of Moses, God's friend (Exod. 33:11), whom the Lord knew face to face (Deut. 34:10).

What would thus be an inconvenient and bold disclosure, namely the fact of Anastasis itself, is now converted by literary alchemy into a necessary obscurity. Mark thus makes the message of the Young Man to the ladies the high point of his whole story. To show further how his mind worked I will imagine him thinking aloud:

The Young Man, who was Jesus's messenger, and therefore functioned as would an angel, barely concealing the deity himself, certified that the risen one was identical with the crucified one (not a metempsychosis on the pattern at Mk. 6:14c-d), and then told those women to give a message to the disciples. He did it as they looked down, through the formerly stoppered opening, into the tomb. Jesus's voice, by his chosen deputy, issued from the cistern-like structure to people who could not have had that experience if they had not had the stone removed for them. Translate all this to biblical terms. Jesus bore still the Spirit of God. The voice was the same that spoke to Abraham, to Elijah, and to Moses. An evangelist must get every scrap of information from the scene as if it had been painted by three eye-witnesses from three different viewpoints. I must go down into the tomb as the Young Man did, and look up [no doubt Mark did]. I must relive the women's pre-occupations, and their reactions. That women mourn (Jn. 11:31, 20:11) and that women mourn apart from the men, as the prophet said (Zech. 12:11-14), was only appropriate. Their presence was what could have been expected. I must know why Jesus's agent said what he did, where he did. The bare fact that Jesus was alive when he gave the message is not to overshadow the significance of time and place. The message to the women carries all the clues that we have, and that we need.

The women were concerned about the stone. The stone was heavy and would have to be moved up an incline for them by someone in the vicinity. Any part of a tomb, including the stone, vertically projected the uncleanness of the corpse within, or of the corpse-blood, unless certain spaces could be ascertained to intervene, and this no one can ascertain. During the Passover week it would not be easy to find someone willing to do this first thing in the morning; perhaps a Gentile or a non-observant Jew might be available, and had they sufficient means to reward him?

Though they did not know it, they were in a situation which called to mind three well known biblical scenes. Moses broke a rock in the wilderness and water flowed out for the people (cf. Jn. 7:37). Prior to that he had sat by a well (Exod. 2:17-21) and by overcoming the shepherds who prevented the shepherdesses from using the well, enabled them to water their flocks. As a result they took him to their grandfather who, *haggadah* says, put Moses in a pit, where he was looked after by Zipporah, whom he subsequently married. It was in her grandfather's house that he obtained the famous rod with which he smote the rock, and so on. Friendship with shepherdesses, wells, and marriage were already connected. Jacob had moved a heavy stone (Gen. 29:2ff.) and so enabled shepherdesses to water their flock, and he subsequently married Rachel, a direct sequel to the kindly action.[4a] The moving of the stone was essential in these cases.

The women were coming in the early morning as women come to a well, about to go down into it as women go down to fill their jars. The excavated tomb is like a cistern, or pit. Moses, we have seen, was imprisoned in such a pit, and so was Joseph. Joseph was put into the dry well (Gen. 37:24) and stayed there three days and three nights[5] until he was sold to the Midianites. Joseph was a forerunner of Jesus, the one 'given up', 'denounced' in order to provide life-giving bread for all his people (Gen. 50:20) (p.10).

The women's jars were already full of ointments. Of course Mark knew that women came in his day bearing censers. This immediately calls up another passage, not from the Law this time, but from the prophets. It provides much

103

of the message. Is. 52:7-15 can be associated with the Crucifixion and Anastasis, for they immediately precede the song of the Servant's redemptive sufferings. 'How beautiful upon the mountains are the feet of him that brings good tidings, and publishes peace . . . they shall see, eye to eye, when the Lord returns to Sion . . . the Lord has comforted his people, he has redeemed Jerusalem . . . all the ends of the earth shall see the salvation of (i.e. provided by) our God;' then:

> *v*.11. Depart, depart, go out thence,
> touch no unclean thing;[6]
> go out from the midst of her,
> purify yourselves, you who bear the vessels of the Lord.

> *v*. 12. For you shall not go out in haste,
> and you shall not go in flight,
> for the Lord will go before you,
> and the God of Israel will gather you in.[7]

The passage continues (*v*.13), 'Behold my servant shall deal wisely, he shall be exalted . . .' It is obvious what Mark has seen. The women are the first to learn of their Redemption. They must depart in cleanness (that is why they did not enter a tomb which might have contained corpse-blood), and go out of Jerusalem, not in a state of panic (Aquila translates with *ekthambēsis* and Symmachus is said to have used *ekthambete* in the same verse), but in confidence that their Lord leads them (as sheep) and God gathers up stragglers (as of a flock). No real flight is being considered; but the union with the shepherd is not visualised as occurring in Jerusalem. As we know already, the 'light' will 'shine' in Galilee.

Now we must pass to Is. 33, where the Messiah is alluded to at *vv*.2,5,10, 15-17,21-22. Is. 33:10 relates, to follow the rabbis, to God's discussion with the angels concerning Isaac. He promises in response to their tears,[8] to be glorified through Isaac, the sacrifice of the latter being accepted to right certain wrongs. The angels are the subject of the next verse which reads (in the LXX) *nun opsesthe, nun aisthēsesthe* (now you shall see, now you shall perceive). The Hebrew is taken to mean 'You will quickly conceive; you will bring to birth altogether', meaning that they will react to God's majesty and vengeance. The rabbis were prepared to deduce from this that whereas the righteous will partake of the Resurrection the wicked shall not.[9] Is. 33:9 in the LXX explains that Galilee is one of the places where the Lord's exaltation will be effective. Now we can see that the 'he' of Mark's 'as he said to you', while it appears to refer to Mk. 14:18, in reality alludes to the pre-existent Christ, the Lord of Is. 52-53!

As it happens, the immediately preceding chapter, Is. 32:9-20 deals with supposedly foolish women, their wealth, their amazement in spite of their 'firmly belonging'. Their own spirit is weak but a spirit will come upon them from on high. Thus, what with Isaac, and the resurrection, Galilee, the movement from Jerusalem, and the vessels of the Lord, we can be sure that Mark applied his mind to Is. 32-33 as well as Is. 52-53.

This experience of the women, linked now with Moses and Jacob, was their theophany, if properly understood. Through the Young Man, and his message, no less a being than God himself showed himself to them, with a charismatic command. This was not enough for Matthew, Luke and John; but it was enough for Mark and seemingly his hearers. The allusion which the first hearers picked up, the allusion to the burial of Moses, was later to set Luke off on a special track of his own (p.111).

2. THE THIRD DAY.

The next question is whether any historical fact can be discovered from the obviously important statement that Christ 'rose' on the third day. Broer, sensing that 'Sunday' minus three days created a 'Friday' myth (Broer, 1972, 283) overlooked that the 'third day' had a symbolic life of its own. Dupont naturally asked from which scriptural source did the 'three days' idea come.[10] Paul tells us that the rising on the third day was scriptural. Is this another case of scripture invading the narrative, and if so, how far has it penetrated it? Before we come to the curious facts at our disposal, one rather important remark must be made in advance. Jewish idiom paid a lot of attention to the number three. If a thing happened three times it could be presumed to be constant. A useful scriptural example is at Is. 33:10: *nun anastēsomai* (cf. Is. 26:19 LXX), *legei kyrios, nun doxasthēsomai, nun hypsōthēsomai*: 'Now I shall arise, says the Lord, now I shall be glorified, *now* I shall be exalted'. A midrash on this verse explains that the three 'nows' refer to three separate hours.[11] But of course they could as well refer to three separate days. And we already know the popular notion that if a body has stayed dead for three days it is indubitably dead. Abraham (according to Test. Abr. Ch. 20) was very properly buried 'on the third day of his dying'.

It was not sufficient that Jesus rose; he had to arise on the third day. This is not explained: obviously, as any experienced New Testament scholar will realise, because the Christians had their own midrash on one or more scriptural texts, in the course of developing their own *haggadah* around their own (novel) traditions. Now we suspect that Jesus's Anastasis must have happened, if the scheme of Mark is to be believed, within about 36 hours of his burial. How does that square with 'on the third day?' It does not. How then can an article of faith derive from a practical improbability? It does not. It has an independent life, as we shall see.

Jesus's predictions of the Passion, which, as we have seen (p.79), reflect a tradition earlier than the church's formula for what happened, do *not* say 'on the third day'. That was an after-thought. They say 'after three days', which does *not* mean immediately after three days on any strict chronology. How can that be squared with what we have surmised about the Anastasis? It fits it even worse. And the disciples must have been aware of that.

Just as the saying that the Son of man 'will rise' did not originally refer to an *anastasis* as a physiological event, so the 'after three days' did not refer to a period of time. It does not mean, 'after a while'. It has quite a clear meaning, given the Hebrew mentality. Suffering is typically a three-day affair. No matter how long it actually lasts it is as if it lasts three days, and then 'on the third day' help comes, by God's saving intervention[11a] When God sent darkness to the land of Egypt it lasted no more than three days (Exod. 10:33). If one searches for a lost object for three days without success one can indeed abandon the search (2 Kngs. 2:17). The troubles of life end after three days (so Lk. 2:46).[12] There are several biblical precedents, namely Gen. 40:13-21, and 42:17-18; and there is Hos. 6:2. This much misunderstood text[13] is valuable not simply because it says 'on the third day we shall arise', which, to the Christians with their new concept of resurrection, *was* immensely important, but because it emphasised the popular notion that, after even the ultimate of suffering, help comes on the third day (Josh. 3:2, cf. *Ant.* 5:17). If people have been with you for three days and are without food they look to God to save them (Mk. 8:2, Mt. 15:32).

One may object that, surely, the discrepancy between the timetable of the Anastasis and the 'after three days' formula must have been obvious to Mark, by whose time the credal formulation, 'on the third day', had long been settled? The answer, fortunately or unfortunately, is that his attention was directed elsewhere. To him the timetable is cosmic. At Mk. 16:2 we have λίαν πρωὶ τῇ μιᾷ τῶν σαββάτων ('and very early on the first day of the week') not simply to emphasise Sunday, the new day of religious celebrations for Christians (*Sabbath* being *over*!), but to insinuate that a new *creation* had occurred (cf. Gen. 1:5—light from darkness), and this suggests that the Anastasis occurred prior to Sunday (as no doubt it did): the rising of the sun (16:2c) recalling Mal. 4:2, a Messianic prophecy, 'But unto you that fear my Name shall the sun of righteousness arise with healing in his wings; and you shall go forth as calves (let loose) from the stall'. It is the moment of Redemption.

For practical purposes the 'on the third day' formula will fit.[14] It is an adaptation of the facts to Hos. 6:2, the meaning of which has at last emerged in Christian history. *On the third day* seeds were created (Gen. 1:13) (for the importance of seed see p.121); Isaac was sacrificed and resurrected (Gen. 22:4); and on the third day God came down 'in the sight of all people' on Mt. Sinai (Exod. 19:11) for the giving of the Law. 'After three days' fits the Jonah story,[15] Jonah the prophet who was in the belly of the whale and emerged after three days and three nights (Jon. 1:17) to deliver a message to the men of Ninevah. Like Jonah, Jesus's life was a sign, a warning.[16] The church looked back on the 'sign of Jonah' in a saying of Jesus as suggestive of the Anastasis (Mt. 12:39, 16:4, Lk. 11:29), but whether it really had that meaning originally is doubtful.[17] However, as if to prove that Jonah is not the precedent for the Anastasis, the church settled for 'on the third day', and, though Jesus probably did not revive on the third day inclusive of his burial, it is *as if* he rose on the third day, because (i) if death is presumed to have closed over a person on the third day it did not close over *him*, (ii) if suffering ends on the third day the suffering endured by the church in the Passion event turns to joy on the third day, (iii) the promise of Hos. 6:2 has come to pass, especially if the church is in solidarity with her Redeemer, and finally (iv) the new Law is brought to the new Israel on the third day as at the original giving of the Law through Moses at Sinai. It is of interest

106

that 'on the third day' is the time when Greek cremations or burials took place,[18] so that the phrase was especially attractive for pagan converts. On the day when *they* would be buried their Saviour rose.

Josephus the historian was born in A.D.37/38 and died about 100, publishing his *Antiquities* in 93/94. By that time it was well known in circles taking an interest in religions that Jesus predicted that he would arise after three days, and that the church believed he rose on the third day. Eusebius in two places cites a passage at *Ant.* 18.63-4 in which Josephus appears to acknowledge that Jesus was the Christ. Origen in two places explicitly states that Josephus did not believe Jesus was the Christ. Thus between about A.D.280 (Origen) and about A.D.324 (Eusebius) some discrepancy in Josephus's text had arisen. The whole passage, notorious for centuries under the name *Testimonium Flavianum,* is extremely curious and intriguing, and most scholars believe that it does not belong to Josephus at all, or if it does it is, in its present form, the result of editorial work by some one unknown. The passage runs:[19]

> About this time there lived Jesus, a wise man, if indeed one ought to call him a man. For he was one who did surprising (i.e., in the popular sense, miraculous) works, a teacher of men who accept the truth gladly, and he won over many Jews and also many of the Greek world. This man was the Christ (i.e. Messiah). When he had been condemned to the cross by Pilate on the accusation of the first men amongst us, those who first loved him did not stop (doing so). He appeared to them alive again in the course of the third day. The divine prophets had spoken of these and myriads of other marvels about him. And the tribe of the Christians, taking their designation from him, has not disappeared to this day.

Since we are interested in the phrase τρίτην ἔχων ἡμέραν πάλιν ζῶν ('alive again in the course of the third day') it is important to have some idea what the passage as a whole can tell us. If it is a Christian forgery it is extraordinarily cunning. Forgers never leave it in doubt what they intend to be understood as genuine. The statement as to the third day does not agree with the 'after three days' formula, or the credal 'on the third day'. It is some sort of compromise. The phrase 'the first men amongst us' is not Josephan. The 'accusation' (*endeixis*) is a non-Christian formulation, for m^esîrâ, the technical term for denunciation, is always rendered *paradosis*. The deliberate avoidance of this term could be due to a Christian's ignorance of it, but this is almost inconceivable: whereas it is quite possible that a Jewish sympathiser with the Christian story would instinctively avoid the verb which has always been a term of infamy amongst Jews. The expression 'works' (=miracles) is a typically Jewish one. My own suggestion is that the passage was written by a Jew during a period when the Christians were under pressure, and were indeed in danger of dying out and could be described as some sort of 'tribe', in other words long before Eusebius's time. Some manuscripts of Josephus probably had an account of Jesus for which this passage survives as a substitute written, I guess, in a more favourable tone. The reference to Jesus's being the Christ is quite possible if the world we are to imagine was not so far from Josephus's own, in which, we know, the Essenes and pious people for whom the *Testament of the XII Patriarchs* were written not only expected a Messiah, but more than one Messiah! The Talpioth ossuaries (p.124) also throw light on this. At that rate there existed in non-Christian circles a century or so after the events a notion that Jesus appeared (ephanē *not* ōphthē; cf. p.98) to those who originally loved him (an interpretation of the 'appearance' stories which the anti-Christian Celsus [c.A.D.170] noticed) alive again (i.e. physically arisen) in the course of the third day from his crucifixion. The theology of Paul, which raised the Anastasis to dizzy heights, had not prevented a widespread impression that, come the third day, Jesus was actually alive, and these and other miracles had been foreseen by the 'divine prophets'. This may well be confirmation of the Pauline credal statements from an independent quarter.

3. THE POST-ANASTASIS APPEARANCES.

Approaching matters as we have to, there seems to us no basis for the view, popular in some quarters, that the 'appearances' occurred prior to, and therefore sparked off, the 'finding' of the empty tomb. This ingenious notion[20] has no textual basis and would ruin Mark completely.

The appearances' convey nothing whatever about Jesus's teaching which is not available to us from stories located *before* the Crucifixion. The current popular notion,[20a] that any episode in the gospels which is incredible as written must be accounted for by a 'retrojection' of post-Anastasis experiences back into Jesus's lifetime, is not in fact an amelioration of the position—one does not remove the problems thereby. On the contrary the scenes in question, e.g. the Feeding of the Thousands, the Walking on the Water, will have to be explained as occurrences revealed in their true (i.e. 'as if') significance. Taking them also into account, *all* Jesus's teaching, save for some fragments to be had from traditions surviving elsewhere, is in the gospels, and *none* of it in the appearances! No comments on Judas or Peter; no discussions of the impending fates of Caiaphas or Pilate; no more prophecies of doom; no injunctions for the structuring of the new church—one would have thought these the most urgent and relevant needs for any revelation, given that revelation was available! A Jewish story of great age tells how a man in a coma for *three days* revived and told what he saw in the other world—how people's standings differed from those they had, at the time, in this world![20b] *There is no halakhic (legal) material, such as Peter once had to obtain from a dream or trance* (Acts 10:9ff.), no panoramas of hell such as Abraham had in the *Testament of Abraham*. If you or I were inventing a resurrection we should have filled the subject's mouth with interesting particulars, and the already highly popular device of the 'testament' would have afforded a ready model. Parenesis is the very kernel and focal point of the Jewish 'testament',[20c] 'Come, my children, listen to the words of your teacher Jesus, who shall tell you about the End Time. You shall sin . . . etc., etc. . . .' As a matter of fact the sediment contains nothing of that sort whatsoever.

The appearances were written to fill a vacuum and to satisfy curiosity. But it does not mean that they did not correspond in some minimal measure to facts.

In spite of the efforts of conservative scholars, the contradictions remain between them, and attempted harmonies are pointless and would amuse their respective authors. My own impression, for what it is worth, is that Jesus did visit his disciples, and ate and drank with them—though not *necessarily* more than once. It is by no means impossible that he expired, 'rose again', 'was taken up' on the third day of his burial! But as soon as rumours of his survival reached those who loved him (not others, as the anonymous Jewish observer shrewdly notices: p.107) they began to have ecstatic visions of him. He was no longer the vagrant holy man, but the risen Lord. That such a shock could cause visions, especially amongst adepts at ecstacies, no one need doubt.[21] A rush of reports of visions coming in (they would not be limited by time or space) met ripples of reassurance from the capital spreading outwards that Jesus was actually setting his business in motion. What we have in the appearance-stories are the results, at second or third hand, of these phenomena meeting and finding expression in more or less artistic shape—given that the authors felt obliged, as I have said, to sacrifice Mark's dramatic conception for the purpose.

(a) MATTHEW.

Matthew seeks to answer the question, 'Why did the women not tell anyone?' Answer: 'They did indeed tell, for otherwise *we* should not know what happened to them.' 'Why did they rest content with a single Young Man's message —for single testimony will not stand up in any court?' 'The Young Man was virtually an angel and appropriately the Lord himself reassured the women and confirmed the message.' Mt. 28:9-10 adds absolutely nothing for the use of a modern detective, save proof of what Alsup has the credit of discovering, namely that in theophanies angels interchange with the deity for whom they are acting!

At this point I think it is desirable to say something about angels. Modern taste finds no room for them. As a matter of fact it was established idiom in the Jewish environment (because it was an established factor of their psychology) to attribute any ideas that arise inside a person to a stimulus from outside. Where they could not be tracked to a human superior to whom it was necessary to defer they were attributed to an invisible source. A similar phenomenon is the belief in evil spirits. One does wrong not because one is wicked, but because Satan put it into one's mind. The phenomenon of attributing intelligent ideas to an external invisible source is extremely commonly illustrated in scripture (see, e.g., 1 Sam. 9: 17, Zech. 4:1, Mt. 1:20, 2:13, etc.). 'To be told by an angel' is the equivalent of having a brilliant notion. After Mark's time the Jewish popular interest in angels increases in the church: Luke has even more of them in his works than had Matthew.

Further, Mt. 28:16-20 answers the question, 'If the Lord told them to go to Galilee why did they not go? And Galilee is a big place: where might they be expected to go?' Answer: 'The eleven remaining disciples *did* go to Galilee and chose the mountain where Jesus had issued his instructions (or injunctions) to them,[22] i.e. the Mount of the Sermon.' The third-day motif of Exod. 19:11 thus becomes real in the form of a verbal icon. Then (as now) some nominal disciples were not really converted by the Anastasis alone. Jesus then declared to them directly that he had received from God (in and by virtue of the Anastasis) all authority. This he distinctly delegated to his apostles, authorising them to baptise all nations, etc.

It is obvious that what we have here as a story depicts what not only could have been worked out, but was worked out by the disciples after the Anastasis. The instruction to make disciples of all the nations (cf. Acts 1:8) is novel, and has been suspected not to be genuine, since it is indeed out of keeping with Matthew's attitude to Gentiles. However, this need not be so. Understandably the command to preach to all nations has been recognised as the climax of the Matthæan resurrection story.[23] Otherwise no new halakhic commandments were given, though the old ones were confirmed. Apart from the sediment (see below) the story adds nothing, in my eyes, to Mark's story but a commentary written out at large.

(b) LUKE.

Luke, a Greek convert, brings an aroma of sentimentality to his gospel foreign to that hard-headed people, the Jews. He allows himself liberties with his material in the interests of the Gentile mission in which, of course, he was much interested (Lk. 9:55).

The women find the regulation *two* witnesses[24] to tell them that Jesus was risen (Lk. 24:6) and then to remind them of his teachings including the proposition that he would rise *on the third day* (they did not positively say that that is what he had done, which was by no means self-evident, and, as we know, the prophecies said, in any case, 'after three days'). The names of the three women are not identical. Joanna has ousted Salome. She was, according to Luke (8:2) a companion of Mary Magdalene. Was there a patroness of the third evangelist with the name Joanna? Or had unpleasant rumours begun to circulate about Salome? We may never know.

By Luke's time the legal problem of female testimony had, somewhat fatuously, raised its head. The obvious answer to it was that women are competent witnesses (and indeed must be so) in matters of childbirth, laying out the dead, and burial and tomb-visiting, in which they have special responsibility and even exclusive responsibility (as suggested at Mk. 15:47). Luke follows indications from elsewhere that the disciples were not content with the message—even a message from the Lord himself (cf. Matthew!)—but saw the facts for themselves. He makes the disciples disbelieve the women, and lets Peter check for himself, lamely departing 'wondering' (24:12). The rather despondent verse naturally slipped out from some early copies of Luke.[24a]

The magnificent story of the Two Disciples at Emmaus[25] is an obvious intrusion into the gospel. 24:13-35 is an independent composition, to which 36-49 is an awkward appendage, to which 51-53 is a sub-appendage. Verses 45-46 are a repetition out of 27 and 32; verse 47 is a repetition of the idea at Mt. 28:19. Two substantive additions are made. As he emphasises in Acts, Luke insists, at 24:48, that the apostles were *witnesses* of the gospel. This is a complex and refined idea and evidently a post-Anastasis development. A witness in the Jewish cultural environment is a passive *participant* in an event. The gospel, which can stand up on its own account, is confirmed and realised in a special way by Christ's suffering and rising from the dead on the third day. They are witnesses of both limbs of the proposition. This speaks to their status and the *practice* of the church recognises this.[25a] To my mind this accurately reflects Jesus's own notion of the situation after the Anastasis. Without them he would be nowhere (Lk. 24:48, Acts 1:8, Jn. 15:27).

At *v*.49 Luke tells us two things, that Jesus conveys a gift to them from the Father and secondly that they must wait in Jerusalem to be further empowered, as if his own empowering were insufficient. Luke's story avoids a static presentation and injects movement into it. We understand from Acts 2 that this further power arrived as a collective ecstatic experience, a corporate possession by the Holy Spirit (Pentecost), to which Luke here looks back. Verses 50-53 link with Acts 1:3-11 which depicts the Ascension. Luke has no time for appearances in Galilee[26] and he alone feels the need to cause Jesus bodily to disappear, or as he puts it '(be) received up' (Acts 1:22). Luke uses some vague expressions at Lk. 24:51 (*diestē*: the last four words are probably spurious) and Acts 1:9 (*epērthē*), and it must be remembered that 'assumption' (*analēpsis*) was a euphemism for death (so Ps. Sol. 4:18(20), Gosp. Peter 19) with overtones of glory (Lk. 9:51, Acts 1:22). John, on the other hand, finds the post-Anastasis Jesus unconfined by space, which is a yet further development away from reality.

In order to appreciate the Ascension story as developed by Luke we must hark back to the question of the death and burial of Moses (p.102), which would have been in the minds of Mark's first hearers. In the time of Jesus the much-loved character of Moses had outstripped (like lesser characters such as Joseph) the biblical text, and bible and *haggadah* marched together. Josephus fortunately tells us about the end of Moses (*Ant*.4.323-6):

> On his going to the place where he was about to disappear (*aphanistē-sesthai*) they all followed him weeping; therefore Moses . . . bade those at a distance remain still, and exhorted those nearer to him not to make his departure (*apallagē*) tearful by accompanying him . . . Only the elders escorted him, with Eleazar the high priest and Joshua the general (cf. Mt. 27:41). But when he arrived on the mountain . . . he dismissed the body of elders. And while he bade farewell to Eleazar and Joshua, and was still conversing, a cloud suddenly descended upon him and he disappeared down some ravine. But he had written of himself in the sacred books that he died, for fear lest they should venture to say that by reason of his excess of virtue he had gone up to the Deity.

Luke obviously did dare, and it may have been a pleasure for him to note, as Josephus apparently did,[27] that Romans liked the idea of their founders disappearing, a feature attributed to both Romulus and Æneas. Meanwhile Luke delights in giving Jesus the rôle of Aaron, dispensing a priestly blessing (Lk. 24:50-1, cf. Sir. 50:20).

The *haggadah* of the burial of Moses supplies fanciful details which (I think) Josephus was too prudent to insert. The angels, led by Michael, buried Moses and Satan attempted to cheat them by stealing the body. The story was a favourite, and an angel-disposal of the body of Abraham was thought up as a pale copy of the Moses story (Loewenstamm in Nickelsburg, 1976, 185-225). Jesus was thus the third (and last) Jewish hero to attract such *haggadah* to the story of his burial. The author of the sensational *Testament of Abraham,* a near contemporary of the evangelists, thought that Abraham was almost as worthy of an ascension as Moses, but he found himself unable to go so far—though he gave Abraham an extensive trip in the other world. What he did permit himself was a scene where the family of Abraham told him that they suspected that he had been 'taken up' from them (ch. 15)! Ascensions are after all familiar in the non-Christian world.[27a]

The *Testaments of the XII Patriarchs,* as we know, are of great relevance. In Test. Levi XVIII.3 the priestly Messiah whom the author expects is the subject of prophecies in his favour. He will be magnified in the world (as we know it) until his ascension (or assumption: *analēpsis*), the euphemism for 'death' suddenly introduced without explanation. The fate of Moses was, in this case, the least the Messiah himself could expect when he came! In all these cases it could be argued that 'taking up' is just a fancy expression for death (as *anelēphthē* seems to be of Christ's dying at *Gospel of Peter,* 19): but it is not. While death is, no doubt, the commencement of the idea there is a special, honorific, addition. It is not sufficient that the spirit has been called away: the whole person is resumed, as it were, into heaven. Such notions belonged to the world in which our evangelists worked, but were already considerably older.

We should now return to Emmaus. The gist of the story is that Jesus was not recognised, after the Anastasis, by his former pupils, though he is still able to teach them through the scriptures—to which they must apply themselves—and is clearly recognised by them only at the breaking of bread (i.e. at the Eucharist), whenever (it is implied) that occurs. It is in this sense they must be open to him and his experience must be internalised.[27b] The personal experience of Christ at the cult meal is quite independent of any actual terrestrial movements of the Lord about his practical business (*vv*.33-35). We are already a long way towards the Johannine position, in which the personal relationship of the risen Lord with the individual believer is intimate, and none the less holy for being private.

(c) JOHN.

The 'bride of Christ' theme[28] emerges with Mary Magdalene's encounter (p.55). It is often suspected that Mary shared with Peter the first 'appearance' of Jesus[28a] but no text says this (everything is against it) and Mary's privilege is a theological construct. The ocular inspection of the tomb by Peter and the Beloved Disciple (representing on the one hand the ecclesiastical organization in its infancy and on the other the faithful Christian, in typical tension: Jn. 21:21-22) was *nugatory* (20:10: 'so the disciples went away again to their own home'), except for *misleading* information suggesting that Jesus divested himself of the grave clothing before leaving the tomb. It looks as if 'documentation' was being 'planted' to 'authenticate' a relic already being exposed for the admiration of the credulous: and John makes the disciples depart from it and Mary turn her back on it.

Jesus's interchange with Mary is interesting.[29] Mary's failure to recognise him parallels the people's failure to recognise Moses when he came down from the Mountain of the Law.[30] The Anastasis is a source of joy and not to be celebrated in ritual mourning (20:13,15). Jesus has clothed himself in the garments of Adam as he was before the Fall (Jn. 20:15, hence the pseudo-eye-witness touch at 19:41!), a theme derived from Mark 1:13. Jesus must not be held down to earth (a belated comment on Mt. 28:9!) even by the most devoted adherents. His purity must be maintained in their interests as well as his—for as he ascends to the Father, who is God, he becomes taboo, like the Mountain of the Law (Exod. 19:11-13)[31] or even the Bush![32] Even on the *third day* she keeps far: Exod. 19:15.

Even though Mary passes on this tremendous message the disciples do not seek to find the Lord of their own accord. His sovereign initiative is preserved. On the Sunday evening, as they hide in the capital, Jesus joins them and consecrates them all to his service, all except one whose literalistic scepticism was removed a week later (20:26-29). This important passage makes the point that there is more merit in being in John's own situation, not having 'seen' the Lord and yet believing than being in the disciples' situation and being able to satisfy themselves of the Anastasis personally (20:31). True enough, to refuse to believe one's teacher is most unworthy in a student (b.B.B. 75a); correspondingly to believe him without physical proof is blessed.

John testifies with this passage that, whether it ought to have done so or not, the Anastasis had overshadowed the rest of the gospel.

The mission-field is the subject of the long passage Jn. 21:1-19, which, with a short appendix on the perpetuity of the Beloved Disciple, i.e. the faithful Christian, closes one of the most remarkable books ever written. It has been argued that 21:1-19 is not John's composition, but an after-thought inartistically tacked on. It could indeed be his work, but a later addition. All the themes come from a synoptic-type gospel, meditated upon, and artistically refurbished. The last vision of Jesus comprehends the entire gospel from Mk. 1:16 onwards.

The scene is the Sea of Galilee—Galilee, epitome of the mission field (p.93). The fishing-expert, Jesus, is on the further shore, and fishes by deputy and at long range. He is recognised, when he shouts to his former partners, by the Beloved Disciple only, who knows that the Lord is not inactive merely because he is no longer in the boat as he was in Luke's story, but walks along the shore as he did in Mark. He knows instinctively that the Anastasis enabled Jesus to be everywhere. The expedition is going so badly that they have not even a snack with them. Jesus prepares one on the further shore, as they arrive at daybreak. Their breakfast consists of the very same food with which he recruited his army in the Feedings of the Thousands. Peter recognises the divinity, and clothes himself, hiding his shame in the presence of God. The recognition that Jesus is the Son of God, which is Peter's prerogative, finds expression once more. The monarchical episcopate was known by John's time, and Peter alone drags the catch on shore. The 153 big fish represent some catch, and from the context it must mean the churches.

153 = QNG in Hebrew cyphers, a Greek word adopted long since into Hebrew, signifying 'the hunt'. As the rabbis will eat Leviathan in the world to come the apostles will have this divine catch both to eat and to distribute. With the aid of Jesus's directions, even from a distance, the hunt goes well. Peter, without that help, is not much of a fisherman; and he is therefore commissioned to be a pastor, to guard and feed Jesus's own flock, as professional pastors do. But his hire, it is understood, is still the recruited man's snack (like the 'King's shilling')—the pastor does not feed off, in the sense of exploit, the souls he has saved from the depths of the underworld. The story is wholly symbolic and tells us nothing new about any of its actors.

(d) THE SEDIMENT.

The sediment amounts to this:

(i) Jesus did not remain in the tomb, and his not remaining there was no banal event, but thoroughly significant,[33] as the earliest accounts themselves indicate.

(ii) The women (who were, in our sense of that word, true witnesses) knew that Jesus was alive, were shocked at the realisation and its possible implications, and did not know what to make of it (the women were not sources of myth).[34]

(iii) People were slow and reluctant to get to grips with the event.[35]

(iv) Jesus did not call the disciples, but went to them and at least physically commissioned his apostles.[36]

(v) Here perhaps we must remain tentative: he emphasised, perhaps only by allusion to scripture, that the latter was fulfilled by what had transpired and was about to transpire.[37]

Even in ancient times the desire was felt to arrive at some sort of 'sediment' by a concordance of discrepant resurrection reports. This is evidenced in Mk. 16:9-22 (the supposititious long ending of Mark, which, apart from this, has no historical value).[38] It was natural to do so, but the hypothesis was false (p.101).

NOTES

1. Evans (1970), 67, 79, 84, 91, 95-6, 117, 123.
2. Ibid., 67, 151. The gospel accounts are 'separate expressions of the Easter faith' (128). 'Whatever the Easter event was, it must be supposed to be of such a kind as to be responsible for the production of these traditions as its deposit at whatever remove' (130) On the burial of Jesus no credit is to be given to material outside Mark (Broer, 1972, 280)
2a. As suspected by Benoit (1969), 261.
3. Evans, 129.
3a. See Walker (1969), 163-5. Brown (1973), 126: the 'appearances' interpreted the empty tomb.
4. *Ass.Mos.* 11:6-8, Mishnah, Avot V.6 E.-M. Laperrousaz, 'Le Testament de Moïse . . .'

Semitica 19 (1970) (an Essene document of A.D.7-30); A.M. Denis, *Introduction aux Pseudépigraphes Grecs d'Ancien Testament* (Leiden, 1970), 135; K. Haacker & P. Schäfer, 'Nachbiblische Traditionen vom Tod des Mose', *Josephus-Studien . . . O. Michel* (Götingen, 1974), 147-74. Cf. Athanasius, *Life of Anthony,* 91; Philostratus, *Vita Ap.* 8.344.

4a. Goulder (1976).

5. b.Shab. 22a, Hag. 2a. Test. Zeb.4.

6. Is this another source for Jn. 20:17a?

7. So Targ., LXX, Vulgate. Not 'shall be your rearguard'.

8. On the angel's tears see J. Mann, *The Bible,* Seder 19. Is. 33:9 LXX. Midr.R., Gen. LVI.5. Ps. 121. Beer (1859), 68. Yalqût, §.438.

9. b.Sanh. 108a; Midr.R., Gen.XXVI.6.

10. Dupont (1959), 753-4.

11. Midr.R., Cant.IV.8,1.

11a. Schubert (1974), 216. Esth. 4:16 would be a good example.

12. Here, obviously, the Jonah story fits.

13. Lindars (1961), 59-72; Cadbury in the *Dodd Volume* (1956), 302-3.

14. Jeremias (1971), 304. The strict chronology of Lev. 7:17-18 is quite different.

15. Jon. 1:4-16 is parallel to Mk. 4:35-41. Jonah was the reincarnation of the son of the widow of Sarepta, Messiah, Son of Joseph.

16. Edwards (1971), 107. Giblin (1975), 415-19.

17. Vögtle (1953), Edwards (1971).

18. Kurtz-Boardman (1971), 144, 145-6.

19. On the whole problem see L. H. Feldman, *Josephus* ix (Loeb. edn., 1969), 49 n. P. Winter in G. Vermes & F. Millar, ed., E. Schürer, *Hist. of the Jewish People in the Age of Jesus Christ,* 2nd edn., I (Edinburgh, 1973), 428ff. (excessively sceptical). Dubarle (1977) has an attitude to this text much like mine.

20. Dodd (1968), 102-33, Enslin (1952), 53-4, Seidensticker (1967), 77-83, Clark (1967), 90-1, 98, Kegel (1970), Fuller (1972), 52, 56, 70; Campenhausen (1968), 60. 76-7, took the other view. So Brown (1973), 127. Delling (1968), 92, took the two experiences to be contemporary. Grass (1971), 93, 180-3, 279, believes that neither the appearances nor the empty tomb were the basis of faith. Braun, 57, suspects all stories from the burial onwards.

20a. At various stages this has got out of hand. For an example see G. Klein at *Rekonstruktion* (1969), 11-48. And M. E. Boring, *Sayings of the Risen Jesus* (Cambridge, 1982) catalogues *spurious* pseudo-prophetic sayings.

20b. Midr.R., Ruth III.1 (Sonc.41); b.Pes.50a.

20c. H. W. Hollander, *Joseph as an Ethical Model* (Leiden, 1981), 6-7.

21. Plut., *Aem.Paul.* 24-5.

22. Chavasse (1971), comparing Deut. 1:6, 13.

23. W. Trilling, *Das wahre Israel* (Munich, 1964), 47.

24. Deut. 19:15. H. van Vliet, *No Single Testimony* (Utrecht, 1955). On women's testimony see Jeremias (1971), 306. Mishnah, Shev.IV.1. Maim., *Code* XIV.II. ix,2, but cf. ibid., IV.II.xii, 16-19, 21-22; III.iii,5-6,11. Jesus's absence from the tomb was neither a civil nor a criminal matter.

24a. Neirynck (1978).

25. Fuller, 113. Wanke (1974). Wilckens (1977), 56. Guillaume (1979), 96ff. Dillon (1978).

25a. Dillon (1978), 225.

26. Steinseifer (1971) seems to share Luke's attitude to the appearances.

27. H.St.J. Thackeray, *Josephus* iv (Leob. edn.), 633 n.(b).

27a. Guillaume (1979), 250ff.

27b. Betz (1969).

28. Jaubert (1963). R. Murray, *Symbols of Church and Kingdom* (Cambridge, 1975) 135. Mt. 28:9. At the risk of incurring ridicule, I point out in all seriousness that the reason why the 'Magdalene's' name is remembered is because she represented 'tower' which recalled

Cant. 4:4, 7:4, 8:10. The Song of Songs is echoed in the story of the Anastasis by the women's spices, brought (unknowingly) for what was *not* a burial: Cant. 1:3, 12, 3:6, 4:6, 10(!), 14, 5:1, 13.

28a. Hengel (1963), 51. Pesch (1980) 50, says Peter 'saw' first in Galilee, and the tradition about Mary is 'younger'.

29. Some scholars regard them as pointing to Mary as the original witness. Hengel (1963), 156; Wilckens (1970); Fuller (1972), 56; O'Collins (1973), 42. But John did not intend to deny the Marcan story.

30. Exod. 34:29-32 as explained by Ps.Philo, *L.A.B.*XII.1. Non-recognition is found in the Test.Abr. also (Alsup, 1978, 262-3).

31. A parallel suggested by Elizabeth Derrett.

32. Alsup (1978), 246.

33. Mk. 16:5, Mt. 28:6,9, Lk. 24:3, 24.

34. Mk. 16:6,8, Mt. 28:8, Lk. 24:5,23; Mk. 16:9.

35. Mt. 28:17, Lk. 24:12,27-31, Mk. 16:8, 11-14, Jn. 20:2.

36. As shown above, passim.

37. Mt. 28:19, Lk. 24:27-32, 44-49. Acts 1:2,8; 1 Cor. 9:1; Mk. 16:15. Marxsen (1968), 33,37. Evans (1970), 91, 94-5.

38. The 'shorter ending' of Mark, a translation of which is inserted as an unnumbered verse after 16:8 in the *New English Bible,* has no canonical status and is accepted as authoritative by no church. The 'longer ending' (16:9-20) is, from its vocabulary alone (for the status of the passage in textual transmission see p.135), recognisable as a conflation foisted upon Mark by unknown harmonisers, perhaps as late as the third century.

CHAPTER X
The Theology of the Anastasis.

The typical Jewish position, that Jesus was an impostor while he lived (Mt. 27:63, Jn. 7:12), and that the imposture was perfected after his death, was soon joined by a more serious reflection. How could the Spirit and Might of God be confined in a single individual and undergo the humiliation of the Cross, followed by whatever happened afterwards? There were Christians who could not bring themselves to believe that the true Christ entered flesh, suffered, and rose. Even within seventy years of the events Ignatius has to congratulate the people of Smyrna,[1]

'. . . for I have observed that you are established in immutable faith . . . being fully persuaded concerning our Lord, that he is in truth of the family of David according to the flesh . . . truly nailed (on the Cross) for our sakes under Pontius Pilate and Herod the Tetrarch . . . that he might 'set up an ensign' for all ages through his Anastasis, for his saints and believers, both amongst the Jews and the nations, in one body of his church. For he suffered all these things for us that we might attain salvation, and he truly suffered just as he also truly raised himself up (*anestēsen heauton*), not as some unbelievers say, that his Passion was merely in appearance . . . For I know and believe that he was in flesh even after the Anastasis . . .'

As a matter of fact the Anastasis had a fundamental effect on the pre-existing gospel, so as to make it unrecognisable. Whereas Jesus's envoys, during his ministry, preached repentance and the coming of the Kingdom, the message spread after the Anastasis was quite different in tone and in impact. From Acts 2:38 and 13:38 we know that the Anastasis carried with it the offer of a (general) forgiveness (or release) of sins. It is really necessary to understand this in order to visualise what the Anastasis meant to those actually involved. But first a simple objection must be removed.

1. THE REDEMPTION DEPENDS ON THE SUFFERING AND DEATH ON THE CROSS.

Paul and Mark were clear that Jesus died on the Cross. We have considered the possibility that this was incohate, i.e. clinical death rather than brain-death which will have ensued after a fairly brief period. That such a brain-death must have been due to the suffering and crucifixion no one will deny. The theological value of that suffering and death is in no way diminished if it appears that between suffering crucifixion and brain-death Jesus passed through a period of revival from reversible death. The pains, in any case, to be endured by anyone who revives from a period of interrupted circulation are bound to be considerable, and Jesus's physical condition would have been one that many might suppose worse than death. The scriptural texts on which the idea of the Redemption hangs do not insist upon a *single* death, and many thought Isaac suffered *two* deaths (p.35).

The idea was simple. A person with relatively few sins could offer his own suffering, particularly his life, sacrificially to expiate vicariously the sins of others. Older than Christianity, the notion is fully outlined in 4 Maccabees.[1a] Admittedly the idea seems strange to us; and Paul had to spell it out for his converts at Rom. 5:6-9:-[1b]

While we were still feeble Christ died, at the right moment, on behalf of the wicked. An ordinary person would hardly die on behalf of a righteous person, though perhaps one might presume to die for a good man. But God proves his love for us in that *while we were still sinners* Christ died on our behalf. And so, since we have now been turned into innocent people (lit., 'justified') through his blood (i.e. his death) we shall *a fortiori* be saved, through him, from the Wrath (i.e. Final Retribution).

Furthermore, God used Christ as a means whereby he would reconcile sinners to himself (2 Cor. 5:17-21). The rôle of the self-given Blood in the 'purchasing' of the church (ecclesia=Heb. *qalāl,* 'community') is emphasised at many levels in the New Testament documents (Mt. 26:28, 1 Cor. 11:25, Acts 20:28, Rev. 5:6,9). Every individual member of the church thus obtained his supersensory status through Jesus's sacrifice. Admittedly Luke prefers to think of Jesus as martyr-saviour, soft-pedalling the very Jewish concept of vicarious sacrifice. But then he had the wider world to cater for, and, without denying it, left the Jewish peculiarity somewhat in the shadow.[1c]

An active mind could make something positive even out of a curse. Anathema in a Jewish context is the equivalent of *ḥerem* and comes to mean 'curse' (so Gal. 1:8-9, Rom. 9:3, 1 Cor. 12:3). But in ordinary Greek it means a *votive offering,* and, since the verb from which it comes, anatithēmi, can be used of nailing a person up on a cross and leaving him to die (Polybius I.86.6), a crucified person is an *anathema.* Therefore Christ was, as a curse according to Deut. 21:23 (so Paul says at Gal. 3:13), an offering to Yahweh precisely as a crucified victim!

The idea after all is founded on two propositions, both non-legalistic and collective, and therefore unfamiliar to Westerners: (i) that suffering is an atonement, and (ii) that the group, particularly the descent group, are solid (i.e. share good and evil) and participate in each others's merits and demerits.[2] According to Luke himself (4:23) Jesus felt the need to explain why he did not exercise his gifts on his neighbours under the unexpected maxim, 'Physician, heal thyself!'

Vicarious suffering, linked long before to the resurrection (2 Macc. 12:38-45), meritorious in the one who offers it, appears in a very remarkable place in Jewish tradition. The well-known heretic Aḥer, whose real name was Elisha ben Abuyah (born before A.D.70), had a devoted pupil, R. Meir, who was subsequently not merely a great sage but also a miracle-worker (his tomb is still resorted to). Elisha was one of the few rabbinical ecstatics. His background was probably Sadducean. Because of his heresies the rabbis judged he would never see the World to Come. Meir spread his mantle over his friend's grave and offered to give his own life in order that Elisha should be judged, and enter into peace, citing Ruth 3:13. It is astonishing that, as a result of Meir's love, figuring as a kind of suretyship, the rabbis believe that the old heretic did enter peace.[3a] The doctrine, therefore, is indubitable.

It is this long-lived Jewish doctrine which serves as the basis of a famous passage in John. John was very learned in Jewish ideas. At Jn. 15:13-14 we have two verses intimately connected, the former often quoted, the second usually passed over. 'No one has greater love than this, that he lays down his life on behalf of his friends. You are my friends provided you do what I enjoin you to do.' As long as they comply with this condition his self-sacrifice is effective for them.

Further quite commonplace notions include what follows: that suffering is an atonement, that undeserved suffering operates as an increase of merit on the part of him who suffers, and that deserved suffering in this life diminishes, i.e. adeems, any suffering otherwise due to one hereafter. A kindred notion is that if miracles are performed for one in this life one's stock of merit, and right to have it recognised, are diminished in the next world. This is why the poor have an advantage and the rich a real disadvantage (Mk. 10:25)!

That one man might dedicate his suffering to release his people from sin and its consequences was proved in the well-known case of Eleazar who committed suicide to do his people good in their war against the heathen.[4]

The basis of the idea is relevant too: the Children of Israel had rebelled. God punished them by handing them over to the Gentiles.[5] A remnant escaped and survived, purified by the sufferings of the others, and resumed their relationship with God, reinstated in his favour. This seemed to be borne out so often by events that the Roman occupation of Palestine called for measures capable of redeeming the people from the sins that had obviously called down this misfortune and so from the misfortune itself. This earthly, superficial notion of redemption did arise in the minds of contemporaries of Jesus: they wanted him to call down heavenly aid to rid them of the Romans and their fellow-travellers.[6]

It does not follow that Jesus hoped to avert the final tragedy, the Fall of Jerusalem, but he could divert attention from the political arena. According to his teaching a pious person *could* be a loyal citizen (Mk. 12:17). But the pursuit of righteousness would be facilitated if the burden of disobedience to God and neglect of his covenant with their forefathers were removed and a new relationship constructed. To put this in Pauline language it amounts to what is stated at Rom. 3:23-25, 1 Cor. 1:30, Col. 1:14, followed in Eph. 1:7:- believers are 'justified' through the redemption they received 'in' Christ Jesus.

Jesus seems to have understood himself as sent by God for this purpose. The Agony in the Garden of Gethsemane is intended to show that Jesus was pursuing no ambition of his own. He acted in conscious obedience to God: Mk. 14:36. Paul puts it clearly at Phil. 2:8-9: Jesus 'being found in the form of a man, humbled himself, becoming obedient even to death, even the death on the Cross, therefore God highly exalted him, and gave him the Name which is above

119

every Name (i.e. made him equal with himself)'.

Thus the martyrdom, his being handed over (*māsûr*) by his own companions to the foreigners for severe chastisement and death, was one way in which the sacrifice of the victim's own life could atone for the sins of the group to which he belonged and/or the sins of any who, by accepting the appropriateness of his sacrifice, could participate in his merit.

Suffering, even at the hands of fellow Jews, for the sake of obedience to God was a classic claim upon God's recognition. God, who feels solidarity with his people all too keenly, loves those who suffer so, and justifies them when the rest are punished. This was thought to be the implication of Zech. 13:6-7 (see MT and LXX). The second verse was applied to the Jewish faithful, who would be separated from the wicked after the Messianic War in the Last Days, by the author of the Damascus Document (c.100 B.C,) (see CD XIX.7ff.,ms.B). The same was applied to Jesus at Mk. 14:27 and both verses were applied to him at Ep.Barn.5:12; while the first verse was applied to Jewish martyrs under Hadrian's persecution by R. Nathan (c.A.D.150) (see Mekilta, Bahod.6=Lauterbach, ii,247). The merit of such martyrs is nothing less than the love of God.

Up to this point Anastasis does not figure. But an actual *anastasis* would call upon the analogy of Isaac and so confirm that the mythical formula, that resurrection was the reward of such obedience, was true. But in Jesus's case it evidently did much more, as we shall see.

2. THE REDEEMER.

Jesus offered his *suffering*. 'Suffering' is at the centre of the creeds on this subject, and has been from the very beginning.[7] It was traditional within the church that the Christ should 'suffer'. His 'body', i.e. the church, would be the true focus of suffering.[7a]

A Jewish Messiah, meanwhile was *not* visualised as a character who would suffer. No doubt rabbis later understood that the Messiah would come in a time of universal suffering, in which he would participate. But the Qumran folk and other pious people of our period would have had the greatest difficulty in understanding a suffering Messiah. That a leader of a new sect should suffer and so lend charisma to his sect would not be so surprising. One gets the impression that many tried (the so-called false prophets) and the Teacher of Righteousness of the Qumran community seems to have suffered. But that it was redemptive suffering is not actually contended.

On the other hand God's Suffering Servant was a figure who would be handed over to death. Jesus seems to have identified the two characters, the Messiah and the Servant, and played both rôles simultaneously. The gospels certainly see Jesus as the Suffering Servant[8] and understand his programme as an example of various atonement. Mk. 10:45 (Mt. 20:28) runs, 'For the Son of man also came not to be served but to serve, and to give (implying to pledge) his life (*psyche*) as a ransom in the stead of many.' This is the oldest interpretation of Jesus's death (Gnilka, 1976).

The genuineness of that text has been questioned. But its Palestinian origin is certain[9] and, though its context may be contrived, it incorporates a genuine Jewish idea characteristic of the whole gospel story. Though many scholars think that 'Son of man' was a title foisted on Jesus later, 'Son of man' (Ps. 8:4) was Jesus's name for himself. It is interesting that Isaac was also Son of man.[9a] Just as the Suffering Servant *was* the righteous remnant of Israel, so Jesus *was* (a new) Adam, and what he did was for humanity's benefit. He was pleased that Peter saw him as Son of God, because he was interested in sonship and to him sonship meant obedience,[10] and therefore likeness. He would restore Eden, Paradise. Since it seems he studied Is. 52-53 we must do the same, using the LXX version as that was the standard text used in Mark's congregation:

Behold my servant shall understand, and be exalted, and glorified exceedingly. As many shall be amazed at thee, so shall thy face be without glory from men, and thy glory shall not be honoured by the sons of men. Thus shall many nations wonder at him, and kings shall keep their mouths shut: for they to whom no report was brought concerning him shall see: and they who have heard, shall consider. O Lord, who has believed our report? and to whom has the arm of the Lord been revealed? We brought a report as of a child before him; he is as a root in a thirsty land: he has no form nor comeliness; and we saw him, but he had no form nor beauty. But his form was ignoble, and inferior to that of the children of men; he was a man in suffering, and acquainted with the bearing of sickness, for his face is turned from us; he was dishonoured, and not esteemed. He bears our sins, and is pained for us: yet we accounted *him* to be in trouble, and in suffering, and in affliction. But he was wounded on account of *our* sins, and was bruised because of *our* iniquities: the chastisement of *our* peace was upon him; and by *his* bruises *we* were healed. All we as sheep have gone astray; every one has gone astray in his way; and the Lord handed him over for our sins . . .
. . . because of the iniquities of my people he was led to death.
. . . The Lord also is pleased to purge him from his stroke. If you can give an offering for sin, your soul shall see a long-lived seed [MT: he shall see his seed, he shall prolong his days]: the Lord also is pleased to take away from the travail of his soul, to shew him light, and to form him with understanding; to justify the just one, who serves many well [cf. Mk. 10:45!]; and he shall bear their sins. Therefore he shall inherit many, and he shall divide the spoils of the mighty; because his soul was handed over to death [MT: because he poured out his soul unto death]: and he was numbered among the transgressors; and he bore the sins of many, and was *handed over* because of their iniquities.[11]

That Jesus as God's Servant was exalted and glorified is stated at Acts 2:33, 3:13, and 5:31. Ps. 22 (21 in the LXX) is exactly appropriate to a crucifixion or impalement, and is quoted and alluded to frequently in the gospels. Incidents are even suspected of having been invented to 'fulfil' Ps. 22 (e.g. Mt. 27:35 seems to be based on Ps. 22:18). The suffering man again says that he had been brought down to the dust of death (*v.*15), and, when God rescues him his seed shall serve

121

God (*v*.30). The psalm can easily be read as promising the resurrection, and an actual *anastasis* could fit it well enough. Not only did the church utilise these texts extensively in the formation of the gospels as literary achievements—it was, in my view, pointed in that direction by Jesus himself.

The Talpioth ossuary inscriptions fit perfectly with a Johannine conception of the relation between the Crucifixion and resurrection (p.127). With typical irony Jn. 12:31-34 makes the point: 'Now is the Judgment of this world; now the Ruler of this World (Satan) will be cast out. And if I am raised up from the earth I shall *draw everyone to myself. He said this to indicate by what death he was about to die.* The crowd replied, "We have heard from the Torah that The Christ (Messiah) remains for ever, and how can you say that the Son of man must be *raised up* [implying an Ascension]?. . .'

The First Epistle of Peter, though the product of Hellenistic culture, and an almost lawyer-like draftsmanship, combines profound meditation with authoritative Christian teaching. At 2:24 we are told, 'He himself bore our sins in his body on the tree, that we might die to sin, and live to righteousness'. The author was not afraid that the death, an accursed one, could not have an atoning quality.[11a] At 3:17-22 he gives a codified account of the relationship between the Anastasis, the baptism of believers, and the subsequent conduct of the latter. At *vv.* 18-19 he says, ' . . . because Christ also suffered once for sins, the righteous for the unrighteous, in order to bring us to God. He was put to death in the flesh, but made alive (again) through the Spirit, through the aid of which he also went and preached to the spirits in prison (i.e. in the underworld) . . .' The author could not believe that in Jesus's short period in what I have called clinical or reversible death he did not have ample time to bring salvation even to those who, like the (drowned) generation of Noah, had forfeited the World to Come: we need not follow him in that fanciful notion. And we must beware of supposing that because Jesus revived because the Spirit so willed it, his Anastasis was not a real and substantial one.

3.   THE OUTCOME IN FACT. HOW FAR DID JESUS PLAN IT?

Jesus cannot be convicted of sin, at least by those sympathetic to him (Jn. 8:46), and thus capable of sharing his merits. He can be a sin-offering, like the paschal lamb, and like Isaac. The offering does not cease to be such when he revives temporarily from incohate death.

In his career he has reproduced the feats of Joseph, Moses, Samson, Samuel, Elijah, Elisha, Jonah: in the obedience to death he has surpassed Isaac. Compelled by the Holy Spirit, his whole life is the working out, in banal fact, of the scriptural scenario he has envisaged. Even the borrowing of an ass has to take on cosmic dimensions.[12] He waits until the Jewish disease, *mᵉsîrâ*, has incubated in the Twelve, his Patriarchs of the new community, his Witnesses of the crossing of the Jordan, and then he knows that all is ready. The actors have assembled, the stage is set; the curtain must go up, the drama must commence.

The Anastasis cannot have been planned by Jesus himself, but when it occurred he knew what it was. Notice this: at Mk. 2:7 Jesus's opponents ask,

'Who can forgive sins, apart from God alone?' As usual, this is gospel irony. At that time and place Jesus could tell by a sufferer's readiness for charismatic cure that God had forgiven his sins, and Jesus confirms by his act of healing that that is what has happened (since people believed at the time that sickness was the result of sin). But after the Anastasis all is changed. The divine power of forgiveness has been irrevocably entrusted to Jesus, and is delegated by him to his apostles. How has this come about?

It is not sufficient to review the case of Isaac. No doubt the Anastasis 'proved' that the case of Isaac was not merely myth, and that the promise made centuries ago to Abraham had at last been earned in right earnest. This could be made out, even if Jesus survived death only for a few hours, But popular notions about the redemptive value of suffering were very much more to the point.

Let us assume that a person who is a sinner accepts his own death as an atonement (p.118). He is entitled to inherit the World to Come. This principle is stated unambiguously at 1 Cor. 5:5: the destruction of the flesh enables the malefactor's spirit to be saved on the Day of the Lord. Let us assume that a person who is sinless suffers and dies without fault on his part: he accumulates merit thereby, and those that love him (i.e. are in solidarity with him) can share that merit if that is his intention, and benefit from the removal of their sins from the account, as it were. Let us imagine that a sinless person voluntarily accepts great suffering, including death, on behalf of others, *and is restored to life*. It is perfectly obvious that God has accepted his suffering, but, by not accepting his life as forfeit, 'justified' him. By his further suffering and death he accumulates, being *ex hypothesi* entirely sinless, an infinity of merit; and by allowing persons nominated by himself or his agents to share his spiritual condition bestows sinless-nes upon them (provided they abide by the conditions of the relationship, of course —as indicated at Mt. 18:27, 31-34). This is a divine quality, and by his Anastasis Jesus acquired that. Not only can God forgive sins, but the risen Christ, who did not have that power in any logical sense previously, now acquires it. He delegates the power, and this gives his teaching a special edge it did not have before.

The teaching of Jesus, as I have said, is a new formula for living, and can be preached as a series of propositions or even precepts without reference to a Redeemer. But a Redeemer who has also risen from the dead is in a position to guarantee those who join him. In addition to the emotional impact of his sufferings voluntarily assumed on their behalf, an intellectual novelty emerges to the effect that so long as they are in solidarity with him they are removed from the Judgement. The Anastasis has conferred on Jesus divine prerogatives, and the apostles have a 'package' to deliver, out of all proportion more interesting than that which they had laboriously acquired in Galilee.

How far could all this be planned? It could not. The reflections I have passed on here would occur rapidly to anyone who had been obsessed with the principle inherent in Is. 52-53, and had actually worked the thing out to the death. But they are reflections that are posterior to the principal event. It seems Jesus realised that the corner-stone had been fitted in the arch. His band of would-be holy men, apprentice *gurus*, mutually jealous status-seekers, braggarts and bluffers, could now put two and two together. Joining with persons like James who had never been parties to evangelisation, but had now become convinced of Jesus's genuineness, they could tread the path of martyrdom themselves—the last thing *they* had planned to do.

4. THE TALPIOTH OSSUARIES.

While we have been discussing theoretical questions, seeking not to reel from side to side as do those theologians who make their way down the road from scepticism towards faith in the Resurrection;[13] and keeping, to some extent, within the limits of a vocabulary in general use, I have been impatient to come to the ossuaries which place the whole question in quite a different light. About thirty-five years ago Sukenik, a celebrated Israeli archaeologist, now deceased, was fetched to a construction site uncovered in the village of 'Talpiot' now a suburb of Jerusalem and within the bounds of the greater Jerusalem of Herodian times. In a publication of immense fascination[14] enriched with plans, sections, photographs, he explained how the underground tomb-complex was discovered, with an antechamber, the tomb proper, the *kukim* or shafts dug horizontally into the walls of the central chamber and, most important of all, the numerous ossuaries that were found *in situ*. There was evidence that tomb-robbers had very early inspected the general contents, moved the slabs which originally closed the shafts, realised that the ossuaries contained nothing but bones, and left. The outer stone not having been sufficiently replaced, sand entered and the whole became silted up. The two Roman Wars had passed over the tomb. The original tomb-robbers were very possibly Roman soldiers.

Inside the tomb was found a quantity of pottery, mostly broken, and a coin dated in the equivalent of A.D.43. It was very worn. Everything pointed to the tomb's having been in use for its normal purpose until approximately A.D.50. There is no question whatsoever of its having been used after A.D.70. We can, for our purposes, put the last normal closing of the outer stone in A.D.60: we cannot guess whether it was by a burial patry inserting a corpse into one of the shafts, or a normal visit by relatives or bone-packers. Bone-packers, professional or otherwise, had been very busy there. One of them may well have dropped that coin. The ossuaries, some of them beautifully decorated, were of various ages, all of course older, and some very much older, than A.D.60. Two attracted attention. Sukenik and his associates and assistants were stunned by them, and theologians have taken advantage of this to discount the discovery for theological purposes: for them it is as if Sukenik had never bobbed down into that tomb.

In his original article Sukenik finds it impossible to account for what he found, and leaves us with very lame suggestions, though his trained archaeologist's memory helps us to see a valuable parallel. In 1956 a historian, B. Gustafsson, repeated the main discoveries[15] and suggested how one of the puzzles could be solved, but he is left helpless with the remainder. We shall set about solving the puzzle with the aid of historical imagination, putting together things which we know from elsewhere.

124

Furthest inside one of the shafts were found two ossuaries together. On them, and on them alone, inscriptions were found. The same large hand had drawn charcoal crosses, with lines of equal length (so-called Greek crosses) in the middle of each side of ossuary no. 8; and had written boldly in charcoal

$$\text{ΙΗΣΟΥΣ ΙΟΥ}$$

clearly in the middle of the back of ossuary no. 7; and had incised with a graving tool of some kind

$$\text{ΙΗΣΟΥΣ ΑΛΩΘ}$$

on the top of the flat lid of ossuary no. 8. He or she tampered with no other ossuary. Several ossuaries occupied the shaft between these two and the entrance to it. Not one of those was similarly marked.

What do those crosses mean? Archaeologists had supposed that the sign of the cross was quite a late invention. But Sukenik remembered that at Herculaneum, which was buried in volcanic ash in A.D.79, the mark of a Greek cross was found on a wall in a position strongly suggesting that a cruciform object of wood had been hastily torn away thence, and a chest was found underneath the matrix, suggesting, conceivably, an altar.[16] No one had connected that cross with Palestine at that very early date.

Sukenik remembered that one Clermont-Ganneau had made extensive notes in 1873 of an enormous cache of ossuaries turned up, not far from Jerusalem, by some Muslims under Ottoman rule, and, quite apart from another discovery, the significance of which now comes to light, took note of four which had Greek crosses on them. Clermont-Ganneau was extremely puzzled by this find and came up with one absurd hypothesis after another to account for it. Sukenik leaves the problem where it lies. We shall return to it.

The next question is what is meant by ΙΟΥ and ΑΛΩΘ. Sukenik thought ἰού meant 'Woe!' (like the Hebrew 'î), and that ἀλώθ might have something to do with aloes and mourning: and that the man or woman who wrote in charcoal, and then (I guess it was afterwards), fearing that it might become illegible, took up the graving implement, was doodling, writing 'Woe to Jesus' or some such thing, mourning a person called Jesus. 'Jesus' in Greek is of course none other than Joshua, and it was a very common Jewish name. For this reason, as well as the crosses, and other unsolved problems, theologians have washed their hands of the Talpioth ossuaries long since. Wrongly.

Gustafsson brilliantly, and obviously correctly, transliterated ΑΛΩΘ into Hebrew word 'ªlôt, which is a 'jussive' or 'cohortative' infinitive meaning 'to rise up'. A perfectly intelligible rendering would therefore be, 'Jesus, (the one who rests here within) is to rise up', or 'Jesus, let him arise!' 'ªlôt is certainly appropriate to the resurrection (2 Kngs. 2:1, the case of Elijah's ascent to Heaven; and Ezek. 37:12-13!). So someone called Jesus is asked to note that the person whose bones have been packed neatly into the ossuary is 'for rising', marked, as it were, to ascend! Now we can set about solving the puzzle of ΙΟΥ. It really is no great puzzle. No great linguist is needed to recognise the intercultural expression ἰού/ἰοῦ/ἰώ/io. It is an exclamation, or shout, whether on an occasion of pain, or of joy, or of triumph. Aquila, the famous bible translator of c.A.D.140, thought that Zeph. 3:18 (where the MT later read *hāyû*) contained the exclamation *hîyû*, which he rendered in Greek *oi*. That exclamation is invariably used by Aquila (says Jerome) not in the sense of 'woe' but as a *call*, or, in particular, a cry for attention. Therefore a scholar of about 140 believed there was a *Hebrew* exclamation almost identical with *iou*. In ΙΗΣΟΥΣ ΙΟΥ the person within the ossuary shouts for joy that he shares in the triumph of Jesus as he rises from the dead! I guess it is a line from a very early Christian hymn. It is already known that the word, or rather sound, can be used to call the attention, e.g. of a divine saviour.[17] Jewish grave inscriptions are found with ὁ βοηθῶν (The Helper), meaning God, at the end.[18] In magical amulettes conjuring by Yahweh Sabaoth Adonai, the Jewish deity is summoned by the repetition of a sound like his name (ιαω), viz. *ia* and *io*.[19] That we are probably on the right track is indicated by Clermont-Ganneau's discovery[20] of an ossuary with a cross followed by what he read as ΗΔ, which is completely unintelligible unless it is (improbably) the Hebrew *'ēd* (witness). Knowing (from our Talpioth examples as from elsewhere) that in the first century the Greek letter O (omicron) was written in a squashed form almost indistinguishable from Δ (delta), we obtain ΗΟ. The barely literate Greek-speaking people of the time pronounced Η and Ι identically and Clermont-Ganneau's ΗΟ becomes *io* (for *iō*, since the Greek O and Ω were pronounced the same).

Since the ossuaries nos. 7 and 8 were together we know two things about them: the deceased were contemporaries, the name 'Jesus' is not their names, and they have been distinguished from all the others by the inscriptions. They were the oldest occupants and therefore probably placed where found even while there were one or more corpses in the shaft. Even assuming many deaths in the family in rapid sequence these two could not have been placed in the remotest position in the shaft less than a good many years before the tomb fell out of use. Let us guess they were put there in A.D.50. Who wrote the inscriptions? Bone-packers? Dutiful descendants in person? Even to pack in the ossuaries meant care and expense; for the average person could not expect his *ossilegium* to do him more honour than to provide a neat bone-pile in a corner or on a shelf. Someone, not necessarily (but quite possibly) a Christian himself, wrote those words, first in charcoal and, when that seemed inadequate, with a metal point. Why? Why should one bother? My guess is that a son or daughter is attending to the last duty (Mk. 7:10, Ex. 20:12) for his parents (we are not told about the bones). All the bones in all the ossuaries were awaiting (indeed they still await) the resurrection. But he or she was carrying out the expressed or tacit wish of the deceased. At the last day Jesus would call forth his own friends from their tombs! The inscriptions, in effect, beg him to remember to do what he promised for them.

We can take it as certain that the two ossuaries carried the bones of a pious person's parents. If he performed his task, a unique combination of melancholy and optimism, in about A.D.50 at the latest, when will they have died? Had they been buried in soil not much more than a year earlier? Or had they been laid in the wall of the family tomb to become desiccated? We cannot be sure. They could have died as long as twenty years earlier. In either case they were almost certainly converts of Jesus's. They could very possibly have been amongst his actual audience! They knew of the Anastasis as a contemporary event. And they could have asked their child to mark their last resting place with evidence that they wanted its implications to be applied to themselves. Jesus, a human being, was the first person since the beginning of the world who could exercise the power of God to cause the dead to rise from their tombs, and the first who could himself be called upon to do just this. Utterly unknown to Judaism, though dimly visualised in pagan notions and hopes, an actual person could guarantee that at the last day he would raise men up, exactly as St. John says (Jn. 6:40,44,54). Jesus was crucified and ascended in order that those that believe in him may have everlasting life (Jn. 3:13-15); at the tomb, after appearing to Mary, he ascends to him who sent him (Jn. 16:5 [cf. Tob. 12:20], 20:17). 'For as the Father raises the dead and causes (them) to live, so the Son also causes to live those whom he wills (to revive)' (Jn. 5:21). At Jn. 14:19 he says, 'because I live you also will live.'

One of Christ's[20a] functions was to comfort, console, or exhort mourners. Is. 61:1-3 develops this theme. We know that Is. 61.1-2 (along with other texts from Isaiah) was applied to one 'anointed', by Jewish scholars before as well as during the time of Jesus.[20b] The Christian message includes the consolation of mourners (Mt. 5:4); it was the one function which Jesus attempted to perform in his lifetime (the cases of the daughter of Jairus and the son of the widow of Nain come to mind) and could be promised emphatically after his death (Jn. 14:16-19, 16:6-7). It was a function which Luke, actually quoting Is. 61:1-2, does not indicate as already effective while Jesus was preaching at Nazareth (Lk. 4:21). There can be no more effective way of comforting mourners than to promise resurrection of their dead.

The sequence of ideas was this. Jesus had himself used the cross as a means whereby he would die, return from death, and be exalted. His immense merit enabled him to share his resurrection- and ascension-power with his friends, those 'solid' with himself. Not all and sundry, but those whom God gave him (Jn. 6:35, 39), whom he would recognise at the last day; those that loved him, had faith, and obeyed his commandments (p.119), and qualified for the resurrection.[21] There is no question of his causing *all* to revive and to ascend to be with him in Heaven. The sinners who do not seek forgiveness will not share in this, and, in archaic fashion, they can be visualised as observing, with chagrin, the triumph of the just.

No one in a tomb could be called upon to revive others—the exploit of Elishah was exhausted—but *he* could be called upon who was ascended and was at God's right hand (an ancient popular Christian notion taken from Ps. 110). Jesus's merit derived from his death on the cross, and this was transmuted into a Jewish symbol by its reproducing in actuality the faggots of Isaac in myth: small wonder that the arms of the cross (two crossed faggots) are of equal length! Jesus's eventual brain-death completed the *'Aqēdâ* which remained in a sense incomplete when Isaac revived and begot his family.[22] Jews already called upon

God to remember Isaac when the time came for him to raise the dead. Now Jesus had both merited and effectuated God's power of resurrection. Of course those disciples knew that Jesus had himself revived from the dead, and had, in some way we do not know, made its theology convincing, and, for them, final. There were even some Christians who believed resurrection occurred *and ceased* with Jesus's experience.[23]

I will be excused for using my historical imagination further. Paul has not yet started his first missionary journey, nor Mark assembled his material. The parents of the writer of those inscriptions need not have survived Jesus long. At least once after A.D.30 they will have been present at the Sepulchre,[24] outside the then wall of Jerusalem. The mother, with a group of women, stands in an inner circle, facing the entrance to the tomb of Joseph of Arimathæa, now probably in the church's hands. The father, with the men, stands in an outer circle. It is dark, but dawn is approaching. The women carry censers, with a small quantity of incense in each; and with a taper the censers are lit. One by one they will soon be bobbing down into the tomb itself, but now it is cold as well as dark; a few persons have just been baptised and shiver in their *sindons*. A trumpeter has been posted at a high point to watch for the first ray of dawn. A cloud of incense rises: all is still. A blast is heard from the trumpet. The boy chanter (cf. Mt. 18:10), dressed in his *sindon,* takes a deep breath (p.136):-

ΚΑΙ ΔΙΑΓΕΝΟΜΕΝΟΥ ΤΟΥ ΣΑΒΒΑΤΟΥ (Mk. 16:1),

and by the time he gets to

ΑΝΑΤΕΙΛΑΝΤΟΣ ΤΟΥ ΗΛΙΟΥ (Mk. 16:2)

it is broad day. There is the stone! They can see, stooping down, into the tomb: there is the place (on the right) where the body was laid! And the story goes on.

Of course Christ rose from the dead, and not metaphorically. Everyone there knew it, long before Mark wrote. Mark may not have been able to question that very couple. That festival may have been the last function they attended: their last Easter, and one of our first.

NOTES

1. Ign., *Smyrn.* I-III.
1a. O'Neill in Horbury & McNeil (1981). On Col. 1:24 see Hooker, ibid., 81-3, and Flemington, ibid.
1b. Kertelge (1976), 114-136. Dumas (1981). On the uncongenialness of the idea today: Schnackenburg (1976).
1c. Zehnle (1969), George (1973). Luke had no objection to the Jewish covenant theory (Lk. 22:20, Acts 20:28) (George, 210-1).
2. *JA*, 44.
3. Ibid. See also Test.Abr.XIV and Neofiti Targ. on Gen. 12:13, 26:24.
3a. Midr.R., Ruth VI.4, Koh.VII.8,1.
4. 4 Macc. 6 *per totum*. Also 17:21-22 ('to be revenged on the tyrant and to effect the purification of the motherland, becoming as it were a ransom (*antipsychon*) for the

sin of the race').

5. Lev. 26:25, Deut. 28:25ff., 1 Esd. 8:77, 1 Sam. 28:19, Ps. 106:41, Jer. 21:10, etc. Dan. (LXX) 3:32, Theod., ibid. 2 Macc. 10:4. Sifre on Deut. §.320.
6. Lk. 1:68, 2:38, 21:28 (cf. Mt. 26:53 and better still 20:21, Lk. 23:42, Acts 1:6, Jn. 6:15)!
7. *pathein* at Lk. 24:26,46, Acts 3:18, 17:3. Ign., *Magn.* 11 (*tōi pathei*), Iren., *c.hær*, 1.10,4 (*to pathos*); *Ap.Const.* 9 (*pathonta*); so the Nicene Creed.
7a. Güttgemanns (1966), 279.
8. *Studies* II, 184ff.
9. Jeremias, 'Erlöser und Erlösung im Spätjudentum und Urchristentum', in E. Pfennigsdorf, ed., *Deutsche Theologie* II (Göttingen, 1929), 106-19; id., 'Das Lösegeld für Viele', *Judaica* 3 (1947), 249-64; id., 'Die älteste Schicht der Menschensohn-Logien', *Z.N.W.* 58 (1967), 159-72, at p.161. For a negative outlook on the tradition see Schmithals (1979).
10. *Studies* I, 76ff.
11. Is. 52:13-53:12 with some omissions.
11a. As feared by Grayston (1981), 653.
12. *Studies* II, 165ff.
13. Above, ch.2.
14. E. L. Sukenik, 'The earliest record of Christianity,' *American J. of Archæology*, NS, 51 (1947), 351-65.
15. B. Gustafsson, 'The oldest graffiti in the history of the church?', *N.T.S.*3 (1956), 65-9. The term 'graffiti', though acceptable in the 1950's, has acquired a disagreeable timbre now and does not represent what the inscriptions are—they are entirely serious and deliberate.
16. Sukenik, ubi cit., 365.
17. See Liddell-Scott-Jones, *Greek English Lexicon*, new edn., *iō*, examples from Æschylus and Sophocles and other related examples. The Greek spoken and written in bilingual Palestine will not have been sufficiently pure for a sharp distinction to be drawn in writing or even in speech between *iou* and *iō* which are, in any case, related.
18. E.g. at *Corp.Ins.Jud.* (ed.Frey), 1539.
19. *Corp.Ins.Jud.* (ed. Frey), I (1936), no. 674.
20. Sukenik, ubi cit., 360.
20a. A. E. Harvey, Jesus and the Constraints of History (London, 1982), 140.
20b. J. A. Sanders, 'From Isaiah 61 to Luke 4', in J. Neusner, ed., *Christianity, Judaism . . . , Fest. Morton Smith* I (Leiden, 1925), 75-106; I. H. Marshall *The Gospel of Luke* (Exeter, 1978), 182-4; Harvey, ubi cit., 152-3.
21. Consider Jn. 5:25,28-29 (see Dan. 12:2, Lk. 21:36, Acts 24:15): 'Truly, truly, I say to you, the hour is coming, and now is, when the dead (literally, corpses) will hear the voice of the Son of God, and those who hear will live . . . Do not be surprised at this; for the hour is coming when all who are in the tombs will hear his voice, and come out, those who have done good to the resurrection of life, and those who have done evil, to the resurrection of judgment.' As for the conditions of being raised up by Jesus, as his elect, see Mk. 8:35,37-9:1, Mk. 13:20, 27; Lk. 12:1-12, and of course that elaborate quasi-parable, Mt. 25:31-46 (cf. Is. 58:6-9).
22. Gubler (1977), 373.
23. The variety of notions about whether, after Jesus's Ascension, there was any reality left in the Pharisaic hope constitute early 'heresies' countered by Paul in 1 Cor. 15 (Spörlein, 1971).
24. It has often been doubted (unnecessarily) whether the Holy Sepulchre is genuine. True enough, there is no proof Paul himself knew the tomb of Jesus. Broer (1972); C. Kopp, *The Holy Places of the Gospels,* 1st edn. (Freiburg & Edinburgh, 1963), 374-394.

CHAPTER XI
Conclusion.

1. THE FIXED POINTS.

In any study of the Anastasis of Jesus certain fixed points must be taken into account. Some of these derive from the factual situation, some from the literary situation. Both are important. The former are in any event decisive. Briefly they can be listed as follows:-

A.   On the factual side we have to contend with these fixed points:

1.   There must have been from the very earliest period a certainty that no bone of Jesus survived.

2.   Since Jesus was a man, whose life and work even as depicted by the gospels was that of a recognisable human innovator and entrepreneur, we cannot entertain seriously any question of his materialising and dematerialising, whatever those words can be taken to mean. Therefore his body must have been disposed of, consistently with fact no. 1 above.

3.   The revival of a person was called in Greek *anastasis,* and only by a metaphorical use could it be applied to resurrection. Resurrection (as a Jewish hope) was a collective experience. To link the *anastasis* of an individual with resurrection is an intellectual innovation which must have occurred to some mind or minds. From the Talpioth ossuaries we know that Jesus having achieved *anastasis* could confer resurrection on individuals (obviously on the last day).

4.   The disciples, who are depicted in Mark in a poor light, and whose behaviour even as recorded some years later by one of their own community (Paul) leaves a great deal to be desired, became, it is said immediately after the event into which we are researching, or in any case within quite a short interval, instruments of a totally new missionary-conversionist endeavour distinctly dangerous to themselves, and of questionable success-potential. None of the disciples had had a training in what we see them doing, and the one about whom we have first-hand information of complete reliability (Paul) had to undergo a self-training as painful as it was prolonged. This development, for which there is no historical parallel, requires explanation.

B.   On the literary side we have additional fixed points:-

5.   There were literary objections to depicting the Anastasis of Jesus (assuming that to be the tradition to hand) as the climax of a narrative of his life. Even if proof had been to hand as to his act which would suit a literary narrative,

the tale would have fallen foul of pre-existing Greek literary genres and motifs. To utter particulars would have risked inconvenience, given that the first persons to be confronted with the miracle were females, including perhaps an unmarried female. To be silent about the particulars would be convenient in another respect. Just as some miracles of Jesus were presented by Mark as a Christian counterpart of the ubiquitous ancient myth of Divine Marriage, and just as two of his companions were presented as Christianised Dioscuri,[1] so the annual visit (which we presume from the festival recitation) of females to inspect an empty tomb was happily congruent with ancient pagan notions of the revival of male counterparts (e.g. Attis) of female fertility deities. Even in Mark's time a Christian 'take-over' of pagan themes was at work.

6. Furthermore, the literary presentation of Mark's gospel sustains a technique of presenting the experience of Jesus as a continuum with the Hebrew scriptures. The strange discovery made by those ladies, placed precisely as they were, at that very time, vibrated with Old Testament parallels. To bring these out was Mark's preoccupation, consistently with the retention of a recitation suitable for, and already appropriated by, a festival. He was not concerned to tell the rather banal story of a mere revival inside a tomb.

7. For several years Mark's technique sufficed. His decision to end at Mk. 16:8 may well have been convenient in another sense also. The broad front of 'explanation' of what had occurred allowed conflicting theories and emphases to emerge, and churches might have been in doubt how any 'continuation' from Mk. 16:8 ought to be devised. Mark's successors 'improved' upon him, and each stimulated his own successor. The queries they set out to answer, and the techniques they utilised to satisfy curiosity, indicate something of the decisions Mark himself could have made and perhaps, in part, avoided. Viewed in that light, the Anastasis did not, by the time of Mark, lend itself properly to satisfying such curiosity. In consequence it was not an articulate part of Mark's gospel at all. Recognition of it informs the whole, but it remains unspoken. The climax of the gospel (the women's experience) takes it for granted. The discovery, and interpretation, of the Talpioth ossuaries, shows for the first time that John was in touch with, and was able to express, theological and eschatological principles alive at an earlier period and by-passed by Mark.

8. In the writings of Paul and later Fathers of the church the Anastasis is a translucent event, important only in respect of having happened. Its consequence from the literal standpoint, is simply theological. No one suggested that it had factual consequences, though it is obvious to us that it must have had.

From these fixed points I conclude that the Anastasis was not a hoax, and that the contemporary non-Christian assertion that it was an imposture was baseless, as well as extremely lame. No third explanation has ever been put forward, except the 'conviction of Peter' formula and other equivocations and prevarications offered by our contemporaries (ch. 2 above).

One is tempted to ask a foolish question: what was the point of the Anastasis? This is as sensible as asking why someone is born with red hair. It

131

happened. One can indeed ask what is the point of the resurrection of Isaac, for there we are in the realm of a literary construct. Isaac himself was mythical, let alone his experience. As a tribal ancestor *de luxe* he was sociologically significant to Jews, whose subjective needs threw up the collective hope of resurrection. This fortunately coincided with the need to rewrite some ancient, pagan stories about human sacrifice, which Judaism, in any form that we are acquainted with, abominated. The sacrifice of Isaac possesses emotional and sentimental themes of value in education, particularly in view of the curious international position of Jewry, which colours, and has long coloured, its self-image, particularly in relation to Jerusalem and the Temple.

We are certainly entitled to ask why the Anastasis was *linked* with the resurrection. This could well have been an event occurring within a particular mind, which had approximately fifteen years of intensive missionary endeavour behind it, and was entirely obsessed with the demands made upon it by the Holy Spirit, whose reality no one could, or would question.

Though my book is, as I said at the beginning, a conjecture, it is a conjecture within some parameters, some of which are fixed, and some of which arise on a balance of probabilities. To me it seems that Jesus is not only the subject of the Anastasis, the person in whom it actually occurred, he is the author of the significance given to it. One is unlikely to accept this if one has not, as it were, moved with him from Galilee onwards, and been captivated by his programme. To this day the same objection is made against him that was made in his lifetime—that he eschewed human discipline (Mk. 7:8) and operated with sovereign originality. But who taught Mozart or Beethoven how to compose? The original mind is autonomous, as John was able to see clearly enough, for he ridicules commonplace people's indignation in the marvellously ironical words at Jn. 7:15, 'How does this man know writings, never having learned them?' If he *had* been someone's faithful disciple, what would Jesus have achieved?

2. FINAL COMMENTS ON THE ENTERPRISE.

In a very few years from the Anastasis Christians are baptising people not simply as initiators into a charismatic apprehension of the divine and of dedication to it, but as agents of a triad, God the Father, the Son, and the Holy Spirit. This is an arrangement, whereby by baptism emerging gasping from a pretend drowning, the neophyte leaves his old nature and becomes a new creature bound by bonds of invisible unity with Christ; Jesus is Messiah and has a divine nature, two propositions which would not have been propounded by Jesus himself in so many words during his ministry, propositions inconceivably blasphemous and absurd to any Jew who remained faithful to his traditional culture. Nor was this unknown to the evangelists themselves. The word for 'to worship' (*proskunein*) is normally reserved for behaviour towards God. It is used freely enough by pagans (who treated idols and outstanding human beings similarly: Mk. 5:6, 15:19, Mt. 2:11—the case of Mt. 4:9 making the point, for Satan by all means wants 'worship'). After the Anastasis Jesus is 'worshipped' by the women in Matthew (28:9) and by the disciples in Matthew and Luke (Mt. 28:17, Lk. 24:52).

132

Yet here, even at the point of entry to the community, the divinity of Christ, unacceptable to Jews, must be confessed.

By his baptism he, the new member, loses his previous sins and their effects, and by his faith in Christ he is saved. Redeemed from sin, the latter has no dominion over him. 'For to this end Christ died, and lived again, that he might be Lord of both the dead and the living' (Rom. 14:9). The baptised Christian lives to the Lord and, when he dies, he is still the Lord's, the Lord who has transcended death. Whether he lives or dies in the physical sense the normal preoccupations with death cease to apply. As expressed in the ancient formula at Acts 2:24, death was *unable* to hold Christ.

I have tried to explain, very briefly, how this extraordinary development could take place. Audacity characterised Jesus's methods in his lifetime. After his death something which even the most audacious could not have envisaged is calmly proclaimed. John the Baptist, who made a fetish of baptising people, did not presume to baptise in his own name. And here the Spirit is given to people who enjoy the authentic baptism in the three names!

So far I cannot be persuaded that this can have come about without a (to them) overwhelming event. Great as its effect on the personalities involved, its effect was even more startling on the gospel, which became, in practically no time at all, attractive to Gentiles in a way that the prevailing schools of Judaism had not been. And within less than that period the hostility of the hierarchy at Jerusalem had developed with a virulence which is, from this distance of time, entirely understandable. It is not at all surprising that the astounding conversion of Paul, formerly one of the Sanhedrin's agents, should have been attributed by him to a vision of the Risen One, whose Anastasis he soon has every reason to expand and develop in his own teaching. This does not impugn the fact of Jesus's revival.

In the light of all this I cannot believe that Jesus did not revive in the tomb. Paul says (1 Cor. 15:13-14),

'If there is no *anastasis* of the dead, Christ cannot have *been raised*. And if Christ was not raised, our proclamation (of the gospel) is vain, and your faith is vain, and we are discovered as false witnesses of God, having borne witness in reference to God that he raised Christ, whom he cannot have raised if the dead are not raised . . .,'

and then (*v.*17), 'and if Christ was not raised, your faith is vain, *and you are still in your sins*'. That was the point. It passes my comprehension how this could be said with a straight face if Jesus experienced no Anastasis, and the Christian religion was started by a 'subjective impression on the part of Peter'—which leaves the initiative with Peter (of all people)—or by an 'existential experience'.

The remarkable thing from our point of view is that all this endurance on Jesus's part should have manifested itself on behalf of the nation revealed to us in Josephus's *Jewish War* and *Antiquities*. If after suffering as he did, reviving (as I envisage it) in the cold tomb, he had asked himself whether he had not already served God as the Servant in Is. 53 would do, the answer must have

133

been positive. Did that unlovely nation deserve still more of him? He had indeed called sinners to repentance (Mk. 2:17). He had played his part (an idea familiar to the early church; cf. Acts 20:24, 2 Tim. 4:7). No doubt his tomb would be visited for a blessing. Thereby his miraculous powers would continue to be effective. He had done enough.

But here the 'precedent' of Isaac (p.35) must come in. His renewal of life was not without purpose. In that culture nothing is without God's purpose. I imagine him pondering over his position, and over the immense merit he had won, and for whom he had won it. Isaiah and Zechariah make it plain that at the End of Days Gentiles will come to worship at Jerusalem.[1a] The Messiah will bring two flocks of sheep and unite them (Jn. 10:16). Jesus lays down his life for his sheep. and not only the Jewish 'sheep' (Jn. 10:11, 15). It is obvious that a tremendous opportunity has been given to him to unite Jew and Gentile. His miserable disciples, constituted apostles by the command of God himself, must go to Galilee and bring the prophecies of Isaiah and Ezekiel to pass.

And, it appears they did, after their fashion.

NOTES

1. Derrett, *Studies* III (1982), 42ff.
1a. The Servant is to be a light to the Gentiles: Is. 42:6 (Lk. 2:32 indicates Luke's preoccupation clearly), so also Is. 49:5-6, where the Servant will be 'my salvation unto the end of the earth. The eventual mission to the Gentiles is mentioned at Is. 49:22, but more plainly at 56:6-7 and 8 ('The Lord God which gathers the outcasts of Israel says, Yet will I gather others to him, beside his own that are gathered.'). Zech. 14:16-17 rather quaintly puts it, 'And it shall come to pass that every one that is left of all the nations which came against Jerusalem shall go up from year to year to worship the King, the Lord of Hosts, and to keep the feast of Tabernacles. And it shall be that whoever of the families of the earth does not go up to Jerusalem to worship the King, the Lord of hosts, upon them there shall be no rain . . .'

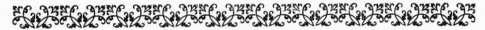

APPENDIX
Mark 16: 1 - 8.

The bogus endings of Mark are only of value in so far as they testify to attempts to keep Mark in use in churches where his successors' success was a threat to his continuing employment. No one who knows anything of textual criticism can deny that Mark ended at 16:8.[1] The research which still debates the question, and holds it to be open,[2] ignores the brilliant and original work of Schenke (1968) who was certainly on the right track. I had apprehended a similar conclusion on different hypotheses; and a pointer in the same direction was given by Moule (1957/8) in reference to the post-Anastasis appearances. The early church's interest in topography (a Christian topology) was stimulated, and for a period sustained, by the possibilities of pilgrimage. Looked at in that light, the beauties of Mk. 16:1-8 assume a new significance. Granted that he has basically adopted and adapted a pre-existing festival-recitation, we find that even before Mark a powerful *apologetic* was at work. The fundamental facts of the first apprehension that Jesus had risen from the dead stood out not in three dimensions, but in four. There was the biblical dimension as well: the story, if composed to be sung on the most solemn occasions known to the church, must breathe in the language of the Holy Spirit, the vivifier, itself. A scholar has already guessed[3] that the form of sentence building, even the recitation, may offer some clues to enable us to enter into the original author's, and perhaps the editor's mind(s). He was right, and below we shall see how this may be done.

It is now established that a gospel can indeed end on the particle, γάρ, 'for'![4] It is already realised that the women's 'fear', the absolute climax of Mark's gospel (in which *awe* still dominates the undomesticated message), is the correct proof of the presence of the numinous. Studying the warp and weft of the gospel as composed, it is quite reasonable to ask whether the presence of the Holy Spirit, as evidenced by the authors, was a fair representation of contemporary Judaism? We are not concerned with that question here, but my drift will have been grasped. The Jesus-religion was not a warmed-up Judaism, whatever its first believers might have supposed: it was something new, unable to clothe itself in entirely new clothing (in spite of what is said in clear terms at Mk. 2:21-22!).

Though Mk. 16:1-8 was composed, as indeed was the whole of the gospel, to be sung, we must envisage a style more simple than the sophisticated methods used in the Byzantine chant or a Sephardi synagogue. If one gives a plenitude of notes to syllables irrespective of their position in the sentence, or indeed irrespective of sense, one assumes that the text is known by heart. If a text itself is valued for its evocative qualities, distortion will be restrained.[4a] Our text itself tells us what we need to know. The poet-evangelist has mastered the problem how to *emphasise* words when they are to be sung, not read, or, if read, then to be read with the peculiar semi-cantillated sound used in reading oriental scriptures. If the text were read silently (which practically no one did in those days) the position of the word in the sentence would give the emphasis, since such flexibility is one of the glories of the Greek language; but this advantage is greatly diminished if the text is sung. A text intended to be sung, moreover, must take into account the lung-capacity of the singer, the resonance of the building (if there is to be one), and so on. The number of syllables to a line is largely determined by such factors, and this is one of the characteristics of gospel style.

Before we go to our passage, we should study some examples. Take Mk. 3:6, which, read as printed, like a newspaper, seems just another unpleasant statement. But this was how it must have been delivered:

καὶ ἐξελθόντες οἱ Φαρισαῖοι	(10 syllables)
εὐθὺς μετὰ τῶν Ἡρῳδιανῶν	(10 syllables)
συμβούλιον ἐδίδουν κατ᾽ αὐτοῦ	(10 syllables)
ὅπως αὐτὸν ἀπολέσωσιν.	(9 syllables)

One expects ten syllables in the fourth line, but it has been shortened by one syllable, so that, at the end of the paragraph, additional notes may be sung to emphasise the punch word, which comes at the end: 'him they might *destroy*.' Apart from the 'soft' words, like 'him', 'his', etc., the word at the end of the line, or before the cæsura, takes the emphasis of the unit, and where a word appears more than once at a cæsura or at the end of a line it is emphatic

Let us take another example, this from the most important part of the gospel (Mk. 14:22-24), which is largely in 9-syllable lines, and one may ask why some lines are different.

καὶ ἐσθιόντων αὐτῶν λαβὼν	(9)	
ἄρτον εὐλογήσας ἔκλασεν	(9)	
καὶ ἔδωκεν αὐτοῖς καὶ εἶπεν,	(9)	
Λάβετε, τοῦτο ἐστιν τὸ σῶμά μου	(11)	} 2 × 9
καὶ λαβὼν ποτήριον	(7)	
εὐχαριστήσας ἔδωκεν αὐτοῖς.	(10)	
καὶ ἔπιον ἐξ αὐτοῦ πάντες,	(9)	
καὶ εἶπεν αὐτοῖς. Τοῦτό ἐστιν	(9)	
τὸ αἷμα μου τῆς διαθήκης	(9)	
τὸ ἐκχυννόμενον ὑπὲρ πολλῶν.	(10)	

One must remember that in syllabic cantillation the singer has it in his power not only to lengthen words for emphasis by dwelling longer on the syllables required, but also to shorten material by running short syllables together. Therefore the difference between a ten-syllable line and an eleven-syllable line may not be so significant as it appears. However the eleven-syllable line in this passage contains words of Christ which are not easily adjusted, and exactly the same can be said of the next two lines. The singer will automatically dwell longer on the word *poterion* (cup), as indeed he should, since 'cup' means 'fate', the fate the speaker and his eventual missionaries will share.

We are now in a position to pass to Mk. 16. The irregularity of the lines is obvious, but more obvious still is the high proportion of lines in regular patterns. If Mark is, as I believe, incorporating an earlier and by his time, traditional recitation, this is not surprising. The cæsura falls in the same place in a significant proportion of instances. Two lines have 6 syllables, three have 8, two have 10, five have 9, but eight have 11 and nine have 13. The thirteen-syllable line is a strain on the singer; it implies small emphasis; the problem is overcome by the cæsura. From the singer's point of view the shifting of the cæsura to provide 9:4 or 8:5 instead of the regular 7:6 is an elegant variation. One must also remember that in accordance with Greek usage vowels may be run together where no loss to the sense is experienced.

I take it that in this passage the very short lines are intended to be very emphatic; that eight-syllable lines are intended to be lengthened by three superfluous notes apiece, whereas a six-syllable line on its own would gain not less than five such. The basic narrative line has eleven syllables. That my discovery is basically correct is proved by an interesting feature. Several manuscripts of Mk. 16:1 read Σαλώμη πορευθεῖσαι. The additional word adds nothing to the sense and has no 'midrashic' significance. The verb is foreign to Mark, but a favourite of Matthew and Luke. How did it get there? This is the effect it produces:-

Μαρία ἡ Μαγδαληνή	(8)
καὶ Μαρία ἡ Ἰακώβου	(8)
καὶ Σαλώμη πορευθεῖσαι	(8)

Instead of having a series of lines running 11-11-9-8-11-11, assuming that Salome was a person of real importance (as she may well have been to Mark's church), we have a nice artistic pattern, 11-8-8-8-8-11-11, which is much easier to learn, and, as it were, takes the 'heat' off Salome, by now perhaps a person of less consequence.

In the text printed below I give the original (so far as we know it) arranged for recitation, with a translation adapted to the singer's purpose. I have indicated the line-lengths and the cæsuras. The footnotes are chiefly to give the (tentative) scriptural allusions so far discovered.

Readers of my earlier studies have accused me of fancifulness. But let us take an example from an acceptable quarter. Luke was not satisfied that the 'Galilee' message meant merely what Mark's Young Man attributed to it. The vital words in Mark, ἠγέρθη, οὐκ ἔστιν ὧδε, semed to require a gloss and he inserts (24:5) Τί ζητεῖτε τὸν ζῶντα μετὰ τῶν νεκρῶν. This is taken from Is. 8:19, utilising both the unpointed Hebrew text and the LXX (τί ἐκζητοῦσιν περὶ τῶν ζώντων τοὺς νεκρούς;) or another translation available to Luke (there were others). The ladies' journey is not on their own behalf: their experience is cosmic. The Lord of Hosts who dwells in Mount Zion is the source to which they must apply themselves. The Spirit (to whom Luke gives very special attention in his works) is not to be found amongst the dead—and that is the message of the Anastasis as he sees it. He might not have had the confidence to build a gospel as he did, had he not Mark's magnificent composition in front of him. I am not fanciful in putting in those footnotes. I am ashamed that I may have failed to supply others which have escaped me. Meanwhile the artistic quality of the present ending of Mark should be obvious.

καὶ διαγενομένου τοῦ σαββάτου	(11)	And when the Sabbath was over
Μαρία ἡ Μαγδαληνὴ καὶ Μαρία	(11)	Mary of Magdala and Mary
ἡ Ἰακώβου καὶ Σαλώμη	(9)	the mother of James, and Salome
ἠγόρασαν ἀρώματα[5]	(8)	bought aromatic oils
ἵνα ἐλθοῦσαι ἀλείψωσιν αὐτόν.	(11)	in order to go and anoint him;
καὶ λίαν πρωὶ τῇ μιᾷ τῶν σαββάτων	(11)	and very early on the first day
		of the week
ἔρχονται ἐπὶ τὸ μνημεῖον[6]	(9)	they come to the tomb
ἀνατείλαντος τοῦ ἡλίου.[7]	(9)	when the sun had risen
καὶ ἔλεγον πρὸς ἑαυτάς,	(8)	And they were saying to each other
τίς ἀποκυλίσει ἡμῖν τὸν λίθον[8]	(11)	"Who will roll away for us the stone
ἐκ τῆς θύρας τοῦ μνημείου;	(8)	out of the door of the tomb?"
καὶ ἀναβλέψασαι[9] θεωροῦσιν	(9)	And they looked up and observed
ὅτι ἀνακεκύλισται ὁ λίθος,[10]	(11)	that it had been rolled up, the stone:
ἦν γὰρ μέγας σφόδρα.[11]	(6)	for it was large, exceedingly.
καὶ εἰσελθοῦσαι εἰς τὸ μνημεῖον	(10)	And they entered the tomb,
εἶδον νεανίσκον[12]	(6)	and saw a Young Man
καθήμενον ἐν τοῖς δεξιοῖς[13]	(9)	sitting on the right side
περιβεβλημένον στολὴν λευκὴν[14]	(10)	wrapped in a white robe,
καὶ ἐξεθαμβήθησαν.[15]	(13)	and they were stupefied. But he says
		to them,
ὁ δὲ λέγει αὐταῖς,		
Μὴ ἐκθαμβεῖσθε. Ἰησοῦν ζητεῖτε	(11)	"Do not be stupefied. Are you
		enquiring for Jesus,
τὸν Ναζαρηνὸν τὸν ἐσταυρωμένον;	(11)	the Nazarene, the crucified one?
ἠγέρθη, οὐκ ἔστιν ὧδε.[16]	(13)	He has been raised: he is not here.
		Here is the place
ἴδε ὁ τόπος		
ὅπου ἔθηκαν αὐτόν.	(13)	where they laid him. But go,
ἀλλὰ ὑπάγετε,		
εἴπατε τοῖς μαθηταῖς αὐτοῦ	(13)	tell his disciples, and Peter
καὶ τῷ Πέτρῳ,		
ὅτι προάγει ὑμᾶς	(13)	that he goes before you into Galilee:
εἰς τὴν Γαλιλαίαν.[17]		
ἐκεῖ αὐτὸν ὄψεσθε,[18]	(13)	there you will see him, as he told you."
καθὼς εἶπεν ὑμῖν.		
καὶ ἐξελθοῦσαι ἔφυγον[19]	(13)	And, coming out, they fled from the
		tomb,
ἀπὸ τοῦ μνημείου,		
εἶχεν γὰρ αὐτὰς τρόμος[20] καὶ ἔκστασις.[21]	(11)	for there held them a trembling and
		ecstasy.
καὶ οὐδενὶ οὐδὲν εἶπαν,[22]	(13)	And to no one did they say anything,
ἐφοβοῦντο γάρ.		for they were afraid.

1. Aland (1974), 469. Paulsen (1980) concurs, so did Pesch and Bartsch (1974).
2. Farmer (1974).
3. Boomershine & Bartholomew (1981), 220-1.
4. Aland (1974), 462; Boomershine & Bartholomew (1981), 213 n.4 (excellent examples). W. L. Knox had ridiculed the idea at *H.T.R.*35 (1942), 13-23, an article now dépassé.
4a. The words of Buddha were soon arranged to be chanted; the disadvantages of an artificial cantillation were observed (*Vinayapiṭaka,* Culla-vagga V.3,1 = Vin. ii, 108).
5. For the significance of *aromata* cf. the references to Song of Songs at p.115, n.28 above.
6. Ironic in view of Cant. 4:10,16 (LXX).
7. Elliott at *R.B.*84 (1977), 10-11 explains that *mnēmeion* is the correct *koinē* form, *mnēma* being atticising. The *mnēma* at Lk. 23:53, 24:1 (cf. Acts 7:16) may well be genuine but those at Mk. 5:3,5 are suspect.
8. Gen. 29:8 (LXX).
9. Gen. 18:2, 22:4 (LXX), Zech. 1:18, 2:1, 5:1.
10. Gen. 29:10 (LXX).
11. Gen. 29:2 (LXX).
12. Gen. 41:12; cf. Exod. 33:11 (Jesus too was a young man).
13. Ps. 141:5 (LXX)!
14. Eccl. 9:8 (LXX).
15. Dan. 8:17 (LXX & Theod.).
16. Is. 26:19 (LXX).
17. Is. 52:11-12 (LXX).
18. Is. 52:15 (LXX), 49:7, 60:2.
19. Dan. 10:7 (Theod.).
20. Ps. 54:5 (LXX), Is. 54:14 (LXX), Hab. 3:16 (LXX)?
21. Dan. 10:7 (Theod.).
22. Is. 52:15b (LXX)!

ABBREVIATIONS

1. BOOKS.

A.N.R.W.	*Aufstieg und Niedergang der Römischen Welt.*, ed. Haase & Temporini.
Ant.	Josephus, *Antiquities of the Jews* in (*Works*), ed. Thackeray, Marcus, Feldman, Loeb edn., 9 vols (1926-65).
Ass.Mos.	*Assumption of Moses,* ed. R. H. Charles (London, 1897).
b.	Babylonian Talmud, ed. L. Goldschmidt, *Der Babylonische Talmud* (Berlin, 1896-1935); English trans., ed. I. Epstein, *Babylonian Talmud* (London, 1935-52); *The Minor Tractates of the Talmud,* ed. A. Cohen (London, 1965).
B.J.	Josephus, *The Jewish War*: see *Ant.*
Enc.Jud.	*Encyclopedia Judaica* (Jerusalem, 1971-2).
Ign.	Ignatius. *The Apostolic Fathers,* ed. K. Lake, Loeb edn., I (1912).
j.	Jerusalemite (Palestinian) Talmud. ed. Wilna, 1922; trans. Schwab (Paris, 1871-1888).
J.E.	*Jewish Encyclopedia* (New York, London, 1901-6).
LXX	The Septuagint Version of the Old Testament (Rahlfs).
MT	The Masoretic Text of the Hebrew Bible (Kittel, *Biblia Hebraica; Biblia Hebraica Stuttgartensia*).
Mann	J. Mann, *The Bible as Read and Preached in the Old Synagogue* I (Cincinnati, 1940).
Mekilta	H. S. Horowitz and I. A. Rabin, *Mechilta d'Rabbi Ismael,* 2nd edn. (Jerusalem, 1960); text and trans., J. Z. Lauterbach, 3rd edn. (Philadelphia, 1976).
Midr.Hag.	*Midrash Haggadol,* ed. M. Margulies and others, 5 vols. (Jerusalem, 1947-78).
Midr.R.	*Midrash Rabbah,* ed. E. E. Halevi, 8 vols. (Tel Aviv, 1953-63); trans. ed. H. Freedman and M. Simon (London, 1939).
Mishnah	Text with English trans., P. Blackman, *Mishnayoth,* 6 vols. (London, 1951-6). English trans. H. Danby (Oxford, 1933).
Neofiti Targ.	Ed., trans. A. Diéz Macho, *Neophyti I,* 4 vols. (Madrid, 1968-78).
P.d.R.El.	*Pirke de Rabbi Eliezer,* trans. G. Friedlander (London, 1916), from a text established from various mss.
Pesiqta Rabb.	*Pesikta Rabbati,* ed. M. Friedmann (Vienna, 1880); English trans. W. Braude (Cambridge, Mass., 1968).
Petrusev.	Ch. Maurer, *Petrusevangelium* in E. Hennecke and W. Schneemelcher, ed., *Neutestamentliche Apokryphen* I (Tübingen, 1959), 118-124. English trans., M. R. James, *Apocryphal New Testament* (Oxford, 1955), 91-4.

140

Philo	Philo, *Works.* Loeb edn., F. H. Colson and G. H. Whitaker, 10 vols (New York, London, 1929-62).
Ps.Philo	*Liber Antiquitatum Biblicarum.* Text and French trans., D. J. Harrington, J. Cazeaux, *Pseudo-Philon, Les Antiquités Bibliques* I (Paris, 1976), commentary by C. Perrot and P. M. Bogaert, ibid. II (1976). English trans., L. H. Feldman, ed., M. R. James, *The Biblical Antiquities of Philo* (New York, 1971).
Tanḥ.	Tanḥuma. *Midrasch Tanchuma,* ed. S. Buber (Wilna, 1885).
Targ.Ps.Jon.	*Pseudo-Jonathan,* ed. M. Ginsburger (Berlin, 1903). English trans., J. Etheridge (London, 1862).
Test.Abr.	*Testament of Abraham.* Text ed. M. R. James, in J. A. Robinson, ed. *Texts and Studies* II/2 (Cambridge, 1892); commentary in M. Delcor, *Le Testament d'Abraham* (Leiden, 1973)
Test.XII.Patr.	Critical edn., M. de Jonge, *The Testaments of the Twelve Patriarchs* (Leiden, 1978). Trans. of uncritical edn. by R. H. Charles (1908) at R. H. Charles, *Apocrypha and Pseudepigrapha of the Old Testament* II (Oxford, 1913), 282-367.
Sefer Hayyashar	*Alias 'Jasher'.* Text, Frankfurt a.M. 1706; English trans., M. Noah (New York, 1840).
Vita	Josephus, *Life,* see *Ant.*
Yalqûṭ	*Yalqûṭ Shimᵉonî,* ed. B. Landau, 2 vols. (Jerusalem, 1960).

Note: Abbreviations not listed here are biblical, classical, or patristic, and these are all given in a conventional form.

2.   ABBREVIATIONS OF PERIODICALS UTILISED.

Am.J.Theol.	American Journal of Theology
Am.J.Arch.	American Journal of Archaeology
B.Z.	Biblische Zeitschrift
Bibl.	Biblica
C.B.Q.	Catholic Biblical Quarterly
E.T.	Expository Times
E.T.L.	Ephemerides Theologicæ Lovanienses
Ev.Theol.	Evangelische Theologie
Hey.J.	Heythrop Journal
I.E.J.	Israel Exploration Journal
Ir.E.R.	Irish Ecclesiastical Record
J.B.L.	Journal of Biblical Literature
J.Q.R.	Jewish Quarterly Review
J.T.S.	Journal of Theological Studies
M.G.W.J.	Monatsschrift für Geschichte und Wissenschaft des Judentums
N.T.	Novum Testamentum
N.T.S.	New Testament Studies
R.B.	Revue biblique

R.É.J.	Revue des études juives
R.I.D.A.	Revue internationale des droits de l'antiquité
S.J.Th.	Scottish Journal of Theology
T.L.Z.	Theologische Literaturzeitung
T.Z.	Theologische Zeitschrift
Theol.	Theology
V.T.	Vetus Testamentum
Vig.Chr.	Vigiliæ Christianæ
Z.D.P.V.	Zeitschrift der Deutschen Palästinavereins
Z.K.T.	Zeitschrift für katholische Theologie
Z.T.K.	Zeitschrift für Theologie und Kirche
Z.N.W.	Zeitschrift für die neutestamentliche Wissenschaft und die Kunde der älteren Kirche.

BIBLIOGRAPHY

BIBLIOGRAPHY OF PRINCIPAL SECONDARY WORKS

USED IN THIS BOOK

Note: the size of this bibliography will surprise no one who is acquainted with the industry and ingenuity, the restless search for improvement, and refusal to accept *Ergebniße* ('results'), on the part of the professional theologian, junior and senior alike. It is the quality of theology that no number of contributions suffices, and no propositions will find contented acceptance.

In Dhanis (1974) one may find a bibliography, provided by G. Gilberti, of 1510 items helpful for the study of the bodily resurrection of Jesus.

In what follows I have, on the whole, omitted any work which receives full references in my Notes to the various chapters above.

1. Non-medical.

Aland, K., 'Bemerkungen zum Schluss des Markusevangeliums', at *Neotestamentica et Semitica. Black Vol.* (Edinburgh, 1969), 157-180.
'Der Schluss des Markusevangeliums', in Sabbe (1974), 435-70 also in *Neutestamentliche Entwürfe* (Munich 1979).

Alsup, J. E. *The Post-Resurrection Appearance Stories of the Gospel Tradition* (London, 1975).

Andresen, C. and Klein, G. *Theologia Crucis—Signum Crucis. Fest. E. Dinkler* (Tübingen, 1979).

Aulén, G. *Jesus in Contemporary Historical Research* (London, 1976), ch.6.

Badham, P., *Christian Beliefs about Life after Death* (London, 1976).

Baldensperger, G. 'Le tombeau vide', *R.Hist.Phil.Rel.*12 (1932), 413-43, 13 (1933), 105-44, 14 (1934), 93-125.

Bammel, E. 'Herkunft und Funktion der Traditionselemente in 1 Kor. 15, 1-11', *T.Z.* 11 (1955), 401-19.

Barrett, C. K. 'The Holy Spirit in the Fourth Gospel,' *J.T.S.* NS.1 (1950), 1-15.

Bartsch, H.-W. ed., *Kerygma and Myth, a Theological Debate* (London, 1953).
'Die Passions-und Ostergeschichten bei Matthäus. Ein Beitrag zur Redaktionsgeschichte des Evangeliums', *Basileia. Fest. W. Freytag* (Stuttgart, 1959).
'Der Schluss des Markus-Evangeliums,' *T.Z.* 27 (1971), 241-54.
'Inhalt und Funktion des urchristlichen Osterglaubens', *N.T.S.* 26 (1980), 180ff.
'Der ursprüngliche Schluss der Leidensgeschichte', in Sabbe (1974), 411-433.

Beer, B. *Leben Abrahams* (Leipzig, 1859).

Benoit, P. 'Marie-Madeleine et les disciples au tombeau selon Jean 20, 1-18,' *Fest. J. Jeremias* (Berlin, 1964), 141-52.
The Passion and Resurrection of Jesus Christ (New York, London, 1969).
'The Ascension', in *Jesus and the Gospel* I (London, 1973), ch.11(=*RB* 1949, 161-203).

Betz, H. D., 'Ursprung und Wesen christlichen Glaubens nach den Emmaus-legende (Lk. 24, 13-32), *Z.T.K.* (1969), 7-21.

Blinzler, J. *Der Prozess Jesu*, 3rd edn. (Regensburg, 1960).

Bode, E. L. *The First Easter Morning, The Gospel Accounts of the Women's Visit to the Tomb of Jesus* (Rome, 1970).

Boomershine, T. E., 'Mk. 16:8 and the apostolic commission', *J.B.L.* 100 (1981), 225-239.

Boomershine, T. E. and Bartholomew, G. L., 'The narrative technique of Mark 16:8', *J.B.L.* 100 (1981), 213-223.

Borgen, P., 'John and the synoptics in the Passion narrative,' *N.T.S.* 5 (1958-9), 246-9.

Bornkamm, G., 'Der Auferstandene und der Irdische,' in *Zeit und Geschichte, Dank. R. Bultmann* (Tübingen, 1964), 171ff; English trans., 'The risen Lord and the earthly Jesus' in *The Future of our Religious Past* (London, 1971), ch. 8.

Braun, H., 'Zur Terminologie der Acta von der Auferstehung Jesu,' *T.L.Z.* 77 (1972), coll. 534-6.

Broer, I., *Die Urgemeinde und das Grab Jesu. Eine Analyse des Grablegungs-geschichte im Neuen Testament* (Munich, 1972).

Brown, R. E., *The Virginal Conception and Bodily Resurrection of Jesus* (London, etc., 1973).

Branton, R., 'Resurrection in the early church,' in A. Wikgren, ed. *Studies in Honour of H. R. Willoughby* (Chicago, 1961), 35-47.

Brüll, N., 'Die talmudische Tratate über Trauer um Verstorbenen,' *Jahrb. für Jüd. Gesch. und Lit.* 1874, 14ff.

Bucher, T. G., 'Die logische Argumentation in 1 Kor. 15, 12-20,' *Bibl.* 55 (1974), 465-86.

Bultmann, R., *The History of the Synoptic Tradition* (Oxford, 1968).

Burney, C. F., 'Christ as the *arche* of Creation,' *J.T.S.* 27 (1926), 160-77.

Campenhausen, H. von., *Tradition and Life in the Church* (London, 1968).

van Cangh, J. -M., 'La Galilée dans l'évangile de Marc; un lieu théologique' *R.B.* 79 (1972), 59-75.

Cavallin, H. C. C., 'Leben nach dem Tode im Spätjudentum und im frühen Christentum. I. Spätjudentum', A.N.R.W.II.19,1 (Berlin & New York, 1979), 240ff.

Charlesworth, J. H., 'Jesus and Jehohanan: an archaeological note on crucifixion,' *E.T.* 84 (1972-3), 147-50.

Chevasse, C., 'Not the mountain appointed,' *Theol.* 74 (1971), 478.

Clavier, H. at W. D. Davies and D. Daube, ed., *C. H. Dodd Vol.* (Cambridge, 1956), 342-55.

Clark, N., *Interpreting the Resurrection* (London, 1967).

Cousin, H., 'Sépulture criminelle et sépulture prophétique,' *R.B.* 80 (1974), 375-93.

Crawford, R. G., 'The Resurrection of Christ,' *Theol.* 75 (1972), 170-6.

Crossan, J. D., 'Empty tomb and absent Lord . . .', in W. H. Kelber, ed., *The Passion in Mark* (Philadelphia, 1978), 135-52.

Cullmann, O., *The Meaning of the Lord's Supper in Primitive Christianity*, in O. Cullmann and F. J. Leenhardt, *Essays on the Lord's Supper* (London, 1958), 8-16.

Cumont, F., *Lux Perpetua* (Paris, 1949).

Cupitt, D., 'The Resurrection: a disagreement,' *Theol.* 75 (1972), 507-19.

Curtis, K. P. G., 'Luke 23:12 and Jn. 20:3-10,' *J.T.S.* 22 (1971), 512-15.
'Three points of contact between Matthew and John in the Burial and Resurrection narratives,' *J.T.S.* 23 (1972), 440-4.

Dahl, N. A., 'The Atonement—an adequate reward for the Akedah,' *Neotestamentica et Semitica* (*Black Vol.*) (Edinburgh, 1969), 15-29.
Jesus in the Memory of the Early Church (*Minneapolis, 1976*), ch.5.

Daniélou, J., 'La typologie d'Isaac dans le Christianisme primitif,' *Bibl.* 28 (1947), 363-93.
'The empty tomb,' *Month* 225 (1968), 215-22.

Delling, G., 'Speranda futura,' (Delling) *Studien* (1970), 39ff.

Denney, J., *'The Death of Christ'* (London, Tyndale Press, 1957).

Dhanis, E., ed., *Resurrexit. Actes du Symposium international sur la Résurrection de Jésus. Rome 1970* (Rome, 1974).

Dillon, R. J., *From Eye-Witnesses to Ministers of the Word. Tradition and Composition in Luke 24* (Rome, 1978).

Dinkler, E., 'Petrusbekenntnis und Satanswort. Das Problem des Messianität Jesu,' *Zeit und Geschichte. Dankesgabe R. Bultmann* (Tübingen, 1964), 127-53.

Dodd, C. H., 'The appearances of the risen Christ: an essay in form criticism of the gospels,' *More New Testament Studies* (Manchester, 1968), 102-33.
Interpretation of the Fourth Gospel (Cambridge, 1968).
The Founder of Christianity (London, 1971).

Drury, J., *Tradition and Design in Luke's Gospel* (London, 1976).

Dubarle, A. -R., 'Le témoignage de Josèphe sur Jésus d'après des publications récentes', *R.B.* 84 (1977), 38-58.

Dumas, A., 'La mort du Christ, N'est elle pas sacrificielle?', *Études Théologiques et Religieuses* 56 (1981), 577-91.

Dupont, J., 'Ressuscité "le troisiéme jour",' *Bibl.* 40 (1959), 742-61.
'Anelēmphthē (Acts 1:1),' *N.T.S.* 8 (1961-2), 154-7.
'The meal at Emmaus,' in J. Delorme and others, *The Eucharist in the New Testament* (London, 1964), 106-121.

Duthie, C. S., *Resurrection and Immortality* (London, 1979).

Duval, Y. -M., *The Nature of Faith* (London, 1964).

Edwards, R. A., *The Sign of Jonah in the Theology of the Evangelists and Q* (London, 1971).

Ehrhardt, A., 'The disciples of Emmaus,' *N.T.S.* 10 (1963-4), 182-201.

Elliott, J. K., 'The text and language of the endings to Mark's gospel,' *T.Z.* 27 (1971), 255-62.

Ellis, I. P., ' "But some doubted",' *N.T.S.* 14 (1967-8), 574-80.

Enslin, M. S., 'And that he hath been raised', *J.Q.R.* 43 (1952), 26-56.

Evans, C. F., ' "I will go before you into Galilee",' *J.T.S.* NS.5 (1954),3-18.
  Resurrection and the New Testament (London, 1970).

Farmer, W. R., *The Last Twelve Verses of Mark* (Cambridge, 1974).

Farrer, A., *The Glass of Vision* (Westminster, 1948).
  A Study of St. Mark (Westminster, 1951).
  The Triple Victory (London, 1965).

Fascher, E., 'Anastasis-Resurrectio-Auferstehung', *Z.N.W.* 40 (1941), 166ff.

Flemington, W. F., 'On the interpretation of Col. 1:24', in Horbury & McNeil (1981), 84-90.

Freistedt, E., *Altchristliche Totengedächtnistage und ihre Beziehung zur Jenseitsglauben und Totenkultus der Antike* (Münster/W., 1928).

Friedrich, G., 'Die Bedeutung der Auferweckung Jesu nach Aussagen des Neuen Testaments,' *T.Z.* 27 (1971), 305-24.

Frey, J. B., 'La vie de l'au-delà dans les conceptions juives au temps de Jésus-Christ,' *Bibl.* 13 (1932), 129-68.

Fuller D. P., *Easter Faith and History* (London, 1965).

Fuller, R. H., *The Formation of the Resurrection Narratives* (London, 1972).

Gaboury, A., 'Deux fils uniques: Isaac et Jésus . . .,' *Stud.Evang. IV* (Berlin, 1968), 198-204.

Gaechter, P., 'Die Engelerscheinungen in der Auferstehung Jesu,' *Z.K.T.* 89 (1967), 191-202.

Gardner-Smith, P. *The Narratives of the Resurrection* (London, 1926).

Garte, E., 'The theme of resurrection in the Dura-Europos synagogue paintings,' *J.Q.R.* 64 (1973), 1-15.

Geering, L., *Resurrection: a Symbol of Hope* (London, etc., 1971).

George, A., 'Le sens de la mort de Jésus pour Luc', *R.B.* 80 (1973), 186-217.

Gerhardsson, B., *The Testing of God's Son. An Analysis of an Early Christian Midrash* (Lund, 1966).

Giblin, C. H., 'Structural and thematic correlations in the Matthaean burial and resurrection narratives,' *N.T.S.* 21 (1975), 406-20.

Gils, F., 'Pierre et la foi au Christ ressuscité,' *E.T.L.* 38 (1962), 5-43.

Glombitza, O., 'Gnade—Das entscheidende Wort,' *N.T.*2 (1956), 281-90.

Gnilka, J., 'Wie urteilte Jesus über seinen Tod?' in Kertelge (1976), 13-50.

Güttgemanns, E., *Der leidende Apostel und sein Herr. Studien zur paulinischer Christologie* (Göttingen, 1966).

Goguel, M., *La foi à la résurrection de Jésus dans le christianisme primitif* (Paris, 1933).

Goulder, M., 'The Empty Tomb', *Theology* 79 (1976), 206-14.

Gourges, M., *A la Droite de Dieu. Résurrection de Jésus et actualisation de Ps. 110:1 dans le Nouveau Testament* (Paris, 1978).
'A propos du symbolisme christologique et baptismal de Marc 16.5', *N.T.S.* 27 (1981), 672-8.

Grayston, K., 'Hilaskesthai . . .', *N.T.S.* 27 (1981), 640-56.

Grass, H., *Ostergeschehen und Osterberichte,* 4th edn. (Göttingen, 1970).

Grimm, W., 'Die Preisgabe eines Menschen zur Rettung des Volkes . . .,' *Josephus-Studien.O.Michel* (Göttingen, 1974), 133-46.

Grundt, F. I., *Die Trauergebräuche der Hebräer* (Leipzig, 1868).

Gubler, M. -L., *Die frühesten Deutungen des Todes Jesu. Eine motivgeschichtliche Darstellung aufgrunde der neueren exegetische Forschung* (Freiburg & Göttingen, 1977).

Guillaume, J. -M., *Luc interprète des anciennes traditions sur la résurrection de Jésus* (Paris, 1979).

Gustafsson, B., 'The oldest graffiti in the history of the Church?', *N.T.S.* 3 (1956), 65-9.

Gutwenger, 1., 'Zur Geschichtlichkeit der Auferstehung Jesu,' *Z.K.T.* 88 (1966), 257-82.

Haas, N., 'Anthropological observations on the skeletal remains from Giv'at ha-Mivtar,' *I.E.J.* 20 (1970), 38ff.

Haenchen, E., *Der Weg Jesu* (Berlin, 1966).

Hahn, A., *Bibliothek der Symbolen und Glaubensregeln der alten Kirche,* 3rd edn. (Breslau, 1897).

Hamilton, N. Q., 'Resurrection tradition and the composition of Mark,' *J.B.L.* 84 (1965), 415-21.

Hanson, A. T., *Studies in Paul's Technique and Theology* (London, 1974).

Hebert, J., 'The resurrection-narrative in St. Mark's gospel,' *S.J.Th.* 15 (1962), 66-73.

Hegemann, W., *Christ Rescued* (London, 1933)

Hemelsoet, B., 'L'ensévelissement selon S. Jean,' *Studies in John. Sevenster Vol.* (Leiden, 1970), 47ff.

Hengel, M., 'Maria Magdalena und die Frauen als Zeugen,' *Fest.O.Michel* (Leiden 1963), 243-56.
'Die Synagogeninschrift von Stobi', *Z.N.W.* 57 (1966), 151-8.

Hengel, M., *Crucifixion in the Ancient World. The Folly of the Message of the Cross.* (London, 1977).
Judaism and Hellenism (London, 1974).

Hertz, R., *Death and The Right Hand* (London, 1960).

Hofius, O., 'Eine altjüdische Parallele zu Röm.iv.17b,' *N.T.S.*18 (1971), 93-4.

Holtzmann, O., 'Das Begräbnis Jesu,' *Z.N.W.* 30 (1931), 311.

Hooke, S. H., *The Resurrection of Christ as History and Experience* (London, 1967.

Hooker, M., 'Interchange and suffering', in Horbury & McNeil (1981), 70-83.

Horbury, W., & McNeil, B., ed., *Suffering and Martyrdom in the New Testament* (Cambridge, 1981).

Hubbard, B. J., (Review of Alsup, Wilckens, N. Perrin (*Resurrection according to Matthew, Mark and Luke*), and P. Lapide (*Auferstehung: ein jüdisches Glaubens-erlebnis*)) Religious Studies Review 7/1 (Jan. 1981), 34-38.

Iersel, B. van, 'The resurrection of Jesus . . .,' *Concilium* 60(1970), 54-67.

Jaubert, A., 'La symbolique du puits de Jacob,' *L'Homme devant Dieu. Mélanges . . . . Lubac* (Lyons, 1963), I, 70-3.

Jeremias, J., '*Amnos tou theou - pais theou*', Z.N.W.34 (1935), 115-23.
    Unknown Saying of Jesus (London, 1957) (2nd edn., 1964).
    Heiligengräber in Jesu Umwelt (Göttingen, 1958).
    'Drei weitere spätjüdische Heiligengräbe,' *Z.N.W.*52 (1961), 95-101.
    New Testament Theology I (London, 1971).
    'Die Drei-Tage Worte der Evangelien,' in G. Jeremias, H. W. Kuhn, H. Stegemann, ed. *Tradition und Glaube* (Göttingen, 1971), 221-9.

Johansson, N., *Parakletoi* (Lund, 1940).

Johnston, G., *The Spirit-Paraclete in the Gospel of John* (Cambridge, 1970).

Kasher, M. M., *Encyclopedia of Biblical Interpretation V* (New York, 1962).

Kearney, P. J., 'He appeared to 500 brothers (1 Cor. xv.6)', *N.T.*22 (1980), 264-84.

Kegel, G., *Auferstehung Jesu—Auferstehung der Toten* (Gütersloh, 1970).

Keller, E. B., 'Hebrew thoughts on immortality and resurrection,' *Int.J.Phil.Rel.* 5 (1974), 16-33.

Kennard, J. S., 'The burial of Jesus,' *J.B.L.* 74 (1955), 227-38.

Kertelge, K., ed., *Der Tod Jesu. Deutungen im Neuen Testament* (Freiburg i.B., 1976).

Kertelge, K. 'Das Verständnis des Todes Jesu bei Paulus', in Kertelge (1976), 114-36.

Kingsbury, J. D., 'The composition and Christology of Matt. 28:16-20,' *J.B.L.* 93 (1974), 573-84.

Klausner, J., *From Jesus to Paul* (London, 1943).

Klein, S., *Tod und Begräbnis in Palästina zur Zeit der Tannäiten* (Berlin, 1908).

Knox, J., 'A Note on Mark 14:51-52', in S. Johnson, ed., *The Joy of Study (Fest. F.Clifton Grant)* (New York, 1951), 27-30.

Knox, W. L., *Some Hellenistic Elements in Primitive Christianity* (London, 1944).
    Sources of the Synoptic Gospels I (Cambridge, 1953).

Koch, G., *Die Auferstehung Jesu Christi* (Tübingen, 1959).

Kratz, R., *Auferweckung als Befreiung. Eine Studie zur Passions- und Auferstehungs-theologie des Matthäus* (Stuttgart, 1973).

Kremer, J., *Das älteste Zeugnis . . .* (Stuttgart, 1966).
    Die Osterbotschaft der vier Evangelien (Stuttgart, 1968).

Kuhn, H. -W., 'Der Gekreuzigte von Giv'at ha-Mivtar,' in Andresen (1979), 303-334.

Kümmel, W. G., 'Die älteste religiöse Kunst der Juden,' *Heilsgeschehen und Geschichte* (Marburg, 1965), 126-52.

The Theology of the New Testament (London, 1974).

Künneth, W., *The Theology of the Resurrection* (London, 1966).

Kurtz, D. C. and Boardman, J., *Greek Burial Customs* (London, 1971).

Lake, K., *Historical Evidence for the Resurrection of Jesus Christ* (London, New York, 1907).

Lambrecht, J., 'The relations of Jesus in Mark,' *N.T.*16 (1974), 241-58.

Lampe, G. W. H. and MacKinnon, D. M., *The Resurrection* (London, 1966).

Le Déaut, R., *Liturgie juive et Nouveau Testament* (Rome, 1965).

Leaney, A. R. C., 'The resurrection narratives in Luke 24:12-53,' *N.T.S.* 2 (1955-6), 110ff.
  'Theophany, Resurrection, and history,' *Stud.Evang.* V (Berlin, 1968).

Léon-Dufour, X., *Resurrection and the Message of Easter* (London, 1974).

Lerch, D., *Isaaks Opferung christlich gedeutet* (Tübingen, 1950).

Lévi, P., 'Le sacrifice d'Isaac et la mort de Jésus,' *R.É.J.*64 (1912), 161-84.

Lifshitz, B., 'Der Ausdruck *psyche* in den griechischen Grabinschriften,' *Z.D.P.V.* 76 (1960), 159-160.

Lightfoot, R. H., *Locality and Doctrine in the Gospels* (London, 1938), ch. 3-4.

Lindars, B., *New Testament Apologetic* (London, 1961), ch.2.

Locker, G. W., 'Der Geist als Paraklet,' *Ev.Theol.*26 (1966), 565-79.

Lockton, W., *The Resurrection and other Gospel Narratives* (London, 1924), pt. 1.

Lohfink, G., *Die Himmelfahrt Jesu* (Munich, 1971).

Lyonnet, S., 'Redemption' in X.Léon-Dufour, ed. *Dictionary of Biblical Theology* (London, 1970), 425-8.

McArthur, H. K., ' "On the third day" ,' *N.T.S.*18 (1971), 81-6.

Macquarrie, J., *Twentieth Century Religious Thought* (London, 1971).

Major, H. D. A., *A Resurrection of Relics* (Oxford, 1922).

Mánek, J., 'The apostle Paul and the Empty Tomb', *NT* 2 (1958), 276-80.

Margoliouth, D. S., 'The visit to the tomb,' *E.T.*38 (1926-7), 278-80.

Marmorstein, A., 'The doctrine of the resurrection of the dead in rabbinical theology,' *Am.J.Theol.* 19 (1915), 577-91.

Martini, C. M., *Il problema storico della Risurrezione negli studi recenti* (Rome, 1959).

Marxsen, W., *The Resurrection of Jesus of Nazareth* (London, 1970).

Mehta, V., *The New Theologian* (London, 1965).

Meier, J. P., 'Two disputed questions in Matt. 28:16-20', *J.B.L.*96 (1977), 407-24.

Menoud, P., *Le sort des trépassés* (Neuchâtel, 1945).

Merklein, H., 'Die Auferweckung Jesu und die Anfänge der Christologie', *Z.N.W.* 72 (1981), 1-25.

Metzger, B. M., 'A suggestion concerning the meaning of 1 Cor. 15.4b,' *J.T.S.* NS.8 (1957), 118ff.

Meyers, E. M., 'The theological implications of an ancient Jewish burial custom,' *J.Q.R.*62 (1971), 95.
  Jewish Ossuaries (Rome, 1971).

Moore, G. F., *Judaism in the First Centuries of the Christian Era* (Cambridge,

Mass., 1958).

Moore, R. G., 'Cross and crucifixion in Christian iconography,' *Religion* 4 (1974), 104-13.

Moore, S., 'An empty tomb revisited', *Downside Rev.* No. 337, Oct. 1981, 239-47.

Morison, F., *Who Moved the Stone?* (London, 1958).

Moule, C. F. D., 'The post-resurrection appearances in the light of festival pilgrimages,' *N.T.S.* 4 (1957-8), 58ff.
'The resurrection: a disagreement,' *Theol.* 75 (1972), 507-19.
ed., *The Significance of the Message of the Resurrection for Faith in Jesus Christ* (London, 1968).

Murray, R., *Symbols of Church and Kingdom* (Cambridge, 1975).

Nauck, W., 'Die Bedeutung des leeren Grabes,' *Z.N.W.* 47 (1956), 243-67.

Neirynck, F., 'Les femmes au tombeau: étude de la rédaction Matthéene,' *N.T.S.* 15 (1968), 168-90.
'La fuite du jeune Homme en Mc. 14:51-52', *E.T.L.* 55 (1979), 43-66.
Miscellanea Neotestamentaria, ed. T. Baarda et al. (Leiden, 1978), 1, 45-60.

Nickelsburg, G. W. E., *Resurrection . . . in Intertestamental Judaism* (Cambridge, 1972).
Studies on the Testament of Abraham (Missoula, 1976).

Niebuhr, R. R., *Resurrection and Historical Reason* (New York, 1957).

Nötscher, F., 'Zur Auferstehung nach drei Tagen,' *Bibl.* 35 (1954), 313-19.

O'Collins, G., *The Easter Jesus* (London, 1973).
The Calvary Christ (London, 1977).

O'Neill, J. C., 'Did Jesus teach that his death would be vicarious as well as typical?', in Horbury & McNeil (1981), 9-27.

O'Rahilly, A., 'Jewish burial', 'The burial of Christ', 'Peter and John at the tomb,' a series of articles in *Ir.E.R.* 1941-2.

Olsson, B., *Structure and Meaning in the Fourth Gospel* (Lund, 1974).

Papanikolaou, A. P., *Chariton-Studien* (Göttingen, 1973).

Pelletier, A., 'Les apparitions du Resusscité en terms de la Septante,' *Bibl.* 51 (1970), 76-9.

Paulsen, H., 'Mk. xvi. 1-8', *N.T.* 22 (1980), 138-75.

Perles, J., 'Die Leichefeierlichkeiten in nachbiblischem Judenthum,' *M.G.W.J.* 10 (1861), 345ff.

Perry, B. E., *The Ancient Romances. A Literary-Historical Account of their Origins* (Berkeley and Los Angeles, 1967).

Pesch, R., *Simon-Petrus. Geschichte und geschichtliche Bedeutung des ersten Jüngers Jesu Christi* (Stuttgart, 1980).

Pesch, R., 'Der Schluss der vormarkinischen Passiongeschichte, und des Markusevangeliums', in Sabbe (1974), 365-409.
'Das Abendmahl und Jesu Todesverständnis,' in Kertelge (1976), 137-87.

Rahnenführer, D., 'Das Testament des Hiob,' *Z.N.W.* 62 (1971), 77-80.

Reardon, B. P., *Courants littéraires grecs en IIe et IIIe siècles après J.-C.* (Paris, 1971).

Reisner, W. H., 'The case of the Tidy Tomb,' *Hey.J.*14 (1973), 47-57.

Rengstorf, K. H., *Die Auferstehung Jesu*, 4th edn. (Witten, 1960).

Reumann, J., *Jesus in the Church's Gospels. Modern Scholarship in the Earliest Sources* (London, 1970), ch.5.

Richards, H. J., *The First Easter. What Really Happened?* (London, Collins, 1976/1980).

Richardson, A., 'The resurrection of Jesus Christ,' *Theol.* 74 (1971), 146-54.

Riesenfeld, H., 'The resurrection in Ezekiel 37 and the Dura-Europos Paintings,' *Uppsala univ. Årsrkr.* 11 (1948), 35ff.

Rigaux, B., *Dieu l'a ressuscité: exégèse et théologie biblique* (Gembloux, 1973).

Robinson, W. C., 'The bodily resurrection of Christ,' *T.Z.* 13 (1957), 81-101.

Rochais, G., *Les récits de résurrection des morts dans le Nouveau Testament* (Cambridge, 1981).

Sabbe, M., ed., *L'Évangile selon Marc* (Gembloux & Louvain, 1974).

Sava, A. F., 'The wound in the side of Christ,' *C.B.Q.* 19 (1957), 343-6.

Schenke, L., *Auferstehungsverkündigung und Leeres Grab,* (Stuttgart, 1968).

Schillebeeckx, E., *Jesus. An Experiment in Christology* (London, 1979).

Schmithals, W., 'Die worte vom leidenden Menschensohn,' in Andresen (1979), 417-46.

Schmitt, A., 'Ps. 16:8-11 als Zeugnis der Auferstehung in dem Apg.,' *B.Z.* 17 (1973), 229-48.

Schmitt, J., *Jésus ressuscité* (Paris, 1949).

Schnackenburg, R., 'Zur Aussageweise "Jesus ist (von den Toten) auferstanden', *B.Z.*13 (1969), 1-17.

  'Ist der Gedanke des Sühnetodes Jesu der einzige Zugang zum Verständnis unsere Erlösung durch Jesus Christus?' in Kertelge (1976), 205-30.

Schoeps, H. J., 'The sacrifice of Isaac in Paul's theology,' *J.B.L.* 65 (1946), 385-92.

Schubert, K., 'Die Entwicklung des Auferstehungslehre von der nachexilischen bis zur früh-rabbinischen Zeit,' *B.Z.*6 (1962), 177-214.

  '"Auferstehung Jesu" im Lichte des Religionsgeschichte des Judentums' in Dhanis (1974), 207-29.

Seidensticker, P., *Die Auferstehung Jesu in der Botschaft der Evangelisten* (Stuttgart, 1967).

  Zeitgenössische Texte zur Osterbotschaft der Evangelien (Stuttgart, 1967).

Shaw, A., 'The breakfast by the shore and the Mary Magdalen encounter as eucharistic narratives,' *J.T.S.*25 (1974), 12-26.

Sider, R. J., 'The Pauline conception of the resurrection body in 1 Cor. 15:35-54,' *N.T.S.*21 (1975), 428-39.

Simon, M., *Forschungen zur Kunstgeschichte und christliche Archäologie* I (Baden-Baden, 1952).

Smith, A. M., 'The iconography of the sacrifice of Isaac in early Christian art,' *Am.J.Arch.*26 (1932), 133ff.

Smith, M., *Clement of Alexandria and the Secret Gospel of Mark* (Cambridge, Mass., 1973).

Snodgrass, K., 'Western non-interpolations,' *J.B.L.*91 (1972), 369-79.

Speyart van Woorden, I., 'The iconography of the sacrifice of Abraham,' *Vig.Chr.* 15 (1961), 214-15.

Spiegel, S., *The Last Trial* (Pantheon Books, 1967).

Spörlein, B., *Die Leugnung der Auferstehung. Eine historisch-kritische Untersuchung zu 1 Kor. 15* (Regensburg, 1971).

Stanley, D. M., *Christ's Resurrection in Pauline Soteriology* (Rome, 1961).

Steinseifer, B., 'Der Ort der Erscheinungen des Auferstandenen,' *Z.N.W.* 62 (1971), 232-65.

Stemberger, G., *Der Leib der Auferstehung. Studie zur Anthropologie und Eschatologie des palästinischen Judentums in neutestamentliche Zeitalter* (Rome, 1972).

Stendahl, K., ed., *Immortality and Resurrection* (New York, 1965).

Stuhlmacher, P., 'Das Bekenntnis zur Auferweckung Jesu von den Toten und die biblische Theologie,' *Z.T.K.* 70 (1973), 365-405.

Sukenik, E. L., 'The earliest record of Christianity', *Am.J.Arch.* NS, 51 (1947), 351-65.

Surgy, P. de, *La Resurrection du Christ et l'exégèse moderne* (Paris, 1969).

Thyen, H., ' "Niemand hat grössere Liebe als die, dass er sein Leben für seine Freunde hingibt" (Jon. 15:13),' in Andresen (1979), 467-84.

Toynbee, J. M. C., *Death and Burial in the Roman World* (London, 1971).

Trompf, G. W., 'The first Resurrection appearances and the ending of Mark's gospel,' *N.T.S.* 18 (1972), 308-30.

Torrey, C. C., *The Lives of the Prophets* (Philadelphia, 1946).

Tzaferis, V., 'Jewish tombs at and near Giv'at ha-Mivtar,' *I.E.J.* 20 (1970), 18-32.

Vanhoye, A., 'La fuite du Jeune homme nu (Mc. 14,51-52)', *Bibl.* 52 (1971), 404.

Vermes, G., *Scripture and Tradition in Judaism* (Leiden, 1961).
 The Dead Sea Scrolls in English, 2nd edn. (Harmondsworth, 1977).

Victorian Larrañaga, P., *L'Ascension de Notre-Seigneur dans le Nouveau Testament* (Rome, 1938).

Walker, N., 'After three days,' *N.T.*4 (1960), 261-2.

Walker, W. O., 'Post-crucifixion appearances and an interpretation', *J.B.L.*88 (1969), 157-165.

Walker, W., 'Christian origins and Resurrection faith,' *J. Rel.* 52 (1972), 41-55.

Walter, N., 'Eine vormatthäische Schilderung der Auferstehung Jesu,' *N.T.S.* 19 (1973), 415-29.

Wanke, J., *Die Emmauserzählung. Eine redaktionsgeschichtliche Untersuchung zu Lk. 24, 13-35* (Leipzig, 1973).
 'Wie sie ihn beim Brotbrechen erkannten,' *B.Z.*18 (1974), 180-92.

Whitaker, D., 'What happened to the body of Jesus? A speculation,' *E.T.* 81 (1969-70), 307-10.

Wijngaard, J., 'Death and Resurrection in covenantal context,' *V.T.*17 (1967) 226-39.

Wilckens, U., *Resurrection. Biblical Testimony to the Resurrection: an Historical*

Examination and Explanation (Edinburgh, 1977) (English trans. of *Auferstehung*, Stuttgart, 1970).

Willam, F. M., 'Johannes am Grabe des Auferstandenen (Jo. 20:2-10),' *Z.K.T.* 71 (1949), 204-13.

Williams, H. A., *Jesus and the Resurrection* (London, 1961).

Williams, S. K., *Jesus' Death as Saving Event. The Background and Origin of a Concept* (Missoula, 1975).

Wilson, S. G., 'The Ascension: a critique and an interpretation', *Z.N.W.* 58 (1967), 269-81.

Wünsche, A., 'Der Auferstehungsglaube . . .,' *Vierteljahrschrift für Bibelkunde* 1 (1903), 195ff.

Zehnle, R., 'The salvific character of Jesus' death in Lucan soteriology', *Theological Studies* 30 (1969), 420-43.

2. MEDICAL, INCLUDING MEDICO-LEGAL.

Albano, E. H., 'The medical examiner's viewpoint,' in A. Winter, ed., *The Moment of Death: a Symposium* (Springfield, Ill., 1969), 19-25.

Arnold, J. D., Zimmerman, R. F., and Martin, D. C., 'Public attitudes and the diagnosis of death,' *Journal of the American Medical Association* 206 (1968), 1949-1954.
'Diagnosis of death': *British Medical Journal* 1979/1, 332.

Heifetz, M. D., 'A definition of death for medical and legal use,' *Bulletin of the Los Angeles Neurological Society* 43 (1978), 27-9.

Isaacs, L., 'Death where is thy distinguishing?' *Hastings Center Reports* 8 (1978), 5-8.

Korein, J., ed. Annals of the New York Academy of Sciences, vol. 315 (1978), *Brain Death: Interrelated Medical and Social Issues.*

Place, M., 'Dying, the ultimate clinical course,' *Practitioner* 219 (1977), 693-6.

Pollock, W. F., ' "Cognitive" and "sapient", which death is the real death?' *American Journal of Surgery* 136 (1978), 2-7.

Sims, J. K., 'Criteria for pronouncement of death and the human brain death syndrome,' *Hawaii Medical Journal* 35 (1976), 11-14.

Skegg, P. D. G., 'The case for a statutory definition of death,' *Journal of Medical Ethics* 2 (1976), 190-2.

Stevenson, I., 'Research into the evidence of man's survival after death. A historical and critical survey . . .,' *Journal of Nervous and Mental Disease*, 165, no. 3(1977), 152-173.

Vaisrub, S., 'Afterthoughts on afterlife,' *Archives of Internal Medicine* 137 (1977), 150.

Walton, D. N., 'On logic and methodology in the study of death,' *Ethics in Science and Medicine* 3 (1976), 135-47.

See also supra, p.46, nn.6a-b.

INDEX OF SCRIPTURAL SOURCES
(in the order of the Jerusalem Bible)

I. OLD TESTAMENT

154

Amos			Jonah			Zephaniah						
2:1	88		1:4-16	115		2:15	97		2:1	139	14:16-17	134
2:11-16	63		1:17	106		3:8	12		3:2	89		
3:3	63					3:18	126		4:1	109	Malachi	
5:24	66		Habakkuk						5:1	139	4:2	106
6:10	88		3:16	139		Zechariah			12:10	50	4:5	12
						1:18	139		12:11-14	103		
									13:6-7	120		

II. FURTHER INTERTESTAMENTAL AND APOCRYPHAL LITERATURE

2 Baruch		1 Esdras		Jubilees		4 Maccabees		Psalms of Solomon	
30:2	32	8:77	129	18:2-19	89	The whole	118	3:12	30
				22:17	88	6	128	4:18(20)	111
		2 Esdras (4 Ezra)				17:21-22	128		
		1:39-40	69						

III. NEW TESTAMENT

Matthew			Mark									Luke				
1:20	109		28:1	31		6:50	69 n53, 97		14:50	63		4:23	56, 118			
2:11	132		28:2-4	65		7:8	132		14:51	8		4:29-30	72			
2:13	109		28:6	116		7:10	126		14:51-52	62, 63		4:30	72			
4:9	132		28:7	65		8:2	106		14:57-59	10		5:10	9			
5.4	127		28:8	116		8:29	99		14:58	81		7:11-17	23			
6:17	69 n40h		28:9	72, 113,		8:31-32	12		14:62	96		7:14	1, 85			
9:18	60			115 n28, 116, 132		8:31-33	79		14:70	55		7:22	85			
10:16	94		28:9-10	109		8:33	83		15:10	26		7:26	57			
11:17	61		28:11-15	75.87		8:35	129 n21		15:17	82		7:28	57			
12:39	106		28:15	72		8:36-37	63		15:19	132		7:32	61			
13:41	69 n52		28:16-20	95, 109		8:37-9:1	129 n21		15:34-35	65, 71		7:38	69			
14:1-2	29		28:17	116, 132		9:5	77		15:37	44		8:2	8, 110			
14:28	97		28:19	94, 110		9:9	8, 12, 85		15:38	50		8:3	77			
15:32	106		28:20	94		9:9-10	96		15:39	7, 44, 45		8:42	60			
16:4	106					9:13	12		15:40	8, 55		9:1-3	94			
16:18	15		Mark			9:15	8		15:41	93		9:7-9	29			
16:19	95		1:11	35		9:31-32	79		15:43	54		9:10	94			
16:21	1		1:12-13	7		9:32	99 n10		15:44	45, 48		9:51	111			
16:27	69 n52		1:13	69 n52, 113		9:33	69 n49		15:45	56		9:55	110			
17:23	1		1:16	9		9:34	95		15:46	51, 53,		9:60	94			
18:18	95		1:28	64		10:25	119			69 n48		10:3	94			
18:27	123		1:39	64		10:32	64, 93		15:47	6, 55,		10:9	94			
18:31-34	123		2:7	122-3		10:32-34	79			91, 110		10:11	94			
19:28	32		2:17	134		10:34-35	96		16:1-8	26, 60,		10:17-20	94			
20:19	1		2:21-22	135		10:35ff.	79			75, 92, 94, 135ff.		10:34	69 n40h			
20:21	129 n6		3:6	136		10:37	95		16:1	6, 56, 68		11:7-8	1			
20:28	120		3:7	64		10:38-39	95			n40h, 128, 137		11:29	106			
21:11	57		3:21	55		10:42	95		16:2	31, 106, 128		11:47-48	80			
23:27	87 n6		3:31-33	55		10:45	120-1		16:3	53		12:1-12	129 n21			
23:29	80		4:35-41	115 n15		11:15-17	81		16:4	53, 55,		12:33	4			
23:37	57		4:40	95		11:17	81			68 n24		13:16	63			
25:31ff.	68 n34		5:3	139		12:13-14	97		16:5	8, 61, 62,		13:32	79			
25:31-46	129		5:5	139		12:17	119			102, 116		13:33	57			
25:34	56		5:6	132		12:23-27	84		16:6	8, 61, 116		14:14	30			
25:35	56		5:17	xi		12:26	1, 97		16:7	61, 104		16:22	33			
26:28	118		5:21-43	26		13	10		16:8	116		16:22-23	33			
26:53	69 n52,		5:22-43	23		13:1-2	10		16:9-20	116 n38		16:27-31	24			
	129 n6		5:23	60		13:6	97		16:9-22	114		16:31	24, 85			
26:63	47		5:36	69 n53		13:7	10		16:11-14	116		21:28	129			
27:18	26		5:38	40		13:20	10, 129 n21		16:12	72		21:36	129 n21			
27:35	121		5:38-40	61		13:27	129 n21		16:14	72		22:15	49			
27:41	111		5:40	88 n10c		13:31	83		16:15	116		22:19	80			
27:52	2		5:42	96		13:33	10		16:15-18	94		22:20	128			
27:52-53	32		6:3-6	96		14:3ff.	4					22:41	83			
27:54	45		6:4	57		14:8	68 n40h		Luke			23:42	129			
27:57	54		6:6-7	94		14:17-21	10		1:68	129 n6		23:43	84			
27:58	60		6:7-13	96		14:18	104		1:46f.	54		23:46	44			
27:59	51, 60, 69		6:12-13	94		14:22	49		2:7	99 n1		23:47	45			
27:61	50		6:13	69		14:22-24	136		2:25	68 n28		23:49	55, 64			
27:62-66	59-60,		6:14	1, 97, 102		14:22-26	80		2:32	134		23:52	60			
	73, 87		6:14-16	29		14:27	120		2:38	68 n28,		23:53	52 60,			
			6:15	57		14:32	83			129 n6			69, 139			
27:63	117		6:29	8		14:36	63, 83, 119		2:46	106		24	90			
27:64	72		6:49	97		14:41	63		4:21	127		24:1	6, 139			

155

INDEX OF AUTHORS' NAMES

157

INDEX OF TOPICS
(including certain literary material not indexed above)

159

burial of Jesus, 52, 114 n2
burial of the dead, a good work, 54; methods of burial, 31, 52
burial, precipitate, 30-1, 54
burning, 82; places of, 85-6
Bush, the Burning, 82, 97, 113

cantillation, 135ff.
canopy, 77
Celsus, 20
centurion, 7
charismatic impression, x
charismatics, 76; and reviving the 'dead', 20, 22, 23, 33, 44-5, 78
charitable acts, 56, 57, 76, 91
Christ, ix, xi, 4, 117; *see also* Messiah
Christianity a 'historical' religion, 15, 16
church, the earliest, its shame, 51; sociology of, 56
Clement of Alexandria, 83, 88
cloth, see *sindon*
comas, 41ff.
commandments, 94, 119; absence of post-Anastasis, 85, 108, 110
commemoration, *see* death-feasts
conjecture, x, 97, 132
conversion, 99
corpse, suffers, 77; mummification of, 59; putrefaction of, 29
'corruption', 29, 30, 77, 84
creeds, xii, xiii, 4, 14, 105, 120
cremation, seldom used by Jews, 81, 85; scandalous, 81, 82; possible indifference of some, 81;
    probable in case of Jesus, 81, 84, 90; *see also* burning
criminals, 57
Cross, the, 56, 82, 117, 127; sign of, 125, 126, 127
crucified dead, 55, 57, 69 n44
crucifixion, age and use of, 25, 47, 48; method of, 41, 48-9
crucifixion of Jesus, 8, 45, 49, 55
cures, 75, 76, 123
curiosity, a factor in gospel-building, 91, 108, 131
curses, 118
custodians of shrines, 74, 78, 80
Cyrene, 8, 11 n7

Dead Sea Scrolls, *see* Qumran
dead, cult of the, *see* death-feasts; tombs, cult of
death, 19; incompetent diagnosis of, 20-1, 38f.; life after, 44
death, incohate or 'clinical', 41, 42, 71, 117; brain-death, 42ff., 71, 117; revival from death.
    19, 20, 38ff., 117
death and atonement, 27
death-feasts, 80, 88
defilement, ritual, 51, 62, 64, 104, 113
demons, 94
demythologising, xiii
Diogenes Laertius, 22
Dioscuri, the, 11 n7
disappearance, 72, 111
disciples of Jesus not summoned, 64, 83, 91, 114
disciples, the, as depicted in the gospel of Mark, 12, 13, 54, 55, 56, 63, 77, 92, 95, 123, 134;
    effect of the Anastasis upon, 95, 117, 123

162

magic, 74
manger, 67 n20
Mark, St., gospel of, xi, 5, 92; date of, 10; climax of, 9, 130, 131, 135ff.; author's methods, xi, 7, 9; his intentions, 7, 13, 19, 26, 31, 60, 64
Marriage, Sacred, 26, 103, 131; *see also,* 'brides of Christ'
Martha, 30
martyrdom, 63, 75, 77, 87, 120
martyrs, 29, 56-7, 59, 73, 82, 120; *see also* athlete
Mary Magdalene, 6, 8, 52, 72, 73, 76, 77, 112, 113, 115-6
Matthew, St., gospel of, 5, 8, 26, 54, 59-60, 63, 65, 73, 75, 87 n3, 94-5, 99, 109
Meir, R., 118-9.
Mekilta, cited, 37
Menippus, 23-4
merit, 30, 35, 75; acquisition of, 87, 118, 119, 120, 123, 134; sharing in, 35, 76, 84, 118, 122, 123
Meron, 72-3
mesîrâ (denunciation), 10, 12, 58, 79, 120, 122
Messiah(s), ix, 104, 106, 108, 112, 115 n15, 120, 127, 132, 134
metempsychosis, 30
Midrash, Haggadol, cited, 37
Midrash Rabbah, cited, 36, 37, 68, 75, 87, 88, 89, 115
miracles, 26, 75, 76, 107, 119; and relics, 77; scepticism about, ix, 17, 45; study of, x
miraculous, 1, 17, 60, 76, 82
Mishnah, cited, 36, 37, 69, 87, 88, 115
missions, 113, 117, 136
money, *see* financial
monotheism, strict, 96, 132
Moses, 4, 66, 74, 82, 91, 97, 102, 103, 104, 111-2, 113
mourners, 127
mourning, 57, 58, 103; signs of, 50, 63, 83; ritual, 40, 50, 61, 64
mummification, *see* corpse

Name, the, 97, 120
nations, all, 110, 133, 134
Nazarene, the, 61, 64
necromancy, 59, 74-5
Nehemiah, 81
New Testament, ix; *see* gospels
Nicodemus, 51, 52, 79
novels, 24-25

obedience, *see* commandements
Œdipus, 49
Old Testament, the, 4, 5, 119, 121, 134; *see also* scriptures
ossilegium, see bone-gathering
ossuaries, 48, 56, 57, 58, 125-6; *see also* bone-packing
othonia (bandages), 51, 52

pagan cults, 80; ideas, 13, 80, 131
partners, 92
Passion, the, of Jesus, 48; predictions of, 78, 79, 83, 96, 105
Passover, 49, 59, 82, 85, 86, 103; *see also* lamb
Paul, St., x, 10, 15, 19, 23, 76, 97f., 133; not interested in details of Anastasis, x
Pentecost, 91, 98, 111
perideipna, see death-feasts
Pesiqta, cited, 87, 88, 89

Peter, Gospel of, 3, 67 n12, 112
Peter, St. (Cephas), ix, 23, 55, 64, 66, 76, 79, 83, 92, 97f., 99, 112, 133
Pharisees, 47, 49, 57
Philostratos, 22
Phineas, 33
Pilate, Pontius, 56, 60, 73, 75, 117
pilgrimage, 4, 9, 75, 94, 102; purpose and frequency of, 74
Pirqe de R. Eliezer, cited, 37
pit, *see* grave for malefactors
Pliny, 21, 22
prediction of the Anastasis, 12, 79
prevarication, 14f., 131
priestly blessing, 111
prophets, 4, 30, 31, 57, 120
propitiation, 82
proselytes, 35, 63
Pseudo-Philo, 88 n15
puns, 93
Pythagoras, 23

Qumran sect, 30, 32, 47-8, 50, 88 n13a, 120; *see also* Essenes
questions addressed to the dead, 23

rabbinical sources, 3; for their use *see also* Mishnah, etc.
rabbis, holy, 73-4
ram, *see* lamb
recitation-text, 60
Redemption, 7, 13, 34, 35, 63, 83, 117f., 119
relations of holy men, 27-8
relations of Jesus, 55, 59, 76, 78
relics, cult of, 74, 77, 81
religious enthusiast, 62
reminiscence, x, 7, 58, 60, 93
rending of garment, 50
resurrection, not an individual experience, 32-3, 130; ideas about, 2-3, 29ff., 33, 84
resurrection of Jesus, 12; mode of unknown, x; mode not an article of faith, x
Resurrection, the hope of the Pharisees, 1, 2, 12, 32, 79, 81, 84, 104; belief in, 32, 77-8; an
      imaginary entity, 2, 32; *anastasis* a token of, 78
resuscitation, 39, 40
revelations of the underworld, 23, 28; of life after death, 24
rich, 119
Rock, 50, 103
rolling, 63, 66, 94
Roman law, 27
Romans, 49, 55, 58, 66, 67 n16, 111, 119

Sabbath (Saturday), 31, 41, 48, 73, 106
Sadducees, 32, 33
'saints', 32
Salome, 8, 137
samādhi, 45
Samuel, 54
Sanhedrin, 32, 59, 133
Satan, 7, 83, 109, 112, 122, 132
sceptics and scepticism, ix; illustrated, xiii, 13, 14ff., 19

scholars, ix, xiii, 13
scourging, 48, 50, 79, 91
scriptural pattern, 85, 114
scriptures, 112, 114, 118, 137
'secondary', 5, 94
secrets, 77, 81
Semachot, 36 n6
Sepulchre, *see* tomb; Holy Sepulchre, 80; not necessarily the genuine tomb, 129 n24
Serapis, 80
sermons, x, 16
Servant, Suffering, 120, 121, 133
side of Jesus, jabbed, 50
Simon of Cyrene, 8
sin, 14, 62, 77, 82, 86, 118, 119; release of sins, 95, 117, 123, 133
sindon, 50-1, 52, 62, 128
Sisyphus, 68
skeleton, concern for, 49
Socrates, 68 n40f
solidarity, 56
Son, the, 4, 132
Son of Man, the, 79, 120-1
spices, see *arōmata*
Spirit, the, *see* Holy Spirit
spirits, 30, 31, 97; consulting, 26
stake, 82
stone, the, 53, 65, 66, 68 n23a, 71, 94, 103, 128
stupefaction of the women, 5, 6, 8, 13, 61
suffering, an atonement, 118, 119, 123
syllabic composition, 136
symbolic story, 113-14

Talmud, Babylonian, cited, 37, 74, 87, 88, 89, 113, 115
Talmud, Palestinian, cited, 36
Talpioth, tomb at, 72, 83, 124; ossuaries found at, x, xi, 14, 96, 108, 122, 126, 130
Targum ps. Jonathan, cited, 67
Temple, the, 10, 33, 81, 82, 86, 132; not built with hands, 81, 86
Temptation, the, 7
Testament of Abraham, 30, 85, 112, 116 n30
Testament of Job, 30, 31
Testaments of the XII Patriarchs, 8, 30, 32, 69 n50, 83, 87 n3h, 108, 112, 115
Testimonium Flavianum, 3, 107-8
theft of the body, possible, 72-3, 75, 76
theologians, professional, tendencies of many, ix, x, 10
theophany, 6, 61
thief, penitent, 33, 84
thorns, crown of, 82
three days, 31, 103, 105ff.
tomb, the empty, xi, 71, 75, 91, 100 n12, 102
tomb of Christ, 5, 52-3, 59, 64, 75, 128; revival in nowhere stated, 13, 19
tombs, cult of, 26, 64, 73, 74, 77, 80
tomb-robbing, 58, 72, 76
tomb-visiting, obligatory after burial, 8, 30-1, 59; as pilgrimage, *see* pilgrimage
tombs, miracles at, 26, 74, 118; sleeping near, 74, 78; custodians of, 74, 78
tower, 18, 115-6
trance, 45, 71

FINIS